JAMES WELDON JOHNSON'S MODERN SOUNDSCAPES

James Weldon Johnson's Modern Soundscapes

Noelle Morrissette

University of Iowa Press

Iowa City

University of Iowa Press, Iowa City 52242

www.uiowapress.org
Printed in the United States of America
Design by Richard Hendel

The University of Iowa Press is a member of Green Press Initiative and is committed to preserving natural resources.
Printed on acid-free paper

Library of Congress Cataloging-in-Publication Data
Morrissette, Noelle.
James Weldon Johnson's Modern Soundscapes / by Noelle Morrissette.
pages cm
Includes bibliographical references and index.
ISBNS 978-1-60938-158-5 and 1-60938-158-0 (pbk.)
ISBNS 978-1-60938-159-2 and 1-60938-159-9 (e-book)
1. Johnson, James Weldon, 1871–1938—Criticism and interpretation. 2. Music in literature. 3. Harlem (New York, N.Y.)—Intellectual life—20th century. I. Title.
PS3519.O2625Z79 2013
818′.5209—dc23 2012041272

For

Robert Burns Stepto

and

Dorothy Franklin

You sang far better than you knew; the songs

That for your listeners' hungry hearts sufficed

Still live—but more than this to you belongs.

— JAMES WELDON JOHNSON,

"O Black and Unknown Bards" (1908)

Contents

Acknowledgments

This book began as a summer 1997 research project in the James Weldon Johnson Papers at the Beinecke Rare Book and Manuscript Archives at Yale University. I was a graduate student deeply inspired by the archival and autobiographical work of my mentor, Robert Stepto, whose ideas and spirit continue to shape my work and to whom this book is dedicated. It was an exciting time at Yale: the interdisciplinary PhD program in African American studies had developed into a department, thanks to the hard work of devoted faculty. The leadership and scholarship of Hazel Carby, Robert Stepto, Paul Gilroy, and others, along with a newly arrived, dynamic junior faculty, facilitated an intellectual closeness between graduate students with diverse and complementary interests. We shared our scholarship in a yearlong research workshop seminar that combined graduate student work with presentations by faculty inside and outside the university. African American studies at Yale fostered a vital intellectual culture that has left a deep mark on my work, and I find myself seeking to model that culture in my current academic context at the University of North Carolina at Greensboro.

Since that beginning, which immersed me in the major repository of Johnson's papers and correspondence, I have traveled to Fisk University's Special Collections, the Library of Congress, the National Archives, the New York Public Library, the Municipal Records of the City of New York, the Harry Ransom Center at the University of Texas at Austin, and Emory University, all of which have significant holdings of Johnson's papers and/or correspondence from or concerning Johnson. The services staff of each of these collections was extremely knowledgeable, helpful, and encouraging. I am particularly indebted to the service staff of the Beinecke Rare Book and Manuscript Library, including Karen Nangle and Adiba Nabiz.

Several fellowships and grants made this ranging archival study possible. The Donald C. Gallup Fellowship in American Literature at the Beinecke Rare Book and Manuscript Library at Yale University, the Andrew W. Mellon Research Foundation Fellowship from the Harry Ransom Center at the University of Texas at Austin, and the Marc C. Friedlaender Award from the Department of English at the University of North Carolina at Greensboro gave me the opportunity to conduct this essential research. A faculty grant from the University of North Carolina at Greensboro allowed me the time necessary to write this book.

Both Patricia C. Willis, former curator of the Collection of American Literature at the Beinecke Library, and Louise Bernard, curator of prose and drama, Collection of American Literature at the Beinecke Library, provided me with invaluable resources and direction. The Beinecke's personal librarian, Heather Dean, was extremely generous with her time and abundantly helpful in assisting me with grounding ephemeral leads. Randall Burkett and Rudolph P. Byrd of Emory University's Special Collections shared their extensive knowledge of the Johnson holdings there and greatly assisted me in my research focus. Beth Howse of Fisk University Franklin Library was patient and generous and shared her deep knowledge of the holdings in the special collections pertaining to Johnson.

This book has benefited from the reception of several conference papers on Johnson's diverse writings presented at the Modern Language Association, the American Literature Association, the American Studies Association, and the Society for the Study of the Multi-Ethnic Literature of the United States. I have been fortunate to receive feedback and encouragement on my in-progress ideas from Michael Nowlin, Amritjit Singh, Joseph Skerrett, and Alex Weheliye, among many others, and from my fellow panelists, especially Monica Miller and Carter Mathes.

Our work as scholars is both ephemeral and practically grounded: it does not become material until it is shared with others. I'm indebted to several of my colleagues at the University of North Carolina at Greensboro for their attentive reading of portions of the manuscript in draft form. Karen Kilcup, Maria Sanchez, and Mark Rifkin patiently read through early versions of my work and offered pointed criticisms and suggestions, from which this book has benefited. Watson Jennison, Tom Jackson, and Lisa Levenstein helped me understand more clearly how sound studies have been pursued in African American historiography. Lorenzo Meachum, Naurice Frank Woods, and Michael Cauthen provided me with the dynamic, interdisciplinary, and rigorous culture of debate that most resembled my environment in African American graduate studies at Yale. I am tremendously fortunate to have these colleagues and friends. The project also benefited from the able contributions of research assistants Dan Burns, Selena Wolf, Will Dodson, Diana Saavedra, and Michael Zinowski.

I'm grateful to the entire staff of the University of Iowa Press for their investment in this book. Special thanks goes to Joseph Parsons, formerly of the press, for believing in my project, and to Elisabeth Chretien, Charlotte Wright, Mary M. Hill, and Jim McCoy for their patience, encouragement, and expertise in guiding this work to completion.

I firmly believe that intellectual community is formed from all aspects of a full, engaged life. Lorenzo and Tomi Meachum inspired me to follow the spirit of Johnson and find where it led me. Ellen Hjerrild Kjerkegaard and I discussed local activism and cosmopolitan culture, both Johnson's and ours, planning ways to provide educational opportunities for our community's children. Manard Brown offered daily encouragement and wisdom from his perspective as a deeply invested community leader and writer. And finally, I drew from the inspiration of my son, a creative spirit to whom James Weldon Johnson is a familiar and a friend. May we take up Johnson's invocation and meet each other in a more just world—a world that is of our creation.

Grateful acknowledgment is made to Jill Jones, executor of the James Weldon Johnson and Grace Nail Johnson Literary Estate, for her kind permission to cite from the Johnson archives at Yale, Emory, and Fisk. I am grateful to the archives and trusts granting me permission to cite from unpublished manuscripts and correspondence: the Manuscript, Archives, and Rare Book Library at Emory University; the Special Collections at Fisk University Franklin Library; the H. L. Mencken Papers at the Manuscripts and Archives Division of the New York Public Library, Astor, Lenox and Tilden Foundations; and Bruce Kellner of the Carl Van Vechten Trust.

JAMES WELDON JOHNSON'S MODERN SOUNDSCAPES

Introduction
The Ragtime Reinventions of James Weldon (William) Johnson

When he died in a tragic train-and-automobile accident in 1938, James Weldon Johnson, an American modern and a racial forerunner whose life and achievements were the embodiment of possibility, was widely viewed as one of the most influential people in American literary and political life. The aspirations of many were tied to Johnson as the chosen agent to effect civic and national changes related to race issues. Johnson's life spanned two centuries and ranged from the recent emancipation of African Americans from the institution of slavery to the radical socialist politics of his younger peers in the midst of the Depression. Beginning with his birth in 1871, just "a few years after the close of the Civil War" and in the midst of America's Reconstruction, Johnson's life, like that of the narrator of his 1912 novel, *The Autobiography of an Ex-Colored Man*, would be shaped by momentous social and political changes for African Americans in their quest for the full rights due them as American citizens. Johnson in turn would shape American life in a biographically rich and complex combination of intention and accident as he grew to national prominence as a writer of national renown and a public figure—one whom many would come to claim as an intimate friend.

Johnson's manuscript notes and drafts of unpublished and published works clearly show the centrality of sound to his aesthetic project as he mediates and directs sound into his written works. Johnson's wide-ranging, diverse writings—modernist poetry, jazz criticism, social editorials, a novel, critical prefaces to anthologies of African American poetry and spirituals, a history of New York, and an autobiography—have not yet received the critical treatment that they deserve, one that treats his cultural production through the modernist and interracial aesthetic of sound.

James Weldon Johnson's Modern Soundscapes argues that sound, broadly conceived—musical and linguistic composition, noise, repetition, silence—functions as a formal aesthetic practice in and between

Johnson's works. Musical comedy, his first career, which propelled him to the national stage, became in Johnson's subsequent works a formal practice of sound as a means of articulating an aesthetic he based on black expressive culture not limited to text. What readers have attributed to Johnson's works—a studied detachment, irony, and objectivism, all text-based terms preoccupied with point of view—inadequately equip us for reading his works. I show that Johnson was in fact demonstrably more preoccupied with the cultural transfer of sound. Using the spirituals as his basis—songs that are derived from the text of the Bible but that represent a distinct creation carried by the voices and experiences of the enslaved—Johnson sought to create an inclusive mode of written expression, whereby cultural transmission is privileged over textual transmission.

Johnson took this idea further to incorporate the idea of interpolation, whereby his works themselves are not discrete entities but are continually transformed and modified by those who enact/perform them. This participation occurs through the incorporation of sound, which enables his writing to be voiced through the bodies of others, and it also occurs between Johnson's works through his technique of repetition. Critics have tended to present Johnson's self-referentiality, repetition, and interplay between his works as if they indexed a single, unchanging viewpoint. Instead, this study emphasizes Johnson's innovative use of these techniques as his distinct, individualized modernist practice, in which sound defines his overall aesthetic: the repetitions aren't merely visual or textual, they are aural. Rather than presenting a tired, unchanging repetition of sentiment or ideology, as critics have assumed, Johnson's repetition establishes an interplay between his works. The repetitions are indicative of Johnson's attitude toward expressive practices, how he wishes his works to be both taken and taken up by others. Such a move parallels that of American musical comedy, where white vocalists sang in the voices of black composers.

Johnson took the American soundscape—an immersive environment of sound inclusive of music and other ambient noise—and evoked the sensations and experiences of its settings in his works. Rather than simply documenting, capturing, and recording this environment, Johnson used it to create an aesthetic based on sound, one that references both its main and lower frequencies. Moreover, Johnson used referencing itself as an act of simultaneously registering different aspects of the soundscape at once. Drawing attention to the simultaneity of sounds in this environment, Johnson also called attention to the *practice* of simultaneity. His simultaneous composition of generically diverse works—such as his poem "O Black and Unknown Bards" and his prose *Autobiography of an Ex-Colored Man*—provides an example of the potential for the controlled use of fugitive or divergent sounds.

As Johnson's works accumulate, they begin to resound with one another, repeating, altering, and extending themselves through an aural reverberation that cuts back and forth in time, content, and selves—and that culminates in Johnson's 1933 autobiography, *Along This Way*. Johnson's elaborate self-referencing in his works accompanied a larger biography of black expressive culture. Providing a story of the experiences of many, a story that was continuously moving beyond its representation in print, Johnson emphasized, more than the events themselves, the *experience* of those events, sonic textures with multiple and simultaneous references within and far beyond the author's own experiences. The bodily experience of those sounds also facilitated their transference to others in this immersive setting. In Johnson's works, writing and reading biography became an active practice of registering bodily experience, privileging the motion of its transference.

The practice of interpolation—the insertion of foreign or unrelated material into a literary or musical composition—underscores the politics of the potential relationship between that material and the composition, as Johnson shows. Using interpolation through the range of his compositions in music, poetry, and prose, Johnson demonstrates that the issue of originality, in claims to authorship and to citizenship and to cultural purity, underscores its opposite: cultural impurities, disruptions, and borrowings. While the stolen creations of black artists remain a pressing concern for Johnson, he also asserts the interconnection of black and white American culture by dissolving the original/copy binary. The interpolations that he presents in his compositions—between musical and textual, racial and gendered, national and international contexts—also demonstrate their connection in a simultaneously playing soundscape.

Those who had known Johnson personally commented on his remarkable charm, grace, and warmth. Colleagues and casual acquaintances were struck by his compelling presence, sometimes attributing it to the glint of his "grey-green eyes" or his "beautiful hands."[1] He was "My Dear Mr. Johnson" in the man-to-man conversation of Henry Louis

Mencken, American literary pundit; he was "Gem" in intimate, poet-to-poet correspondence with Anne Spencer. He was even considered a cherished friend as well as an icon and a model for black aspiration to those who had never met him. In 1930 a young single mother in Harlem named her child James Weldon Johnson, although the elder outlived him. And in his lifetime, women civic leaders in Harlem formed the James Weldon Johnson Literary Guild, an organization devoted to leadership, example, and literacy among urban black youth.

These observations about Johnson, including practices of naming and claiming him, demonstrate his remarkable skill in forging the diverse friendships and conversations that have created this expansive, larger-than-life portrait of him. Following his death, these portraits became contentious, with differing perspectives on the meaning of his life emerging from discrete sectors of the population, each demonstrating its individual claim on Johnson in relation to its needs. Although the portraits generated by these groups appeared to be contentious, taken together they complete the picture of a man who appeared to be all things to all people. In addition, Johnson became a symbol not only of what had been accomplished through his leadership and example but also of the unfinished project of civil rights and equality, the unfulfilled dreams and aspirations of many. As Oswald Garrison Villard, his former colleague at the National Association for the Advancement of Colored People, wrote of him in the *Nation*, at the age of sixty-seven "Johnson was much too young to lose, and the country—both whites and colored—could not spare him, for there are too few comparable with him."[2]

Following Johnson's untimely death, his publisher and friend, Alfred A. Knopf, recalled him as "a man of great personal dignity."[3] The versatility and charm exhibited by Johnson in almost any setting were perceived to be a reflection on his character and his background, and his presence in previously segregated forums held the promise of wider social possibilities for African Americans. In many ways, it seemed as if Johnson lived a charmed life. His life story reads almost like fiction, conveying not simply geographic and social mobility and the extraordinary breadth and scope of his accomplishments but also the extraordinary character of the man behind them, the hero of the story. How else had he been able to position himself at the center of so many important currents in American life, from its modern arts cultures to its national-scale civil rights movements? It is undeniable that Johnson had achieved extraordinary things in his lifetime despite the predominating racism of the times. From his founding of a daily newspaper for Jacksonville's black readership to his weekly editorials for an urban black audience in the *New York Age*, Johnson demonstrated his belief in the reach of journalism, the importance of a black newspaper readership, and the power of his journalistic flair. From passing the Florida bar—the first African American to do so—to getting an antilynching bill through the United States House of Representatives, he demonstrated his unflagging commitment to and faith in the American legal system and the framework it provided for according legal rights to all Americans. Whether in his role as principal of Stanton School, Jacksonville's grade school for black children, or serving his nation as American consul, first to Venezuela and then to Nicaragua, Johnson demonstrated his adeptness in forming local alliances while defusing explosive conflict. And from song lyricist of the infectiously popular tunes of the Cole and Johnson Brothers trio to his role as the field secretary of the National Association for the Advancement of Colored People who built and expanded its southern base by over two hundred branches, Johnson proved his skill in popularizing and coalition building.

Johnson's writings from this period encompass all of these accomplishments, for he was not only a statesman of many causes but also a distinguished author. His statesmanship and writing were intertwined with each other in complex ways, since his writing was far more than simply the cumulative effect of his multiple careers. A host of American political and cultural currents broadly and aesthetically shaped his life and writing, encompassing the international, national, and local. The domestic Progressive Era politics of anticorruption and American expansionism in Latin America at the turn of the twenty-first century, the local cultures of New York's Black Bohemia and Greenwich Village, all of which he participated in, shaped his writing. And Johnson was equally taken by the newness of H. L. Mencken's "American Language"—its distinct vocabulary and spellings, employed by such prominent Americans as Theodore Roosevelt—and the influence of Latin American Spanish and its culture. Looking closely at Johnson's writings permits us to see the complex negotiations of a man placed at the center of different but overlapping modern movements—in both popular culture and literary modernism—that often were viewed as exclusive to each other. Johnson, it seemed, was the perfect interpreter, the one to explain them to each other. Recognizing these overlaps, Johnson positioned himself as their interpolator, using his changing experiences as the basis of his unique role.

Johnson was drawn to New York City by his younger brother, John Rosamond Johnson ("Rosie," his middle name, reflected his mother's wish for a daughter), who had resettled in New York after completing his musical education at the New England Conservatory, traveling abroad with a popular musical show, *Oriental America*, and briefly teaching music to schoolchildren in Jacksonville. While it may seem unlikely that Johnson pursued civil rights through the musical comedies he subsequently authored with his brother, his experience in this field made him a unique leader for the cause while affording him the opportunity to shape a new, modern self. Johnson's immersion in the world of improvisatory black music enabled him to develop a new discourse on race in tandem with a new theory of literary composition afforded by his exposure to musical composition.

Moving from Jacksonville to New York City, Johnson stepped out of his former familial identity in Jacksonville as "Young Jim"—so called to differentiate him from his father, James Sr. He was now thirty years old and in New York; he would invoke his father often in his writing to recall the elder's familiarity with an earlier New York, which he had occasionally visited, and, one suspects, to speculate on the kind of life his father could have lived in this new, modern city of possibility. From 1901 on, Johnson would link his life with this city, forming his new identity by assuming the role of the city's cultural biographer through the presentation of its soundscape.

Coinciding with his new role as biographer, Johnson would begin using a new middle name in early 1913, when he "made the 'W' in [his] name stand for Weldon instead of William."[4] Between 1913 and 1914 he wrote compositions for theater and film bearing the names Johnson James, Jay Johnson, J. Johnson, and Weldon Johnson. These names indicate Johnson's experimentation with both the shifting roles of an interlocutor and various popular idioms and forms. Accustomed to blackface stereotypes of the minstrel and vaudeville stage, American audiences did not usually align musical theater with dignity—this was an arrangement that Johnson made, inspired by the spirited cultural productions of black artists whom he recognized as innovative because they broke the mold of expectation. As the city's self-appointed biographer, Johnson became black expressive culture's interlocutor, explaining the city's value and significance to a wide-scale American audience.

Biography is improvisatory, a theme that I develop further in chapter 1, "Biography of the Race: Musical Comedy and the Modern Soundscape of *The Autobiography of an Ex-Colored Man*."

According to Knopf, Johnson understood "the romantic and always poignant story of the black man in America . . . this story, this struggle, in all its sadness and bravery."[5] That story was his and many others'. For Johnson, documenting the life of the city was also the process of telling a story. In it he was but one of the characters, and the central one was not a person but black expressive culture in the context of the American nation. It was a story seemingly without boundaries, stretching from Latin America and the Caribbean, particularly, northward to the black cultural "capital"—New York. And it was a story without an end, constantly "in the making"—borrowing a phrase from Johnson's 1930 history of black New York, *Black Manhattan*—and expansive in possibility. By aligning his new life with a story of the metropolis that had infinite variations and possibilities, Johnson created an unconstrained, liberated self, one that was unknowable because it too was always in the making.

Born in Jacksonville, Florida, Johnson described his hometown in the years of his youth as generally atypical of the widespread southern culture that claimed the racial inferiority of African Americans, an attitude that was used to deny their economic and political advancement and to justify violence against them. Johnson's father, James Johnson Sr., of Virginia and freeman heritage, held the position of head waiter at the Jacksonville Hotel, a resort that catered to a white clientele. His mother, Helen Louise Johnson, a Bahamian, was the first black teacher to be hired at the Stanton School, of which Johnson was to become principal years later. His mother's origins outside of the United States gave Johnson a sense of a birthright broader than the nation, both a strong affiliation with modern black identity of the Americas and a desire to seek opportunities not limited to national borders. While his parents' lives of relative privilege might be considered atypical of black Americans in the late nineteenth century, as was the city of Jacksonville of Johnson's description, his parents were not entirely free. Everyday life was informed by racial distinctions and restrictions that were sometimes starkly defined. By the time he was a young man, Johnson had been both victim of and witness to the worst of white southern practices in an event that profoundly informed his self-concept.[6]

In Jacksonville, in 1901, a great fire that required the assistance of the

National Guard made clear the underlying racism governing the small southern city. As the fire swept across Jacksonville, it became clear that the fire department would prioritize putting out the blaze in white neighborhoods, letting the flames run their course in the black part of town. The National Guardsmen who were drawn from the closest available southern states to enforce martial law as a precautionary measure, since the town's infrastructure was all but destroyed, reinforced these racist sentiments, propelling them to the point of violent racial conflict. Johnson found himself at the center of this conflict. During a meeting with a woman journalist in a park that had been untouched by the fire, he was brutally assaulted by a band of Guardsmen who had appointed themselves enforcers of the southern law banning interracial encounters of any kind, especially those between a white woman and a black man. A terrified Johnson recognized the magnitude of racial hatred just under the surface of life in this small southern city, a hatred that could at any time erupt with violent consequences. No matter his education or standing in the community, these qualities were rendered mute to those who saw only his exterior and what it symbolized to their prejudices and fears. In any case, the course of his life was suddenly and dramatically altered, for Johnson was profoundly shaped by this incident, which occurred when he was beginning to settle into a life in the city as principal of Stanton School, a position he had assumed after graduating with a bachelor's degree from Atlanta University in 1894. Shortly after the event, he took a leave of absence from his post, resigning from it just months later.

When he arrived in New York City in 1901, Johnson found himself in the middle of the artistic ferment of Black Bohemia in the Tenderloin district, an area of mid-Manhattan roughly stretching from 42nd Street to 23rd Street running north to south and Fifth Avenue to Seventh Avenue running east to west.[7] Its theatrical and musical culture was an important part of the quickening of national black culture beginning at the turn of the twentieth century. As an active agent in Black Bohemia, Johnson helped to shape the first black cultural renaissance of the modern century. Here, Johnson, his brother, John Rosamond Johnson, and Bob Cole formed the Cole and Johnson Brothers trio in 1901, with Rosamond and Bob as performers as well as composers and James as the unseen lyricist. The center of black musical and theatrical talent from the turn of the twentieth century well into the teens, Black Bohemia was lined with clubs catering to different clienteles: boxers and jockeys, performers, and an interracial crowd partly composed of white sightseers and performers. Among these clubs, one stood out to Johnson as the most "professional" and also the most popular; to Johnson it characterized the accomplishments and larger significance of the arts movement of which he was a part. Ike Hines's club featured photographs and lithographs of accomplished, well-known blacks—from the nineteenth-century abolitionist Frederick Douglass to the twentieth-century jockey Peter Jackson—on the walls of its parlor. According to Johnson, there were so many portraits of black men and women who had ever "done anything" that they covered the walls. Many of them were autographed, thus summoning their subjects' presence as appreciative audience members in Hines's club. The space was set up for entertainers in the front and dancing in the back, and it encouraged a kind of art from its black artists not yet permitted beyond its walls, virtuoso performances in theater and song that allowed those artists to forget the limiting stereotypical roles imposed upon them by popular taste.[8]

Cole and Johnson Brothers walked a fine line, unsettling the prevailing taste for the racist stereotyping of the minstrel show with bold, innovative compositions that mocked American jingoism while exploiting the perceived exoticism of African and "other" cultures of darker complexion. (Their unproduced, unpublished musical comedy, "The Czar of Czam," is one such example, featuring the American opportunist Dr. Hocus Pocus in a location closely resembling the Philippines.)[9] They also strategized to produce universally appealing numbers that could be sung by and addressed to anyone, regardless of their racial identity. The trio aimed to entice some of the most popular vocalists of the day, from May Irwin, Anna Held, and Faye Templeton to John McCormack, Arthur Collins, and the duo of George Walker and Bert Williams, to perform these songs (fig. 1). Their "Under the Bamboo Tree" became so infectiously popular that it was taken up by Yale students as a football chant with altered lyrics, and it was also incorporated into T. S. Eliot's "high modernist" *Sweeney Agonistes*. Whether or not those who sang its lyrics recognized the tune as the spiritual "Nobody Knows the Trouble I've Seen," they were stirred by its catchy melody and lyrics: "If you like-a me like I like-a you . . ."[10]

Borrowing well-known tunes that belonged to everybody, ragging them up, and infusing them with playfulness was a frequent practice of the trio and allowed them to draw on their individual talents as com-

1. Sheet music, Cole and Johnson Brothers, "Lindy." Faye Templeton, emerging darling of the theatrical stage, starred in this 1903 performance. Oddly, Johnson never again mentioned the trio's work on this early Broadway success. Photograph courtesy of the James Weldon Johnson and Grace Nail Johnson Papers, Collection of American Literature, Beinecke Rare Book and Manuscript Library, Yale University.

posers. While Rosamond was cautious about making this practice their hallmark, James was proud of the appropriative measures that such borrowing facilitated, for not only were the spirituals and work songs given new voice by their compositions, they were sung enthusiastically by white as well as black people. The trio as a whole had differing ideas about the future of music and of black culture in the United States. Bob Cole was convinced that Latin American and Caribbean culture would strongly inflect and fuse with black culture here, that ragtime and habanera rhythms would merge, and he wrote this idea into one of their earliest hits, the production *The Evolution of Rag-Time*.[11] Rosamond saw great opportunity in operatic interpolations that elevated black composition as a whole, and he inserted arias from operas by Giuseppe Verdi and others into ragtime, much as Antonín Dvořák, Frederick Delius, and other European classical composers inserted spirituals into their symphonies.[12]

These differences in outlook among the members of the prolific, popular trio were productive ones and reflected the artistic ferment of Black Bohemia. The Marshall Hotel, run by proprietor Jimmie Marshall, became a meeting place where artists convened to discuss their roles as authors, artists, and performers. It was located about ten blocks north of what was considered the uppermost boundary of Black Bohemia and drew aspiring black artists uptown to West 53rd Street between Sixth and Seventh Avenues. Johnson and his brother rented rooms there that served as a social hub for some of the most notable composers, performers, and poets of the day: Harry T. Burleigh, Will Marion Cook, Theodore Drury, Paul Laurence Dunbar, and Bob Cole, who lived just a few doors away from the hotel. In their conversations, they often considered their roles as artists in changing the world of music and theater in order to advance the status and regard of black people as a whole. Their positions were unique and diverse, and there were differences of personality and opinion that led to formal rifts, such as between Cook and Cole concerning artistic originality and whether to imitate white performances. Yet the diversity of opinion demonstrated a vital intellectual culture. According to Johnson, even with their differences, the group agreed on the importance of convincing managers that a black company could play a first-class theater, even Broadway. All of these composers aspired, optimistically, to use their artistic talent as a means of breaking through constraints that were both an artistic and a social reality.[13]

Black Bohemia's cultural force took on widespread significance in late December 1908 with Jack Johnson's triumph as heavyweight champ of boxing—a victory that helped form a national black culture and consciousness.[14] Jack Johnson's victory propelled a collective sense of the "New Negro" that encompassed popular *and* political culture. African Americans recognized in this physically powerful black man a compelling image of a collective, modern black culture that insistently and tenaciously demanded acknowledgment of ability—and mastery—in the context of supremacist calls for a white boxer to take back the title. After winning the title, Jack Johnson would become embroiled in controversy through his marriage to and involvement with a series of white women, emblematizing the perceived threat of miscegenation as the logical consequence of equality for blacks, for which he would pay with time in prison in 1920. Defiant of white supremacist idolization of pure white womanhood, he exploded the myth that only black rape, and not white choice, formed interracial liaisons.

The New Negro Renaissance, the black modernist movement in the arts and concomitant pursuit of civil rights, has often been defined by scholars as emerging in the decade of the 1920s, understood to have been propelled by the Great Migration, the conclusion of World War I, and the summer of racial violence that followed close on its heels in 1919, with more than twenty riots in cities across the United States, what Johnson referred to as the "Red Summer."[15] What constituted the New Negro culture of the twentieth century, however, should be seen as a new century's inclusion of and continuous claim to black culture that commenced in Johnson's Black Bohemian milieu. It must be remembered that blacks generated this positive aspect of national and cultural identity in the context of white supremacist rallying calls, in which Jack Johnson's body became emblematic of the black body's overpowering of the white, the savagery of civilization, and the rapaciousness of black Americans demanding equal treatment. Although most middle-class blacks disapproved of Johnson's activities as a clubgoer, jazz lover, and interracial lover, he nevertheless emblematized the main masculine-centered claim to autonomy of the New Negro era. As Gerald Early writes, "The black badman was now, through Johnson, bestowed with a political and cultural meaning, and his defiance was no longer simply psychopathic. Middle-class blacks, who in large measure were responsible for the nationalistic formation of the concept of the New Negro, rejected many aspects of Johnson—notwithstanding, his simple act of assertion, his refusal to accept his place became an element of the New Negro."[16]

The public perception of the emerging music of ragtime was part of this fear, too. Ragtime was often seen as either mechanized and soulless or excessively primitive; in either case, it seemed to overtake the body involuntarily through the "syncope"—a loss of consciousness as well as the loss of unstressed vowels from within a word. In the ragtime debates, the syncope was both the rhythm of syncopation, which includes pauses and elisions of stress, and the moment in which the heart literally skips a beat.[17] Because of the widespread reception of ragtime as a physical phenomenon with real consequences of racial transference, it is crucial to consider its culturally and politically shaping influence on the more familiar 1920s Renaissance. The New Negro Renaissance of the 1920s emerged from this earlier decade of modern black life and black popular culture and from the fascination, fear, and violence in American reception of this culture. The 1920s Renaissance gained direction and force from Black Bohemia's newness and self-concept, of which both Johnsons were a part. James W. Johnson personally knew Jack Johnson from the clubs of Black Bohemia before the latter had garnered his boxing title. Unlike most other middle-class African Americans of the time period who sought to distance themselves from working-class folk and popular culture—and anything that might be construed as stereotypically black, such as physical strength alone—James Johnson had embraced the successes of black jockeys and prizefighters before Jack Johnson's victory. Because of his experience as a popular songwriter, Johnson also recognized the force of popular culture in shaping social and political attitudes, for better or for worse.

As a mere visitor to the city in August 1900, before his permanent move, Johnson witnessed the riot in New York and saw firsthand the repercussions of the dehumanizing stereotypes of the minstrel show that were popularized and perpetuated by such hits as Ernest Hogan's "All Coons Look Alike to Me." The three-day riot, begun after the death of a white plainclothes policeman in the Tenderloin, demonstrated how popular lyrics, even those intended as parody, easily became "epithets of derision," in the words of Johnson. Hogan, a skilled veteran performer of the minstrel stage with a dazzling set of teeth and a hit song "Love, Love, Love," for which he had been best known, found a minor composition preempting all his prior work as it was appropriated for the purpose of the white mob in New York City. The policeman, Robert Thorpe, had attempted to arrest a woman as she waited on a street corner for her boyfriend, Arthur Harris. Harris emerged from a saloon to find a white man grabbing his girlfriend and fought with Thorpe, stabbing him twice—wounds from which he died the next day. Using the names and lyrics it knew of black performers—including Johnson's brother, Rosamond, and his partner, Bob Cole—the mob conducted a "brutish orgy," resulting in an undocumented number of brutal beatings by the mob and the New York police, who were accused of fomenting violence rather than dissipating it. New York lawyer Deborcey Macon Webster would seek legal redress for black citizens from the police following this riot.[18] About eighty black New Yorkers later submitted affidavits stating that they had been attacked.[19] The white mob of hundreds conducted their violent assault on streetcars, in businesses, and on the street, and the riot appears to have dissipated only after foul weather on the third day, August 16. A musician who was a friend of Johnson, his brother, and Cole was badly beaten during the riot, suffering blunt force trauma to the head from which he never recovered. Rosamond, who had taken to the street to bring his friend to safety, had the uncanny experience of hearing himself referenced by the angry mob, along with the names of the most popular musicians of the day, including Bert Williams and George Walker. "During the height of the riot," Johnson would later write, "the cry went out to 'get Ernest Hogan and Williams and Walker and Cole and Johnson.'"[20]

The culture of Black Bohemia began a northward move in 1910, resulting in a developing local theater scene in Harlem during the teens. The move uptown wasn't a conscious choice—it was an obligation. Exiled from Broadway partly as a result of the riot, black performers had no choice but to survive by their own wits. If white theaters would not have them, they would make their own. In later years, the result of this move was described as a developmentally necessary shift. By the 1930s, it had become common to describe the move from the Tenderloin north to Harlem, and from earlier forms of music into ragtime, as a process reflecting black culture's maturation—as music publisher Edward B. Marks would claim in his memoir, *They All Sang*. But the Tenderloin's move northward coincided with black culture's exclusion from Broadway, just as the heyday of the Renaissance period of the 1920s coincided with black theater's return to Broadway, with the unprecedented hit *Shuffle Along* in 1921. Therefore, the forced exile of black theater from downtown, as well as its warm reception there almost a decade later, describes not simply black culture's maturation but also a profound shaping by its reception by mainstream and predominantly white venues and audiences.

Johnson told this story in *Black Manhattan*, published in 1930 by Alfred A. Knopf. His working title for the composition was "The Story of the Negro in New York," and in addition to being the story's narrator, Johnson was one of its participants. Giving himself a diminished, almost silent role, like his part in Cole and Johnson Brothers' performances, Johnson described the centrality of modern theatrical experience to the continued quest for civil rights and full artistic expression by black agents. According to Johnson, black artists' innovations of the modern century in theater were extended into other areas of expressive culture, such as ragtime. Modern American culture and modern black culture, mutually produced, needed to understand each other in order to understand the century culturally and historically. Johnson grounded his artistic identity and work in this larger biography of the city of New York and the American nation. He was fond of NAACP colleague W. E. B. Du Bois's review of *Black Manhattan*, in which Du Bois wrote: "There are few more fascinating stories, and Mr. Johnson tells it from the point of view of one who, in its most important years, helped to make it; who was personally acquainted with its chief characters, and *who felt perhaps more than others, its rhythm and meaning*."[21]

Johnson's preference for Du Bois's review suggests not only his investment in the physical experience of black expressive culture (and his approach to this experience in his writing, in this work and others, as variation, improvisation, and mutability) but also his ear for the music and rhythm of modern life, an ear that Johnson was to make use of in the composition of his literary works. He believed in, and composed his works to convey, rhythm and vibration as a scientific rather than a purely empathetic connection between bodies. Speaking to the Georgia State Industrial College for Colored Youth in June 1916, Johnson stated: "The things I want to say to you are written in no book, they are the things that are in my heart, the things that are sure to find a vibrating response in yours."[22] He later confirmed the "science" of physical connection through sound. In his annotations in the 1920s to the 1912 edition of his *Autobiography of an Ex-Colored Man* as he contemplated its revision and republication, Johnson thought he should "explain the scientific basis" of the ragtime introduced by the novel: "This was ragtime music, then a novelty."[23] When the novel was reissued in 1927, Johnson decided to leave the passage as it was, since it sufficiently referred to the unavoidable physical response to ragtime by any listener: "It was music that demanded physical response, patting of the feet, drumming of the fingers, or nodding of the head in time with the beat." In making this argument, Johnson embraced rather than rejected negative evaluations of ragtime, redirecting attention toward the mutuality of the listening experience while asserting that "modern music and modern dancing are both Negro creations."[24]

The value and influence of black culture in American life, hotly contested, was demonstrated by the first decade of the new century's so-called ragtime debates, during which time Cole and Johnson Brothers wrote their most popular musical numbers. Was ragtime primitive or mechanical? Ragtime's critics often contradictorily described it as both. Either way, it was strongly felt to be irresistible to the body of the listener, governing bodily response and movements while preempting the mind. The intense hostility to ragtime as an art form in some quarters acknowledged the fear of black cultural presence, manifested in the physicality of the music as it was described as a threat to—or invasion of—the body. Finely attuned to this response, Johnson saw theater, inclusive of musical comedies, musical performances of ragtime, and other forms of expressive culture, as a profound enactment by black performers of American citizenship, claimed against the cultural violence and demeaning roles that were forced upon them. While Johnson observed that "sound has a wider appeal than sense"—reasoning, narrative—it also had the potential, when combined with the material of a "word writer" like Johnson, to alter contexts of American racism, one body at a time.[25]

As Ronald Radano astutely observes, for modern black writers such as Du Bois and Amiri Baraka, "music, and particularly song . . . symbolized a body claimed; arising out of the body, it offered a kind of realness amplified by its material relation to the truth of one's enslavement."[26] Johnson, taking up Du Bois's *The Souls of Black Folk*, a text that deeply influenced Johnson as he began to write what he called "more serious work"—his *Autobiography of an Ex-Colored Man*—explored whether the assimilation of black Americans could be traced through the evolution of its music. Decades later, Baraka in *Blues People* (1963) and Albert Murray in *The Omni Americans* (1970) also took up this question, confirming that the music's relation to the political presence of black culture in the American nation has been a lasting, crucial exploration from the time that Du Bois initiated it in 1903. But, as Radano makes clear in his groundbreaking work on race and black music, there has been a tendency to answer this question in a uniform way. "The listening public has remained remarkably committed to a particular story about black music," one that affirms its aesthetic value as "the last bastion of authenticity," formed in isolation and out of distinctiveness. He cautions against this inclination to narrativize and render uniform the wide range of music's expressive capacities and meaning: "Black music's dynamism and heterogeneity become not limitations but sources of potency. . . . That is, the qualities that define black music grow out of a cultural ground that is more common than many may realize, and this commonality is all the more so in racial circumstances, where practices literally exist in the air and are thus accessed more easily than in other forms of cultural expression."[27] Writers like Du Bois and Johnson affirmed the ironic relationship between desire and deprivation voiced through music, which was perceived by the authors more as a social phenomenon than a natural occurrence. Johnson in particular, as a writer and a lyricist, saw tremendous possibility in the use of sound as a means of generating a new subject position for black artists and modern black culture as a whole. "The highest contribution made by the race to art is Negro music," Johnson wrote in 1916 during the Great War.[28]

Both as an artist and a political leader, Johnson was acutely aware of the great attention that was given to his physical presence despite his many achievements in public life and as an artist. He used this attention to place emphasis on the incongruity of public focus on his exterior, given his considerable accomplishments, by cultivating a gentlemanly persona and entering settings that were previously racially exclusive—white hosts' homes and women's clubs, for example—and sending his books to white readers and the White House's Presidential Library. For this he was confirmed as a cultural diplomat who could put anyone at ease while speaking his mind. Johnson's diplomacy in broaching hotbed issues surrounding interracial relations in American political and domestic life was unsurpassed, his dynamism as a public speaker on these concerns widely remarked. He was appointed to provide biographies of major political and artistic figures by Knopf and Viking Press and by influential whites such as Edwin M. Embree, head of the Julius Rosenwald Fund. Observing the import of his too-short life, Johnson's publisher Alfred A. Knopf called him "the most distinguished Negro in the United States."[29] On June 28, 1938, the *New York Times* called him "one of the foremost of Negro leaders." Oswald Garrison Villard observed:

> Always he was supremely modest and usually of quiet demeanor until he was aroused. There was nothing servile but also nothing aggressive about him. He was the personification of good manners and courtesy, whether receiving a president of another republic, or American naval authors astounded to find a Negro who spoke both French and Spanish in charge of an American consulate, or some ill-mannered, overbearing Southerner. But there was a limit beyond which no man could go with him and not pay well for it. He could fight. Here was no coward, no toady—just a fine gentleman, as well bred and cultured as any man who ever came out of a Southern manor-house, or a mansion on Washington Square.[30]

This public impression of Johnson's gentlemanliness was tied to his visual, physical presence—he manifested at all times an acute awareness of his relation to others that observers always considered in creating a profile of the man. Slight and not quite tall, Johnson still came across as authoritative, manly, and suave. Public reception of him reveals a preoccupation with his "rhythmic" physical movements, the "tonal harmony" of his attire, the "half-closed eyes of the visionary," demonstrating the white and black public's preoccupation with his authority in relation to black manhood.[31] For blacks, those perceived rhythms were controlled movements in a precariously disordered and hostile American political context. For some whites, Johnson's grace and rhythm in his physical presence similarly represented his physical control, a comforting marker of his difference and distance from whites and from the out-of-control movements of prizefighter Jack Johnson.

And James Weldon Johnson responded to this bodily preoccupation, an overwhelmingly visual cultural force, playing to the role of black male authority. Photographs of Johnson from throughout his life attest to this: the Black Bohemian, a well-dressed, goatee-and-watch-chain-wearing portrait taken after his arrival in New York (fig. 2); the diplomat in Nicaragua, pictured beside his lower-ranking white American subordinate; the literary man of the *New York Age*, sporting a pearl tie pin and with cigar in hand (fig. 3); the NAACP field secretary, a publicity head shot where he looks straight into the camera, almost seeming to address it confrontationally while leaning on his fine fin-

2. *"To my lifelong friend J. D. W." Portrait of Johnson circa 1903 inscribed to Judson Douglas Wetmore, Johnson's close friend and the basis of the narrator of his* Autobiography of an Ex-Colored Man. *Photograph courtesy of the James Weldon Johnson and Grace Nail Johnson Papers, Collection of American Literature, Beinecke Rare Book and Manuscript Library, Yale University.*

3. James Weldon Johnson. Photographed by Patton Studios, circa 1914. After leaving his post in the American consulate, Johnson redoubled his efforts at musical comedy. He also began to write a regular editorial column for the New York Age. *Photograph courtesy of the James Weldon Johnson and Grace Nail Johnson Papers, Collection of American Literature, Beinecke Rare Book and Manuscript Library, Yale University.*

gers (fig. 4); and, finally, the author at his desk and at home—again featuring his sartorial flair and delicate features—in photographer Doris Ulmann's portrait (fig. 5). Black and white viewers' physical scrutiny of Johnson indicated their preoccupation with black mastery of roles previously understood as the exclusive domain of whites: Bohemian, American Diplomat, even Author. Jack Johnson's heavyweight title in boxing in 1908 had merely underscored the idea of black physical mastery, power, and presence in American life. James Weldon Johnson, as NAACP executive, author, and university educator, drew a similar amount of attention, yet he was the focus of interest quite distinct because of his involvement in literary and political realms that reached beyond the prizefighter's range.

By 1938 Johnson's reputation as a civil rights leader, both within and outside of the NAACP, was unparalleled. Progressive whites such as E. George Payne, dean of New York University's Teachers College, and Thomas Elsa Jones, president of Fisk University, believed their friendship with Johnson to be indicative of a future of respectful understanding between blacks and whites—so much so that, starting in 1934, Johnson was hired by Payne to integrate the faculty by joining it and the curriculum of NYU Teachers College with his lecture course titled Negro Contributions to American Culture. From 1934 until his death, Johnson brought several artists to his NYU classroom to guest lecture, ranging from the widely anthologized poet Countee Cullen to the young and aspiring visual artist Romare Bearden. Johnson had made a distinct practice of advocating on behalf of their rights as American citizens while championing the value of black culture to American life, a platform that black civic leaders expected Johnson to continue in the lean years of the Depression. From the 1930s until his untimely death, younger black artists sought Johnson's approval of and participation in their creative endeavors, hoping that he would facilitate and promote their publication and review. These efforts encompassed their entrance into venues ranging from new literary magazines to a new theater arts guild.

Johnson's death was keenly felt by such artists because "perhaps no one of the so-called intelligentsia among the Negro group was more a friend of the stage and the Negro actor than James Weldon Johnson"—and, taken more broadly, of the black artist—wrote his eulogizer William E. Clark in the *Negro Actor*, the organ of the newly formed Negro Actors Guild. As an influential political leader whose past

4. James Weldon Johnson. Publicity photo, National Association for the Advancement of Colored People, 1926. Three different "head shots" were taken of Johnson. This one features his fine fingers, which were admired by Carl Van Vechten, Mary White Ovington, and others. Photograph by James M. Allen. Photograph courtesy of the Author Publicity File, Alfred A. Knopf Papers, Harry Ransom Center, University of Texas at Austin.

5. James Weldon Johnson at his writing desk. Photographed by Doris Ulmann, 1929. Ulmann visited Five Acres, Johnson's summer home in Great Barrington, to produce publicity photos of the author for the publication of Johnson's Black Manhattan. *Photograph courtesy of the Author Publicity File, Alfred A. Knopf Papers, Harry Ransom Center, University of Texas at Austin.*

careers included a life centered on the stage, Johnson recognized both the artistic wealth and potential of black performance and "some of the hazards of the stage," as Clark put it.[32] Well aware of the power of sheer physical presence as well as the importance of diplomacy effected through contact, Johnson had garnered a reputation among blacks of "bringing people in," a practice he had begun when he became the first black member of the previously all-white executive committee of the NAACP and continued at Fisk and New York Universities. For example, Walter White, William Pickens, and others assumed critical positions in the NAACP as a result of Johnson's influence. During the Depression, Johnson used his position as distinguished chair of creative writing to attempt to persuade Fisk University to hire artist Romare Bearden, poet Sterling Brown, and a Haitian acquaintance as instructors in art, literature, and French. Johnson, an appreciator of fine art by African Americans—he owned woodcuts by Horace Pippin and had viewed painter Archibald Motley's New York exhibit in 1926—also "brought in" portraits of black artists to cover the walls of his study at Fisk University, replicating the cultural world of "The Club," which he described in his 1912 novel, *The Autobiography of an Ex-Colored Man*, and observed as an artist at Ike Hines's club in Black Bohemia.

Nevertheless, for Johnson, physicality had to be understood and to operate as more than mere bodily presence. Therefore, while engaging visual culture—Johnson's imperative referencing of the American cultural preoccupation with visual, physical difference—he uses sound to bridge that presumed separation. As Salomé Voegelin observes, "The ideology of a pragmatic visuality is the desire for the whole: to achieve the convenience of comprehension and knowledge through the distance and stability of the object. Such a visuality provides us with maps, traces, borders, and certainties, whose consequence are communication and a sense of objectivity. The auditory engagement however, when it is not in the service of simply furnishing the pragmatic visual object, pursues a different engagement. . . . Listening discovers and generates the heard."[33] Hearing thus became for Johnson a bodily experience representative of the physical and material conditions of the modern soundscape as well as a dematerialized transference of culture through auditory exposure. Physicality became for Johnson a practice of creating and sounding out what otherwise could not be said, making the visual presence of black artists on his wall at Fisk resound with his writings, ranging from *The Autobiography of an Ex-Colored Man* and

Black Manhattan to his autobiography, *Along This Way*. The reverberating effect of these works in chorus with each other creates an aural composition, directing image and text into sound.

James Weldon Johnson's Modern Soundscapes attends to the author's literary representation of sound and to his body of works as the site of new sounds, as cultural productions of sound running counter to those of mainstream American culture. Johnson's writings represent the American soundscape in order to present the imperative that it be mastered by its auditors, self-mastery of sound providing a judgment of and orientation to one's cultural-sonic environment. However, while presenting an ideal, uniform relation of the self to sound, Johnson represents these American sounds as a source of multiplicity and diversity, often developing a framework for the interracial transfer of sound. Never precisely fixed to the page, sound can operate as either cultural violence or creative force. Johnson uses sound—noise, speech, languages, music—to register the multiple stories of African American expressive culture through their extremes of sonic experience. For Johnson, the import of these stories is that they draw attention to the mutual contingencies and interdependence of American and African American culture. He took advantage of sound's inherently contradictory and transgressive nature in the naming and framing practices of his works, using "Aframerican" to situate black culture as foundational to and fused with American national culture while referencing "American" as the Americas, indicating the overriding presence of black culture beyond national boundaries. Johnson used sound as a formal aesthetic practice in and between his works, presenting its multiplicity and repetition as an unbounded, interracial cultural practice as much as it is a racially distinct cultural history.

Ragtime was one important site for the negotiation of Johnson's varied public personae, from American diplomat to Broadway composer. Ragtime offered Johnson the testing ground for his developing aesthetic of sound in his writings, and it explained black culture to Americans while helping Johnson understand himself through popular culture. Johnson's relationship to ragtime and popular culture was a vexed one, though, as we shall see. Leaving off lyric writing for Broadway musicals in an official capacity in 1906, the year in which he became diplomat to Venezuela, Johnson still had a hand in composing works that helped him stay connected to the theater, as evidenced in a number of unpublished manuscripts from this time period. Numerous incomplete compositions on ragtime, including "The Story of Ragtime," "The Origin and Development of Ragtime," "The Contents of a Name: Mozart Jackson, Composer," in addition to the finished work by Cole and Johnson Brothers, *The Evolution of Rag-Time*, composed between 1902 and 1916, indicate ragtime's centrality to Johnson's writing as not just a modern idiom but a systematic approach to black expressive culture as a whole.[34] In this period, Johnson began to formulate personae to carry this culture and these compositional ideas; he named them Mose Jenkins and Jasper Johns. At the same time, he experimented with authorial personae, naming and renaming himself in a series of improvisations. The ragtime variations of James William Johnson reflected the larger cultural history out of which ragtime emerged, informed by psychic and physical violence directed at black Americans.

Oddly, Johnson, who in 1902 had authored the lyrics to the lavishly produced show *The Evolution of Rag-Time* in collaboration with Bob Cole and Rosamond Johnson, never again acknowledged this work in any of his writing. One of their earliest group efforts, it was produced by the New York theatrical moguls Klaw and Erlanger in 1903 and featured the emerging theatrical star Faye Templeton. Its final act included a richly clad chorus line that brought the work to a grand conclusion with an elaborate cakewalk. The production was an overwhelming success, with positive reviews in major New York newspapers such as the *New York Times*.[35] The composition of this work, and ragtime more generally, was central to Johnson's creation of himself as an author, with subsequent drafts such as the short stories "The Contents of a Name: Mozart Jackson, Composer" and "The Story of Ragtime" indicating Johnson's desire and commitment to work through sound in his writing.

As archival materials demonstrate, after leaving the consulate in 1913 he redoubled his efforts in composing musical comedies and romantic operettas, remaining an author and an audience member of such performances for the rest of his life. There is no explanation for Johnson's thoroughgoing silence about *The Evolution of Rag-Time*. This early and successful work was obviously pivotal to Johnson's developing career as a Broadway lyricist, and yet he fails to mention it in any of his works, indicating that it was suppressed by him as thoroughly as his near lynching. It could be that Johnson, although he promoted and repeated everywhere his assertion that black culture had made its central and defining contribution to American culture through music—

major works from 1912, 1915, and 1922 bear this claim in roughly the same phrasing—felt the pressure to respond to and be a part of jazz criticism in particular and felt uncomfortable having his musical affiliations and assertions reduced to the example of ragtime, which bore such a strong association with lower-class people and behaviors. While undercutting these presumptions and the association of ragtime with the low-down by affiliating its musical form with composition and its "classically trained" composers and performers, Johnson still felt uneasy with the reception of his message by an audience with the potential to reduce and diminish its significance as an intellectual *and* popular form. Despite his silence about *The Evolution of Rag-Time*, the archives show Johnson's deep investment in sound as the central mode of production for his writings. *James Weldon Johnson's Modern Soundscapes* demonstrates his continued involvement through careful attention to Johnson's many unpublished manuscript drafts, outlines, and scripts as well as to the subtle references to popular culture in his published works.

This study not only explores this unexplained silence but also reveals how Johnson's autobiography, *Along This Way* (1933), has often been taken at face value, resulting in the virtual repetition of his representation of his life in its pages—even to the extent that phrases from this work often appear verbatim in critical works about him. Rather than understanding that work to be a figurative presentation of his life, scholars have used Johnson's autobiography to "explain away" rather than embrace the complexities of the author and his works. While Johnson is partly responsible for this obscuring—so that, as I show, his silences in the published works and his experimentation in the manuscript drafts are important—I discovered that he also intentionally presents something more complex, leaving it to readers to "hear." The key to this more subtle hearing resides in attention to Johnson's intentional repetition of passages from work to work, which results in a reverberating effect that uproots the notion of discrete works/creations or indeed generically distinct works, such as poetry or prose, fiction or nonfiction.

Indeed, Johnson favored biography and sound, generically impure forms, as the vehicles for the delivery of his works. I argue that Johnson's innovation was to create a distinct narrative of modernism through the use of sound in his works, a narrative that initiated dialogues about modern black identity and black modernist practices. Reflecting the contingencies of African American culture and expression, the foregrounding of sound permits Johnson to address modern black experience through the embodied and ephemeral, through individual and communal voice, and through the productive tension—not binary—of sound and print. Unbeknownst to his readers—existing only in manuscript draft—and a full forty years before Albert Murray coined "Franklin Delano Jones" to underscore the perceived anomaly of black culture in America, Johnson had invented "Mozart Jackson."[36] Johnson's name both references the perception of the anomaly of "Negro" and "American" and appeals to the notion of sound and musical composition to assert black expressive culture's centrality to Americanness.

For Johnson, I argue, biographical practice is in many ways a practice of sound. A life is, after all, improvisatory, never complete, and never fully known; it is shaped by contingency, a series of interpolations. Biography is at once the self and another self, the life and its interlocutor. Much as Johnson regards his works as biography and sound to be taken up by others, I intend to replicate Johnson's modernist practices of sound and biography; that is, I am aware that the archives have been used to "authenticate" arguments, and I intend a rather different use of them here. It is precisely because knowledge about Johnson has become rigidly codified by claims to ownership of his image and legacy that it has become necessary to listen intently and re-sound his compositions.

Rather than present an exhaustive biography of Johnson's life, I have selected the most productive, pivotal years of his artistic output in order to privilege his formation of an aesthetic based on sound. His works between 1900 and 1938 are treated roughly chronologically here, but they resound through each other. As this study moves from work to work, a more complex, reverberating aesthetic emerges. Each chapter begins with a little-known fact or suppression, whether experiential or textual, Johnson's or his critics', and locates this alongside a creation by Johnson. I initiate this structure with Johnson's thirty-year silence on his experience of a near lynching in his native Jacksonville, the central event that shaped his life and creative output. Images of Johnson are included as a competing narrative to sound, the overwhelming visual presence of Johnson representative of his iconic (and sometimes caricatured) status as a public figure, a profile that, while informing our understanding of him, has overshadowed his modernist creation of a sound-based aesthetic.

There is a sound accompaniment to this work, available through the

University of California at Santa Barbara's cylinder preservation and digitization project, where many of these compositions are available through streaming. Here, the cylinder recordings of Johnson's compositions as part of Cole and Johnson Brothers are brought to life, directing his lyrics through the voices of popular white and black vocalists such as May Irwin, John McCormack, and Bert Williams.[37] As such, this Website is a partial embodiment of Johnson's aesthetic project and an essential companion to this study.

Calling *The Autobiography of an Ex-Colored Man* (1912), his first published book, "a biography of the race," Johnson used the biographies of Rosamond Johnson, Bob Cole, and other performers in the musical world of New York's Tenderloin to shape its soundscape. Chapter 1, "Biography of the Race: Musical Comedy and the Modern Soundscape of *The Autobiography of an Ex-Colored Man*," shows how Johnson created a text-based soundtrack by borrowing the technique of musical interpolation from Cole and Johnson Brothers' compositions, creating musical and biographical interpolations in his innovative text. In his initial formation of a sound-based aesthetic in his writing, Johnson suggests the necessity of music's alteration and reinvention through performance. The novel's innovations in sound break with the visual culture usually associated with black identity in early twentieth-century America and instead emphasize an interracial framework of American sound that is based on musical interpolations between black and white cultures.

Chapter 2, "Cultures of Talk: Diplomacy, Nation, and Race in *The Autobiography of an Ex-Colored Man*," extends this discussion through the novel's privileging of linguistic heterogeneity, as the novel performs black expressive culture at the margins of the nation. An early Cole and Johnson Brothers composition, *The Evolution of Rag-Time*, initiated this practice of articulating a heterogeneous modern black identity through multiple discourses and locations. The novel's linguistic framework suggests the continuous alteration of black culture through the conversation of the novel itself.

For Johnson and his intimates, the body was the source of modern experience, conveying meaning not through the visual but rather through the internal experience of the body—especially through sound, which, by emphasizing its transference, inhered difference. Chapter 3, "The Interpolated Body: Passing, Same-Sex Talk, and Discursive Formations in *The Autobiography of an Ex-Colored Man*," discusses the way in which sound significantly relates to these practices of bodily interpolation and crossover, showing that auditory exposure necessitates the alteration of its listeners.

In the late 1910s and 1920s, Johnson composed such a work as could be altered and carried forth by performance and musical composition. *God's Trombones* (1927), Johnson's collection of sermonic verses, was his interpolation of the music and rhythm of "the old-time Negro preacher." In emphasizing this work's continuation through alteration, Johnson sought its adaptation through musical and dramatic compositions and its translation into French and Norwegian. These adaptations encouraged Johnson to reissue *The Autobiography of an Ex-Colored Man* in 1927, which was translated into German in 1928. Chapter 4, "Cosmopolitan Travels: Diplomacy, Translation, and Performance in *The Autobiography of an Ex-Colored Man* (*Der weisse Neger*, 1928) and *God's Trombones*," shows how, speaking *through* Johnson, these creative alterations and extensions respond to the interpolation introduced by the author in his work. Johnson develops the idea here that biography and sound are constantly expressed but are not contained within the pages of a print text; they are a series of unending extensions, from the folk to the preacher, the preacher to Johnson, the author to other composers and performers.

From 1917 to 1927 Johnson was simultaneously writing poetry and groundbreaking prefaces to anthologies of black poetry and spirituals, both of which formed the basis of his black modernist poetics. Chapter 5, "Framing Black Expressive Culture: Prefaces to *The Book of American Negro Poetry*, *The Book of American Negro Spirituals*, and *God's Trombones*," shows how Johnson created his poetics by extending the boundaries of black cultural expression from nation to hemisphere, English to Spanish, even from poetry to prose in order to encompass the vernacular, linguistic, and performative registers of black culture. His preface to *The Book of American Negro Poetry* (1922; revised edition, 1931) and his prefaces to *The Book of American Negro Spirituals* (1925), *The Second Book of American Negro Spirituals* (1926), and *God's Trombones* (1927) show this work of continuous reframing.

Chapter 6, "'The Creation': *God's Trombones* and Johnson's Formation of a Black Modernist Poetics," discusses the composition of this work as the initial basis of *God's Trombones* and the site of Johnson's formation of a black modernist poetics. Although a linguistic project that seems to resemble the work of white modernist contemporaries of Johnson, this work underscored the resistance of black expressive culture to notation by focusing on the transmission of language through sound rather than image. The sounds *God's Trombones* conveys are elusive, in-between, unrecordable except by their transmission through the voices of others.

Black Manhattan (1930), a text shaped by intimate oral histories far more than its readers realized, presents theater as an expansive notion, shaped by performers' and audience members' experiences, not just Johnson's, as evidenced by his research, composition, and attribution of source information through others. Chapter 7, "From Noun to Verb: Black Phonographic Voice in *Black Manhattan*," shows how, using the combined forms of biography and autobiography, the text evolved to become a work distinct from Johnson's subsequently published autobiography, *Along This Way*. Addressing multiple performative registers through the figure of the black performative body in the American theatrical world, Johnson enunciates and practices an aesthetic of modern black identity that can be called black phonographic voice: sound and graph (or recording) are connected through the body of the performer that is Johnson's subject and through the author Johnson.

In Johnson's autobiography *Along This Way*, his self-referencing is more complex than it at first seems: this work uses all of Johnson's prior autobiographical references in his other published works in the new context of his lead role, effectively creating an autobiographical collage that is sound-based and contingent upon prior, now simultaneous, selves and their expressive forms. Chapter 8, "Not the Story of My Life: *Along This Way*," shows how Johnson's autobiography becomes the story of modernity told through sound-based collage. Johnson uses sound to convey experience as reverberation, using the corporeal and sensory registers of sound to emphasize its interracial cultural transfer. Reaching beyond print, Johnson used his autobiography as a diplomatic gesture, sending the work to President Franklin Delano Roosevelt for inclusion in his library.

The afterword, "Remembering James Weldon Johnson," describes how, responding to his sudden, unexpected death, Johnson's memorial service in Harlem, a mass ritual of grieving, dramatized his aesthetic of sound as shared experience and appropriately extended his works into acts of remembrance—in sermons, song, and performance. At the same time, his estate and some of his most ardent admirers began a process of archiving Johnson that would stretch well into the twentieth century (it may still be going on). As a result, his interpolated biographical practices were hardened into concepts like "tradition," "progress," and "original," which have led to his rigid categorization by the critics who succeeded him, from Sterling Brown on, and by the efforts of his widow, Grace Nail Johnson, to control the use of his name and image. Meanwhile, the competing acts of the public continue to call upon Johnson in the present tense, as if he is still living, and to celebrate his works' investment in interplay and sound. Reverend Joseph E. Lowry's benediction at the inauguration of President Barack Obama pointedly demonstrates Johnson's continuing active presence as a creative force in American politics and life, from his opening lines, taken from Johnson's lyrics to "Lift Ev'ry Voice and Sing"—"God of our weary years, God of our silent tears, Thou who has brought us thus far along the way"—to his concluding ones—"Lord, in the memory of all the saints who from their labors rest, and in the joy of a new beginning, we ask you to help us work for that day when black will not be asked to get back, when brown can stick around—(laughter)—when yellow will be mellow—(laughter)—when the red man can get ahead, man—(laughter)—and when white will embrace what's right."[38] The interpolation of the people's experiential wisdom, a biblical proverb, and Johnson's lyric sounds resounds in Reverend Lowery's inaugural benediction, creating a timeless tribute to Johnson and his aesthetic.

Biography of the Race
Musical Comedy and the Modern Soundscape of *The Autobiography of an Ex-Colored Man*

Sound is an intrusive phenomenon: we can avert our eyes from sights we wish to ignore, but sounds enter our ears whether we want them to or not. If sound contributes to the shaping of the self, then control of the acoustic environment—the "soundscape"—becomes an issue with real social and political consequences.
—David Suisman, *Selling Sounds*

Jacksonville, Florida, 1901. It was a sunny May day, the kind with a playful breeze that shifts direction north, east, south, and west. Midday found most laborers at the Cleaveland Fiber Factory returning to work from their lunch break, only to discover the entire city block, including the factory, aflame. By the time the playful breeze had turned into gusts and gales, the fire had spread through the neighborhood, where most of the city's black residents lived, and was heading south along the coast through the business district. Eight hours later, the fire had done most of its damage: the business district was destroyed, and an estimated ten thousand people were homeless. Jacksonville's Great Fire of 1901 proved to be one of the worst disasters in Florida's history and was the largest urban fire in the southeastern United States.

Johnson recalls of the incident that the firefighters spent "all of their efforts saving a long row of frame houses just across the street on the south side of the factory, belonging to a white man named Steve Melton."[1] Narrating the event in his autobiography, *Along This Way* (1933), Johnson repeats: "By nightfall more than one hundred and fifty blocks are smoldering ashes. But the row of frame houses belonging to Steve Melton, across the street from the fiber factory, is still standing" (*ATW*, 164).

When the fire engulfed Jacksonville, Johnson, age thirty, and his brother, twenty-eight, were riding their bicycles from the eastern part of town toward the west. As they rode in the early afternoon light, they noticed a dark curl of smoke that, as they grew closer, "spread wider and grew darker" (*ATW*, 163). Johnson continues: "Now, under and through its mass we could see the lurid glow, and now, the vivid, darting tongues of the flames" (*ATW*, 163). As people fled, the Johnson brothers attempted to save Stanton School, the all-black grade school of which Johnson was principal, in order to make it a refuge. Not one fireman has been spotted in the area of the school, however. Johnson writes: "Where are the firemen? We haven't yet seen a single stream of water. We run down into the street, where we find a half-dozen firemen pulling on a line of hose. We appeal to them. . . . [T]hey look at us listlessly and make no answer" (*ATW*, 163). Concluding that the school "is to go," Johnson and his brother take out the principal records of the school and rush home, where they find their house, located in a predominantly white neighborhood, safe, "whether due either to the reported race prejudice of the fire chief or to the direction of the wind" (*ATW*, 164).

For two weeks, the Johnson household was a temporary shelter for about twenty-five friends and acquaintances—"our family," as Johnson calls them (*ATW*, 165). Displaced and destitute families needed relief in the form of money, food, clothing, and lodging, which the Johnsons and others provided. In the meantime, civil law had been replaced with martial law, drawing state militia from western and central counties to form a "provost guard," in the words of Johnson. Tensions were high, as journalists descended to capture incidents of "looting" by making black men and boys pose for pictures. According to Johnson, he was forced to move on by members of this guard when he attempted to persuade the men and boys not to pose for the pictures.

This would not be Johnson's last confrontation with one band of the roving militia. His second clash had far more serious repercussions because it involved the taboo of black male interaction with a white woman. The beautiful woman journalist Johnson met two weeks into Jacksonville's occupation by National Guardsmen had dark eyes and hair that "blanched the whiteness of her face" (*ATW*, 165): she was a black woman who appeared to be white. Seeking Johnson's advice as a prominent black citizen of Jacksonville and as a fellow journalist, she brought an article she had written on the fire that addressed its impact on the city's black population. They met on a hot afternoon in June after one of Johnson's long days of work as director of a commissary distributing provisions. Taking the streetcar to Riverside Park, Johnson searched for the journalist at the waiting station; not finding her, he reboarded the car, only to see her approaching from a distance. His abrupt exit from the streetcar just as it had begun to move away from the station was noted by the conductor and motorman, as was the appearance of the woman he was meeting.

Describing this incident, which propelled his northward migration, thirty-two years after the event, Johnson shifts from the past tense to narrate his immersive experience with the militiamen—and "Death"—in the present tense. This chapter falls roughly at the center of Johnson's life narrative and effectively splits his story—his life—into a before and an after. Johnson describes his near lynching in 1901 as an experience in which the sense of sound preempts the visual:

> I became conscious of an uneasiness, an uneasiness that, no doubt, had been struggling the while to get up and through from my subconscious. I became aware of noises, of growing, alarming noises; of men hallooing back and forth, and of dogs responding with the bay of bloodhounds. One thought, that they might be hunters, flashed through my mind. . . . And yet, what men would hunt with such noises, unless they were beating the bush to trap a wild, ferocious beast? . . . The noises grew more ominous. They seemed to be closing in. My pulse beat faster and my senses became more alert. . . . I lose self-control. But a deeper self springs up and takes command; I follow orders. . . . They surge round me. They seize me. They tear my clothes and bruise my body; all the while calling to their comrades, "Come on, we got 'im!" And from all directions these comrades rush, shouting, "Kill the damned nigger! Kill the black son of a bitch!" . . . As the rushing crowd comes yelling and cursing, I feel that death is bearing in upon me. (*ATW*, 166–67)

Reasoning dialogue is not permitted in this scene ("There is the truth; but there is no chance to state it; nor would it be believed"): the mob will not know that they have not captured the wild beast of their imagination but rather a pillar of the community, educated, esteemed, a school principal and civic leader, until "a quivering message from intelligence to intelligence has been interchanged" with the officer who brings Johnson for judgment before "Major B——," a member of the Florida bar, of which Johnson too is a member. Johnson stresses that he "felt the waves of mental affinity" with this young lieutenant (*ATW*, 168). It is Johnson's brother, Rosamond, only "to whom I confided what had taken place." "I never mentioned it to my parents," he wrote (*ATW*, 170). His father and mother, who passed away in 1912 and 1919, respectively, never knew of the incident. Describing the impact of the trauma, Johnson writes that he was years in healing "this horror complex": "For weeks and months the episode with all of its implications preyed on my mind and disturbed me in my sleep. I would wake often in the nighttime, after living through again those few frightful seconds, exhausted by the nightmare of a struggle with a band of murderous, bloodthirsty men in khaki, with loaded rifles and fixed bayonets. It was not until twenty years after, through work I was then engaged in, that I was able to liberate myself completely from this horror complex" (*ATW*, 170).

The work to which Johnson refers was both political and literary. In 1917 Johnson's work on the Dyer antilynching bill carried him to the nation's capital, where he advocated for it amongst political leaders. While it narrowly passed in the House of Representatives, it failed in the Senate through filibuster. Johnson was deeply disappointed in this outcome and felt personally betrayed by the senators who had promised their support and then declined to defend the bill. In this same year, Johnson wrote and published his antilynching poem, "Brothers," in which the lynch victim is permitted an observation prior to his burning that is only heard by his murderers once the event has transpired and he is dead: "What did he mean by those last muttered words, / 'Brothers in spirit, brothers in deed are we'?"[2]

Johnson's silent, reverberating experience of a near lynching, known only to him and his brother, suppressed and internalized for years, finally formed the stunning soundscape of modernity that he presents in his first book-length publication, *The Autobiography of an Ex-Colored Man* (1912). The dominance of sound in the depiction of his near lynching in his autobiography, *Along This Way*, thirty years after the fact testifies to Johnson's privileging of sound throughout his lifetime and his major works as expressive of individual feeling and of an ethos linked to social, political, and cultural attitudes toward sound at the turn of the twentieth century. Johnson's near lynching was a pivotal moment in his life and provided the catalyst not only for the shape and content of his writing but also for the evolution of a new aesthetic, one based on sound and incorporating multiple voices. His experience furnished a deeply personal and emotional imperative for enabling the voices of black people to be heard in national and international conversations.

In 1901, "shortly after" Johnson's horror with the Jacksonville militia, both brothers moved to New York permanently (*ATW*, 170). Some three years prior, Rosamond Johnson, or "Rosie," the impetus to his brother James's entrance into the world of musical comedy at the turn of the century, had drawn Johnson into the composition of their first musical comedy, *Toloso*, in 1898. Rosamond had just returned from his studies at the New England Conservatory and a year touring in musical producer John W. Isham's *Oriental America* (New York to London, 1896–97), a "forerunner" production that called upon the talents of "the best trained Negro singers and musicians then available" (*ATW*, 146). The brothers, traveling to New York City in the summer of 1899 during James's vacation from his position as principal of Stanton School, met the influential publisher of "light opera" Isidore Witmark but decided against publishing with his office for fear their comic opera would be stolen (*ATW*, 150). The brothers didn't find a market for *Toloso* as an opera, but, according to James Weldon Johnson, they "ultimately adapted most of the single numbers, and they were produced in one or another Broadway musical show" (*ATW*, 151). In the meanwhile, Rosie's composition of "My Castle on the Nile" for Bert Williams and George Walker's *Sons of Ham* in 1900 led to a partnership with seasoned composer and performer Bob Cole. The collaboration between Cole, Rosie, and James resulted in the composition of over two hundred songs, many of them the hits of the day sung by the most famous vocalists of the day—May Irwin, Anna Held, Marie Cahill, Lillian Russell, Arthur Collins, John McCormack, and others. The brothers, together with Cole, made a name for themselves in Black Bohemia's Tenderloin district, composing, among other hits, "The Maiden with the Dreamy Eyes" (1900), "When the Band Plays Ragtime" (1901), "Oh, Didn't He Ramble" (1902), "Under the Bamboo Tree" (1902), "Nobody's Lookin' but the Owl and the Moon" (1902), "Congo Love Song" (1903), and a setting of Johnson's poem "Sence You Went Away" to music (1906). They also knocked out "You're Alright, Teddy" (1904) for Theodore Roosevelt's presidential campaign, perhaps riffing on Isidore Witmark's "President Cleveland's Wedding March" of 1886 and Axel Christensen's "popular rag version" of Mendelssohn's "Wedding March," published in 1902. The former was a moderately successful tune that marked the beginning of the Witmark brothers' success as publishers and commodifiers in the sheet music industry, while the latter was an already-established institution of ragtime instruction books by the well-known "popularizer" and "mercenary" who "dwarf[ed] the efforts of serious composers."[3] The "Wedding March" reappears in a prose composition that was forming in Johnson's mind in this imaginatively fertile and briskly competitive period, set to paper beginning in 1903–4.

Johnson, Rosie, and Cole took part in the creation of musical compositions that targeted the American mainstream by virtue of their universal appeal—the invocation of "dreamy eyes" without reference to race, for example.[4] But their compositional practice also included parody and musical quotations, as in Rosie's composition "Tell Me, Dusky Maiden"—in his view, "a 'travesty' on the song 'Tell Me, Pretty Maiden' by Leslie Stuart," a Gilbert and Sullivan production that had been performed just a little over one year earlier.[5] This combination of compositional practices underscores the trio's awareness and manipulation of popular songs as commodity, their success measured by the sale of sheet music, the sheet music promoted by the publishers through images of the songs' performers.[6] Moreover, as David Suisman notes, "by the 1890s, modifications in typeface and graphics and the increased use of chromolithographic printing made sheet music covers livelier" than its earlier forms had been and were used in the printing of Cole and Johnson Brothers' lyrics such as "Congo Love Song," which features a lithograph portrait of the popular Broadway performer Marie Cahill on its title page.[7] Cole and Johnson Brothers' compositions entered the publishing world as sound and text and as a commodity that rendered them both physically present (in the title page's acknowledgment of the composers' names) and absent (in the transferring of vocal presence to the popular performer inscribed on the page).

Cole and Johnson Brothers' parodic treatment of and allusion to other popular tunes of the day, while representative of the vast musical array of the modern soundscape at the turn of the century, also indicates the dialogic and innovative nature of Rosie's compositional practices as part of the trio. Speaking of their "curious partnership," in which "the three of [them] sometimes worked as one man," James noted that "there was an almost complete absence of pride of authorship" (*ATW*, 156). While James characterized their unique compositional practice as one in which ownership was shared, musicologist Thomas Riis has since described Rosie's skills as a pianist and a composer as peerless, indicating his distinct contributions to the trio's compositions.[8] Riis describes Rosie's "harmonic language" as "consistently richer than that of his contemporaries, Will Marion Cook excepted." According to Riis, Rosie "speaks a sophisticated harmonic language and varies his forms. . . . [T]he general style of several of [his] songs suggests the cultivated flow and high-toned romantic sentiments of some operetta tunes."[9] For example, in Cole and Johnson Brothers' "My Castle on the River Nile" (1901), Riis finds an approximate quote of a "brief chord progression from 'Su! Del Nilo al sacro lido,' a chorus from Verdi's *Aida* about the River Nile."[10] In his "gestures beyond the typical use of the tonic, dominant, and subdominant"—"the movement to a triad on the flatted-third scale degree," "deceptive cadence," and "varied series of chords to arrive at the dominant," in Riis's examples—Rosamond demonstrated his extraordinary care as a composer, even in "light" tunes for Broadway.[11] More than this, Rosamond "had a penchant for incorporating art-song elements—arpeggiated chords richly larded with sevenths and chromatic passing tones, and numerous expression and tempo markings."[12] Indeed, Rosie's skills as an original composer and arranger call for greater acknowledgment than they have been given.

Working from the knowledge that every parlor had a piano, Cole and Johnson Brothers—and sometimes just Rosie and James—wedded catchy lyrics to irresistible melodies. Cole and Johnson Brothers' immediate predecessors in America's popular music tradition, it should be remembered, had authored works that had fallen exclusively in the minstrel tradition. According to Johnson, the transformation effected through their compositions was twofold: a class takeover and transformation of black art's status, and a racial and aesthetic alteration of the American soundscape. As James described it, their compositions were a distinct departure from "the Negro songs then the rage . . . known as 'coon songs'": Cole and Johnson Brothers made a conscious "attempt to bring a higher degree of artistry to Negro songs, especially with regard to the text" (*ATW*, 152).

But it was much more than this. Most significant was the trio's compositional practices of text *and* harmonics as well as what Alexander Weheliye calls "the repetition *of* difference, wherein the original/copy distinction vanishes."[13] Not only in "musical quotation" or "outright parody," which suggest the unmodified or explicit presence of "original" musical numbers, but also in the more complex practice of re-sounding and reinscribing prior works, the trio altered the aesthetics of sound both in their practice of collaborative authorship and in the songs they produced.[14] It is well to remember that Cole and Johnson Brothers often "stole" the spirituals and well-known folk songs, syncopating, arranging, and rewording them as modern tunes, as in the case of "Under the Bamboo Tree" ("Nobody Knows the Trouble I've Seen").[15] As artists, they engineered the "parlor takeover" of American musical sensibility to include and, indeed, begin to sing in the voice of its black composers.

This chapter is a story of the radical alterations in musical composition, performance, publishing, and recording between 1900 and 1912 of which the trio Cole and Johnson Brothers was a part and in which it was commercially successful. But it is also a story of sound as an innovative expressive mode and code in Johnson's novel, used to reference feeling and the shaping of larger social attitudes about music, race, and American culture. Johnson composed *The Autobiography of an Ex-Colored Man* with a veritable soundtrack. While the presence of music in the text has often been treated thematically as representing the narrator's loyalty and right- or wrong-mindedness as an aspiring composer and performer through his affiliation with classical (white) or spiritual (black) music, the text offers something far more complex, if only Johnson's readers will hear it.

The Ex-Colored Man of Johnson's novel is born to a formerly enslaved, fair-skinned woman and her master's son in Reconstruction Georgia, "a few years after the close of the Civil War."[16] Removed to Connecticut when his father marries a well-to-do southern woman, the narrator attends a grade school that instructs blacks and whites and discovers his talent and proclivity for musical expression. He is classically trained as a pianist. When he is nine years old, a shaming event at school reveals the narrator's racial status as a Negro to him. Suddenly he begins to read on the "theory" of being a Negro and an American—and on "what my nation thought of me" (*AECM*, 47, 27)—through W. E. B. Du Bois's *The Souls of Black Folk* (1903) and Harriet Beecher Stowe's *Uncle Tom's Cabin* (1852).

The narrator's early exposure to music through his mother's singing of the spirituals with piano accompaniment provides the counterbalance to his publicly shaming exposure as a Negro in the school classroom. The spirituals form a powerful emotional bond between the narrator and his mother, even before he knows the name or significance of these songs.

When he later masters ragtime, which excites his mind and body, the narrator seems to have found a vehicle for his creativity that also pays well, as he performs in the clubs of Black Bohemia and for hire at leisure-class white parties; his signature piece, Felix Mendelssohn's

"Wedding March," is a hit in both settings. After being party to an unfortunate incident at the club in which a white woman is murdered by her black lover, the narrator is easily exchanged with his white patron's servant, Walter, and travels with him to Europe as his attendant and for-hire musician; he is asked to play all hours of the night, although he is paid "liberally" for doing so (*AECM*, 73).

While in Paris, the narrator attends the opera—Charles Gounod's *Faust*—and discovers by his side his father and a never-before-seen half-sister of ethereal and compelling beauty. Distraught and unable to force their acknowledgment of him, he stumbles into the street and seeks "oblivion" through alcohol.

Seeking his life purpose, the narrator is struck by a revelation in Germany, where, as he is exhibited by his patron, a German musician forces the narrator from the bench and plays the narrator's ragged classical piece "varied and developed . . . through every known musical form." The narrator decides that he will "take ragtime and ma[ke] it a classic" in much the same way (*AECM*, 85).

In pursuit of black expressive forms, the narrator returns to the American South, attending camp meetings and gathering sermons, spirituals, and work songs. In this setting, he bears witness to the lynching of a black man, an experience that roots him to the spot in horror and mirrors his public shaming in his northern classroom. This event permanently resounds in the narrator's psyche, even as he abandons his pursuit of the dream of becoming "a great colored man" through "varied and developed" musical compositions incorporating black expressive culture (*AECM*, 29, 85). Instead, he becomes an Ex-Colored Man.

In the North, the narrator courts a seemingly white lover to whom he must tell his secret if he is to marry her. He meets his lover through her voice, which he hears from another room; when he enters and beholds the singer, he is astonished by her "dazzlingly white" beauty, and more especially by the "tones of such passionate color" that emanate from her frail body (*AECM*, 117). Together, they write and perform Chopin and "Chopinesque" compositions, and while they are temporarily separated by the trauma of the narrator's racial revelation, they are also reunited by their dual performance of Chopin's thirteenth nocturne. They are married and have two children; his wife dies giving birth to their second child, assuring that the secret of their racial status is kept from the children and continuing the cycle of experience that the narrator himself has endured in the modern soundscape. He is but an observer, not a composer, of the spirituals as they are given a name and significance in their performance before him at Carnegie Hall as the novel closes.

The Autobiography of an Ex-Colored Man was published anonymously in 1912 by Sherman, French and Company, a Boston publishing house. Its sales were small, its reviewers vocal and opinionated in their pronouncements on whether the matter of the work was truth or fiction. The work was presented as a "human document," an autobiography of the child of a former slave and her master's son who is light enough to "pass" as white. Reviewers were taken in by Johnson's provocation, a sensationalist staging of the life-narrative confession of a man claiming to be "ex-colored." Weighing in on the side of fiction were reviewers who found that the narrative was prone to "embellishment," as was "the African" who ostensibly had authored the story as well as those who declared outrageous the claim that any black person could pass as white. On the side of truth, reviewers found the autobiography similar in substance if not in spirit to Booker T. Washington's autobiography of progress and uplift, *Up from Slavery*, while others found that the narrative attested truthfully to the internal "black peril"—the "threat" of black access to white strongholds of political power and social and economic opportunity, often articulated through the stereotype of black males as sexual predators. The "black peril" was considered a greater threat to the American nation than the "yellow peril" of Chinese and Japanese immigrants, the "threat" of an unwanted population of Asian immigrants who were perceived as a danger to national stability.

Johnson's decision to publish the work anonymously had to do with his desire for it to succeed. He wrote his brother, Rosamond, his wife, Grace Nail Johnson, one of his literary mentors, William Stanley Braithwaite, and his Atlanta University classmate George A. Townes that the secret of his authorship had to be kept so that the book would not "fall flat" when it became known that the author and the narrator were not the same and that the work was therefore fiction.[17] Nonetheless, behind the scenes, Johnson was its tireless promoter. He convinced Brander Matthews, his former professor of dramatic literature at Columbia University, to write a review of it in *Munsey's Magazine*, a popular, fiction-oriented monthly in which Matthews extended Johnson's ruse of authenticity by feigning ignorance of the author's identity. Johnson's work, informed by post-Reconstruction sentiment toward blacks, also anticipated the wave of eugenics-oriented works that would articulate fear and hatred of a changing social fabric brought on by an upwardly mobile black population and the influx of immigrants of the "wrong sort" (Irish, Italians, eastern Europeans), such as Madison Grant's *Passing of the Great Race* (1916) and Lothrop Stoddard's *The Rising Tide of Color against White World Supremacy* (1920). The "Negro question" had a particular urgency to the American nation at the time of Johnson's composition of *The Autobiography of an Ex-Colored Man*, and Johnson profited from it, if not by actual sales, then by the discussions that ensued from the most provocative elements of the work: interracial romance, interracial marriage, and "the dangers of race amalgamation," as one reviewer put it.[18]

Although the preface to the work is signed "The Publishers," Johnson wrote it himself. It sets the terms that are developed by the narrative and advances the claim that "prejudice against the Negro is exerting a pressure, which . . . is actually and constantly forcing an unascertainable number of fair-complexioned colored people over into the white race" (*AECM*, xlv). In the preface, Johnson anticipated and even defined the reception of the novel by his white audience. Johnson used the preface to echo the significance of such introductory material in African American slave narratives, in which the preface traditionally was authored almost exclusively by whites and served as a paternalistic, controlling, and authenticating document.[19] In these prior works, white spokespeople and/or publishers attested to the truth of the life narratives, disclaimed intervention in the telling of the story, and yet competed with the life story for control of—authority over—the work as a whole. Johnson's preface continues this tradition on the surface, competing with the life story of the narrator, but its fictitiousness also dismantles the custom; it is mastered to facilitate the reception of the work as a real life story, a "human document." Indeed, it is possible to read Johnson's preface as a tacit gesture toward the crisis of the narrator within the work's pages: to possess the sonic literacy that would enable him to identify, interpret, and understand the creative, artistic experience of being black and locate (and value) himself as an authority within this culture, or to dissolve, rather than build, his self outside of this. For nineteenth-century slave narratives, the acquisition of the subject's literacy paralleled his or her claim to human, and not object, status and thus his or her emancipation. The theme of literacy, a prevalent feature of nineteenth-century slave narratives, is here transformed to a twentieth-century struggle to acquire sonic literacy that the narrator shares with his white reading public—the ability to recognize, reveal, and value black culture and appreciate and cement its bond to American culture. The invisible preface writer, Johnson, like his invisible narrator at the conclusion of the work, challenges his audience to read—or hear—between the lines, to investigate the work's method and values of interpretation. The reader is asked to travel this distance with the narrator of the work.

The narrator not only translates Spanish, French, and German, evidencing his own claim of the "adaptable" nature of "the Negro" to his various national homelands, such as the "black West India gentleman in London" who is "in speech and manners a perfect Englishman" and "natives of Haiti and Martinique in Paris" who are "more Frenchy than a Frenchman" (*AECM*, 91). He himself must, in the words of the preface, be "initiated" into "the freemasonry . . . of the race" (*AECM*, xlv), moving from racial ignorance to a "theory" of race and then its "practice" (*AECM*, 47). Thus, even while the preface claims the narrator as a representative of untold numbers of blacks, he has more in common with his white readers as an outsider in terms of the experience of it. As he himself is inducted into the "freemasonry" of the race, into "the inner life of the Negro in America" (*AECM*, xlv), the narrator similarly promises to "initiate" his readers by revealing his discoveries and experiences to them. In the preface and the narrative itself, Johnson drew from the nation's tradition of letters—from the slave narratives, American autobiography, and abolitionist speeches and a novel—to forge this connection. Writers such as Booker T. Washington, Josiah Henson, Benjamin Franklin, Harriet Beecher Stowe, and Wendell Phillips, to name a few, were drawn together (explicitly and implicitly) in *The Autobiography of an Ex-Colored Man* to mediate racial experience while creating a new, intervening literature about race in American letters by improvising on their stories through the use of sound.

In *The Autobiography of an Ex-Colored Man* Johnson deliberately chose the symbolic elements of slavery and Reconstruction, North and South, to develop and transform the full range of literary antecedents that spoke to race. Foremost of these were the slave narratives, which themselves borrowed from American variants of autobiography—"rags to riches," self-improvement, and captivity narratives—to weave their life stories into the nation's literary fabric. They created metaphors and personae that spoke to the reality of their condition as enslaved, fugitive, and free people in the American nation, a model that Johnson acknowledged and developed by introducing the living paradox of the "ex-colored" man and the metaphor of invisibility. The narrator, born "a few years after the close of the Civil War" (*AECM*, 3) and unaware of his racial identity as a "Negro" until its public revelation in a school classroom when he was nine years old, speaks to this metaphor of invisibility. Suddenly he notices the black children with whom he attends school; he has "a very strong aversion to being classed with them" (*AECM*, 15), but he also realizes and appreciates the difficulty of their—and his—position. As the narrator learns of his new identity as a black man, he learns also "the dwarfing, warping, distorting influence" that forces "each colored man" to inhabit the outlook forced upon him by "other eyes," the "viewpoint of a *colored* man" rather than that "of a citizen, or a man, or even a human being" (*AECM*, 13). This form of invisibility means that while blacks must know what whites think of them, "the colored people of this country [are] a mystery to the whites"; "there is one phase of him which is disclosed only in the freemasonry of his own race" (*AECM*, 14). Johnson's metaphor of a self who was simultaneously conspicuous and invisible to the American nation shifted racial discourse by attempting to concentrate on the as-yet-unknown perception of blacks as citizens, men, and human beings.

The first sentence of the preface that Johnson sent to Sherman, French and Company in draft form stated that "*The Autobiography of an Ex-Colored Man* is a document that reads stranger than fiction (or—romance?)," effectively referencing both Josiah Henson and Harriet Beecher Stowe in their appropriative exchanges.[20] In this draft version, Johnson specifically alluded to the slave narrative of Henson, a narrative that went through several editions and was revised and expanded by the author in 1849, 1858, and 1876. The second edition was significantly revised to announce as its title "*Stranger than Fiction: Father Henson's Story of His Own Life*" (1858) after Stowe revealed that Henson's life story had been one of the sources of her Uncle Tom in *Uncle Tom's Cabin: or, Life among the Lowly* (1851). Henson gradually appropriated Uncle Tom's character, introducing himself as "Mrs. Harriet Beecher Stowe's Uncle Tom" on the title page of the third edition of his narrative.[21] Stowe and Henson engaged in an elaborate staging of mutually authenticating works. Johnson drew Stowe into *The Autobiography of an Ex-Colored Man*—another "stranger than fiction" representation—in an act of appropriation and distancing, simultaneously claiming and altering her story of America.

Johnson referenced the abolitionist movement through Harriet Beecher Stowe and Wendell Phillips, both of whom the narrator reads or listens to as he defines himself and his ambitions. The choice of Stowe's text is significant in this act of self-definition. The narrator, after all, largely defines his perception of self through others' eyes—his mother's, the school's, the lynch mob's—and so *Uncle Tom's Cabin* allows the narrator, at the tender age of nine, to see "who and what I was and what my country considered me; in fact, it gave me my bearing" (*AECM*, 27). This emphasis on the perception of a black man by the outer world—through a national perception that sees him as an outsider, standing in contrast to a black man's perception of himself, his capabilities—is Johnson's exploration of Du Bois's concept of double consciousness (his narrator calls it "dual personality"). The narrator's search for the right sort of hero—he becomes "impatient and disappointed" that, "notwithstanding the great power [Christ] possessed, he did not make use of it when . . . he most needed to do so" (*AECM*, 16)—mirrors Johnson's dispensation of the martyred Uncle Tom as a feasible contemporary race hero. It is possible to argue that at the close of the work the narrator himself is a martyr, a potential race leader whose vision of racial uplift, involving his heroic role as a black composer in the public sphere, is buried by the impossible odds of mob terror. And yet the narrative contains abundant examples of race leaders, including Booker T. Washington as well as the narrator's classmate "Shiny," whose heroism runs counter to the narrator's action, revealing his cowardice.

Moreover, in referencing *Uncle Tom's Cabin* Johnson defines his work in relationship to Stowe's. As Johnson later told his New York University students in his course titled the Negro in Literature, he "would mark the beginning of vital literature based on Negro life with *Uncle Tom's Cabin*." Stowe, Johnson observed, drew her material from previously published slave narratives. According to Johnson, Henry Bibb's narrative, and Josiah Henson's, "went far in providing inspiration and material for Harriet Beecher Stowe's *Uncle Tom's Cabin*, which, after all, is a slave narrative done on a grand scale in fiction."[22] In coming to the defense of Stowe against critics who find her work "fiction" and "direct misrepresentation," his narrator controversially agrees with the extremes of goodness and badness, which could easily be defined as stereotypes, represented in her work's pages. "I believe that there were lots of old Negroes as foolishly good as [Uncle Tom]," he writes while also observing, "I do not think it takes any great stretch of the imagination to believe there was a fairly large class of slaveholders typified in Legree." He calls *Uncle Tom's Cabin* "a fair and truthful panorama of slavery" (*AECM*, 27) because it presents multiple types of slaves and slaveholders. The ambition of Johnson's narrator, emphasized by the preface, is to present a portrait of the race that is "composite and proportionate"—that is, balanced and comprehensive (*AECM*, 1). Rather than emphasize "either his virtues or vices," Johnson's work claims that it will choose no sides in the "race question" but rather present "conditions as they usually exist between the whites and blacks to-day" (*AECM*, 1). Thus, *Uncle Tom's Cabin* is positioned as a precursor and *The Autobiography of an Ex-Colored Man* as an improved and updated version of it.

Johnson knew of the imbalanced use of propaganda in relationship to blacks, which defined the limitations of *Uncle Tom's Cabin*. Stowe's work was, after all, the nation's first best seller after the Bible. In his 1915 essay "*Uncle Tom's Cabin* and the Clansman," Johnson noted the public welcoming of the debased stereotype of a black man in a work adapted to film (*The Birth of a Nation*), whose dissemination also justified the brute violence enacted against him in Jacksonville: "Here comes a stupendous moving picture play that seriously attempts to hold the American Negro up before the whole country as a degraded brute, and further, to make him the object of prejudice and hatred." The essay concludes with a plea that colored citizens not allow the film to "misrepresent and vilify us as a race." Observing that a dramatic production in Atlanta of *Uncle Tom's Cabin*, coinciding with a reception for *The Birth of a Nation* at the White House, was forced to transform itself into an "Old Plantation Days" piece, its "offensive parts . . . expurgated," Johnson makes a strong statement that extreme stereotypes of either sort—good or bad—do a disservice to the race, as they can be misused, and either extreme can be ignored in favor of the other.[23] The narrator, traveling through the South a second time, observes that "log cabins and plantations and dialect-speaking darkies are perhaps better known in American literature than any other single picture of our national life. . . . It is almost impossible to get the reading public to recognize [the American Negro] in any other setting" (*AECM*, 91). It is no mistake that the narrator calls this a "picture" and "setting." The popular reception—either praise or vilification—of *Uncle Tom's Cabin* led to the production of "Tom Mania"—trinkets, illustrations, broadsides, and novels in response that rendered Uncle Tom as a spectacle and an object. Responses to Stowe's work also came in the form of countless stage adaptations, including minstrel numbers that had nothing to do with Stowe's original intent or character.

A young Johnson had been witness to this rage for Uncle Tom. Johnson later recalled: "*Uncle Tom's Cabin* was the first play I ever saw," under the stars on his first trip to New York City in 1884 at the age of twelve or thirteen.[24] Johnson's recollection was made known nowhere in any publication; it was his New York University Teachers College students with whom he shared this significant milestone in a course called the Negro in American Literature. The concept of this course and the context of this disclosure of personal experience with popular culture reveal Johnson's view of his work in *The Autobiography of an Ex-Colored Man* as a contrast to stereotypical presentation, as one that altogether dispenses with it by engaging the American soundscape.

Imagine for a moment the shaping influence on a future lyricist, librettist, aspiring dramatist, and novelist of seeing his first play, *Uncle Tom's Cabin*, at an outdoor tent show in New York City. No doubt, this early image was a compelling one for him. Just ten years later, Johnson began collaborating with his brother on their first musical comedy, *Toloso*, and in 1916 Johnson began work on a dramatic production of Uncle Tom based on George Aiken's stage adaptation of Stowe's work (the work was never finished). In all of Johnson's compositions, beginning with his *Autobiography of an Ex-Colored Man*, music and sound generally work to counteract the all-pervasive image of the Negro in the "picture" and "setting" of the log cabin on the plantation so starkly drawn in American literature. In *The Autobiography of an Ex-Colored Man*, this challenge of getting the public to recognize the Negro "in any other setting" entails listening before seeing.

This crucial framework of sound had been introduced by Du Bois's *The Souls of Black Folk*, which featured poetry by British and American authors alongside a musical bar from a spiritual as epigraphs to each chapter. Du Bois did not provide lyrics or titles to the musical notations of the spirituals, forcing his readers to "sound out" their meaning and thematic connection to the poetry. The intellectual parity of each composition was located also in uneasy tension, the spirituals calling for a recognition of humanity and citizenship not yet achieved. Johnson had read Du Bois's *Souls* when it was first published and met the author at a speaking engagement in Atlanta in 1904. What Du Bois had initiated through the spirituals as the basis of his work, Johnson took up in *The*

Autobiography of an Ex-Colored Man as an even more broadly constituted concept of music and sound composition.

As the narrator listens to black performers in a New York club discuss "the time they would compel the public to recognize that they could do something more than grin and cut pigeon wings" (*AECM*, 64), his author's characterization of their dilemma becomes clear. At a time when "no manager could imagine that audiences would pay to see Negro performers in any other role than that of Mississippi River roustabouts" (*AECM*, 64), these artists must "compel" their audience through sound. Experiencing sound as both sensory and corporeal, black performers' sounds are taken into the bodies of their listeners. Johnson's emphasis on ragtime in *The Autobiography of an Ex-Colored Man* facilitates this dual approach to sound, with the ultimate result of its physical entry. The "syncope" of the syncopation that defined the musical form of ragtime during Johnson's era was a pause in the body, or an elision of sounds, in which something else could enter in.[25] Johnson takes this central feature, which propelled the "ragtime debates" about ragtime's value and influence as a cultural form, and embraces it. A novel form of interracialism that does not demand the "loss" of racial claims in its transference, ragtime instead demands, according to Johnson's text, physical interaction through sound. In *The Autobiography of an Ex-Colored Man*, the narrator's first experience of ragtime music brings forth the observation that ragtime "was music that demanded physical response, patting of the feet, drumming of the fingers, or nodding of the head in time with the beat" (60). The dexterity of the player is matched by the physical response of his listener, wedded together in "a most curious effect" as he plays "barbaric harmonies, the audacious resolutions often consisting of an abrupt jump from one key to another, the intricate rhythms in which the accents fell in the most unexpected places, but in which the beat was never lost" (*AECM*, 60). That Johnson wished to emphasize the "science" behind this response in *The Autobiography of an Ex-Colored Man*'s revision for reissue in the following decade underscores his developing commitment to sound as an aesthetic in his works.[26]

By embedding a soundtrack in his 1912 novel, Johnson used the increasing presence and power of sound and music in people's lives at the turn of the twentieth century to force attention to two distinct issues. First, he drew attention to the new musical culture taking shape through which sound was made into musical commodity, which paradoxically would begin to be "*de*materialized at the same time, severed from the tangible realm by the metaphysics of sound recording and by copyright law, which came to recognize property rights in music that were unconnected to physical forms."[27] Second, Johnson's novel forced attention to the experience of sound in the modern world—chosen and imposed auditory exposures, their entry into and impact on the self, and the self's struggle to control this modern soundscape. This is a story about emotion and interiority: "Through the ear, you hear the world in your head, it enters *inside you*; you perceive the world from the inside out, as it were. . . . No matter how rationalized the production of sound going into the ear, it remains an organ conditioned first and foremost by emotional response."[28] (Ragtime, and the debates about its merit or corrupting influence on American culture, would characterize this disembodiment and its attendant cultural [and racial] fears through the "syncope," as Katherine Biers has shown.)[29] These emotions are connected, in turn, to the collective perception of emotional response to sound, to the shaping of the experience of sound through a shared sensibility. However, "hearing more than one piece of music at a time" produces "cacophony, aural chaos," which demands acknowledgment of the presence of multiple sensibilities in the modern soundscape.[30]

In attempting to control aural experience, many forums sought to distinguish between music and noise, and ragtime music often entered these debates. Indeed, as Emily Thompson has observed, "The connection between jazz and the sounds of the city was evident to virtually all who listened in":

> Critics of jazz articulated their disdain for the new music in a curious conjunction of racism and antimechanism. Jazz was attacked "not only for returning civilized people to the jungles of barbarism but also for expressing the mechanistic sterility of modern urban life." It was perceived to reflect "an impulse for wildness" even as it was "perfectly adapted to robots." It stimulated "the half-crazed barbarian to the vilest deeds" while simultaneously constituting "the exact musical reflection of modern capitalistic industrialism." This curious conjunction of things seemingly primitive with those technologically advanced drove not only the critics, but also the most fervent enthusiasts of a culture defining itself as modern. . . . The change that such arguments focused upon was both racial and technological.[31]

The modern soundscape and conversations about it were inflected with the modern American racial landscape, both cultural fears and cultural possibilities. Sound, and debates about it, articulated the paradox of embodiment and invisibility, the cultural and social presence and nonpresence of black Americans. Medical diagnoses of neurasthenia and the syncope—the former considered by historians at the turn of the century to be an "epidemic"—evidenced a "crisis in masculinity" and a "plague of effeminacy." These alarmist cultural observations were responses to the "New Woman" and the threat of "anarchic sexual modernism" as much as they were reactions to the increasing presence of black culture, manifested in the sounds of ragtime.[32] Here, sound and the body merge, willingly or through coercion. The white (male) body, perceived as ailing, weak, effeminate, and subject to the lapses and mental gaps of the syncope, was vulnerable to the entry of black musical sounds and culture. This vulnerable, disembodied, or dispossessed state, contrasted with the literal disembodiment of black Americans in the act of lynching, at its peak in the 1890s (this same period of weakened white men—and women), creates a contradictory, cacophonous modern soundscape in which experiences of sound compete with one another.[33]

James William Johnson's activities as a composer and lyricist of musical comedy at the turn of the century put him at the center of these debates about sound and sensibility. Odd advantages arose for aspiring black composers from the changing state of sheet music publishing and of mechanized recording, as Johnson later recalled in his autobiography. The voice of the composer of works, whether racially ambiguous or specific, was carried by leading vocalists of the day, whose portraits were printed on the sheet music. Suisman writes that this act became the standard for "the systematic promotion of popular songs around the country": "For the publisher, printing the picture of a well-known performer on the cover of the sheet music took advantage of the performer's existing popularity; for performers, having their image on the cover of such sheet music enhanced their reputations."[34] Black composers' disembodiment in this instance could make for greater dissemination of their work.

Johnson's anonymous authorship of *The Autobiography of an Ex-Colored Man* modified this tactic by insistently demanding that its readers hear before they see the author of the narrative. This work uses a soundtrack to address these contradictory, appropriative features of sound, featuring a disembodied performer (the Ex-Colored Man) who is at once a listener and the teller of the tale—its biographer. Critical treatment of Johnson's text has focused on the problematic nature of the narrator and the question of ironic distancing between the narrator and his world, Johnson and his character. But characterizing the interpretative problems of *The Autobiography of an Ex-Colored Man* as exclusively textual issues may not be the most appropriate way to read Johnson's novel—although criticism of the novel rests on this foundation.[35]

More recently, in an effort to free up discourse on the novel, critics have argued for the reading of visual culture in Johnson's work: the "terrible real" of lynching and lynching photography, the "camera works" of new media in the modern age of segregation.[36] These works have deepened our understanding of the novel, but, because they employ a visually oriented framework, they cannot begin to account for the primacy of sound in the novel—the way in which it governs physical responses of the body, cultural crossovers in performance, and the way in which emotion as sensibility and sentiment is used to chart the biography of the narrator, in effect using the "ear" to privilege meaning.[37]

Johnson's work comes with a soundtrack of the narrator's aural experiences, a sequence that might look something like this:

Track 1: A hymn "from the book" (*AECM*, 5)
Track 2: "Some old southern songs," a spiritual with the "freer" female voice of the narrator's mother (*AECM*, 5)
Track 3: "That's Why They Call Me Shine" (1907), lyrics by Cecil Mack (R. C. McPherson) and music by Ford Dabney (*AECM*, 9)
Track 4: A waltz by Chopin (*AECM*, 22)
Track 5: "Toussaint L'Ouverture," Wendell Phillips's abolitionist speech (*AECM*, 28)
Track 6: Sonata in C Minor, op. 13, "Pathétique," by Beethoven (*AECM*, 32)
Track 7: An aural performance of Spanish as "reader" in the cigar-making factory ("badinage," *AECM*, 43) (*AECM*, 46)
Track 8: Ragtime at the club (*AECM*, 60–61)
Track 9: Mendelssohn's "Wedding March," ragged, attributed to white interloper Axel Christensen (*AECM*, 70)
Track 10: "Avant de quitter ces lieux," Valentin's aria in C minor from Gounod's opera *Faust* (*AECM*, 80)

Track 11: Spirituals, sermons, and camp songs, Singing Johnson and John Brown (*AECM*, 103–7)
Track 12: "Chopinesque" compositions (*AECM*, 119)
Track 13: Nocturne in C Minor, op. 48, no. 1, by Chopin (*AECM*, 121)
Track 14: Concert of spirituals performed by the Hampton Institute at Carnegie Hall (*AECM*, 125)

In this soundtrack, speech, silence, and noise matter as much as music does. For example, the narrator's enforced silence in his recognition of his father and half-sister—"I knew I could not speak" (*AECM*, 81)—against the operatic performance of brother and sister in Gounod's *Faust* informs this musical soundscape. It's also evident from this soundtrack that oratory and talk—what the narrator amongst Cubans in Florida calls "badinage" (*AECM*, 43)—are privileged by the narrator and the work as a whole. The imposed aural experience of the man who is lynched—"He . . . gave out cries and groans that I shall always hear" (*AECM*, 111)—constitutes the noise that runs counter to linguistic and musical experience, informing the narrator's modern soundscape by forcing his exposure to the aural. Noise and silence, then, account for much of the novel's exploration of sound and experience. Johnson uses sound—music and linguistic practices, silence and noise—and the conflicts between its central and marginal uses as the basis of modern experience.

Within *The Autobiography of an Ex-Colored Man* and many of his subsequent works such as *Black Manhattan* and *Along This Way*, Johnson characterizes linguistic and musical variety and conflict through sound, using it to describe individual and collective aural experiences of the modern world. His innovative incorporation of spirituals and hymns, classical and romantic scores for piano and opera, abolitionist oratory and Broadway-era songs from New York's Tenderloin, and especially ragtime is used to show their imperative and continuous alteration, both through performance and the conversation of the novel itself. In *The Autobiography of an Ex-Colored Man* and in Johnson's subsequent works, the author uses a biography of the American soundscape—sound and biography—to shape each other, confounding the idea of discrete formal representation through realist or sentimental modes, truth or fiction.[38] What emerges instead is the interplay and conversation among the works themselves as well as their reach beyond to the varied, continual composition of modernity through sound and interpolation and through songs that his novel's narrator is only beginning to hear.

The Autobiography of an Ex-Colored Man brought Johnson's sonic experience of mob violence into one of the first fictive autobiographies in African American letters—although the generic category is somehow inadequate to the task of describing the complexity of this work, which Johnson characterized in a letter to his publishers as "a biography of the race." Written in the first-person point of view, the *Autobiography* uses music and a musician who can "pass" for white (or black) to explore the cultural meaning and value of blackness in the American nation. At the same time, Johnson placed this national assessment of black cultural contributions in an international context by including the perception of American cultural practices—from ragtime to lynching—by European nations such as France, Germany, and Britain. *The Autobiography of an Ex-Colored Man* included these national and international aspects to underscore its relevance to contemporary discussions of how American art, language, and civilization were distinct from British, Nordic, and Teutonic cultures—the so-called stocks from which many white Americans were descended. Such early twentieth-century debates about American cultural heritage and its inheritance bore a direct relationship to ways of perceiving the American social fabric: simultaneous to the discussion of what constituted distinctly American art, there were dialogues about issues of wide-scale immigration, especially from eastern Europe, and the migration of blacks from the South to the North. In Johnson's work, America's international reputation rested on two opposing practices, one constructive and foundational to American civilization, the other destructive to this groundwork for the nation's greatness: the profound art of black America, and the unspeakable brutality of lynching.

This experiential landscape of sound informs Johnson's novel, which he began writing in 1905. There is a compositional practice at work in Johnson's novel that echoes Rosamond's complex, appropriative referencing of the American musical landscape. Indeed, Johnson describes his "job" of attending the theater alongside "jott[ing] . . . down ideas for new work" (*ATW*, 192)—perhaps what would become *The Autobiography of an Ex-Colored Man*—indicating not linear influences on his compositions but the simultaneity of expressive practices. Attending dramatic literature courses at Columbia University under Brander Matthews, Johnson began more extensive writing of the *Autobiography*, producing the first three chapters (*ATW*, 192). Yet critical attention to Johnson's incorporation of the musical landscape in *The Autobiography of an Ex-Colored Man* has flattened out its significance by characterizing musical meaning as a racial distinction between original and copy and treating the references to music in the text as thematic and character-driven, as seen in scholarship as various as Cristina Ruotolo, Eric Sundquist, and Katherine Biers. Rather, Johnson's soundscape offers a theory of narrative through sound. In a process quite similar to how Johnson and Rosie composed many of their hit songs using the tunes of spirituals, the model of the Ex-Colored Man involves more reciprocity and intertwining than critics have attributed to it, and his actions cannot be so readily condemned as the ironic opposite of best-foot-forward racial heroics. As Daphne Brooks has persuasively shown, black performances during the years of Johnson's activities as songwriter and novelist strategically presented the bodies of their subjects in complex relational patterns and through a variety of gestural techniques as a means of renegotiating their marginalization, using their bodies as the site at which "blackness" could be reinscribed and reappropriated from mere spectacle.[39] Within Brooks's study of this remarkable era—one in which she "seeks to make the work of various marginalized cultural performers more audible and . . . 'legible'"—there is ample room to discuss sound and musical composition in Johnson's and Rosamond's works as performative acts that draw attention to the construction of blackness as spectacle as much as to the continual reworking of blackness and whiteness in performance, making a kind of living biography repeated differently each time it is performed.[40]

Suisman observes of the nature of the emerging modern soundscape: "Modern music publishing and commercial sound recording both had strong patriotic accents from the time of their inception. . . . [T]he history of the republic echoes with sounds that have united, sustained, succored, fomented, cajoled, and galvanized in times of both calm and crisis."[41] The performance history of these sounds significantly articulates how these sounds' emergence worked within a culture—if only to recognize, as Joseph Roach has emphasized in his work on performance, that "a fixed and unified culture exists only as a convenient but dangerous fiction":

> The key to understanding how performance worked *within* a culture . . . is to illuminate the process of surrogation as it operated *between* the participating cultures. The key, in other words, is to understand how circum-Atlantic societies, confronted with revolutionary circumstances for which few precedents existed, have invented themselves by performing their pasts in the presence of others. They could not perform themselves, however, unless they also performed what and who they thought they were not. By defining themselves in opposition to others, they produced mutual representations from encomiums to caricatures, sometimes in each other's presence, at other times behind each other's backs.[42]

The performance of these sounds and their reception complicate the idea of sound inhering a single ethos, unless that ethos is defined in part by contradiction, inconsistency, and discrepancy. Steven Feld's study of the Kaluli in *Sound and Sentiment: Birds, Weeping, Poetics, and Song in Kaluli Expression*, for example—a study that writer Nathaniel Mackey cites as foundational to his inquiry into sound and poetics—introduces the idea that sound delivers a prevailing ethos, articulating a collective response to one's environment that develops and shapes individual emotional responses into collective sentiment. But when we discuss sound as a sonic environment in which an ethos—or competing "ethoses"—articulates collective experience, we are talking about power and control of that soundscape as well, including the commodification of music and the abstraction of sound in developing legal discourse such as local noise ordinances and copyright law.[43]

As Roach reminds us of the visual performance of difference, so we may apply it to sonic performances of difference:

> A number of important consequences ensue from this custom of self-definition by staging contrasts with other races, cultures, and ethnicities. Identity and difference come into play (and into question) simultaneously and coextensively. The process of surrogation continues, but it does so in a climate of heightened anxiety that outsiders will somehow succeed in replacing the original peoples, or autochthons. This process is unstoppable because candidates for surrogation must be tested at the margins of a culture to bolster the fiction that it has a core. That is why the surrogated double so often appears as alien to the culture that reproduces it and that it repro-

duces. That is why the relentless search for the purity of origins is a voyage not of discovery but of erasure.[44]

Johnson's use of a ragged Mendelssohn's "Wedding March" in *The Autobiography of an Ex-Colored Man* demonstrates the author's use of performance as biography rather than as a distinction between original and copy. On the one hand, Michael North describes this execution of Mendelssohn's composition as "producing arch parodies of semiclassical chestnuts like [it]."[45] On the other, Biers contrasts the narrator as composer to the black ragtime musician who composes all his works "by ear": "To those in the know, the narrator's transcription of the 'Wedding March' would have provided a stark contrast. It was in fact a real tune published by the leading white popularizer of ragtime, Axel Christensen."[46] While Biers and North do not fall into the trap of discussing music through its characterization in the *Autobiography* (as fully as the others mentioned above), there is still (especially in Biers's example) a presumption that a conversation is being had about original and copy. Contrasting this is North's argument, where he argues that claims to originality within the logic of the work are easily and conspicuously undercut by the inconsistencies facilitated by ragtime.[47] Indeed, there is little certainty that Axel Christensen was the "originator" of the ragged "Wedding March": the pattern the narrator describes, of taking set classical pieces and ragging them, does not point to the extreme polarities of black and white compositions and the misguided, inadvisable act of the narrator in working from the classical rather than the racial (of the spirituals) in creating his ragtime.[48] In Johnson's *Autobiography of an Ex-Colored Man*, Mendelssohn's "Wedding March" was not simply the composer's march but a creation of Bert Williams and Will Marion Cook for their 1906 show *Abyssinia*, in which their composition "The Tale of the Monkey Maid" appropriated Mendelssohn's "Wedding March" from the incidental music for Shakespeare's play *A Midsummer Night's Dream* and perhaps the ragtime composition of Christensen.[49] Johnson, with Cole and Rosamond, would carry the biography of this composition through its multiple enactments of difference, where origins are not so much invented as obscured by quoting, interpolation, and just plain theft of sound—of what could not be owned or controlled but that nonetheless had "real social and political consequences."[50]

Therefore, in this example of Mendelssohn and many others in Johnson's novel's soundtrack, the emphasis of musical composition is on its enactments and performances, whereby difference is emphasized. For example, Shiny is the interlocutor of Wendell Phillips's "rhetorical . . . even . . . bombastic" abolitionist speech, and in its performance he forces the physical response of his listeners, who "actually rose to him" in an "electric" response; and while Shiny is "a natural orator," it is more the juxtaposition of voices, performances, and realities that, when recognized, "loosed the pent-up feelings of his listeners" (*AECM*, 28). More pointedly, Shiny's name alludes to a popular song of the Tenderloin period in black musical production: "That's Why They Call Me Shine" (1907), a song that referenced the New York City riot of 1900.[51] Johnson had been present in New York when the riot occurred, as he later described in his autobiography, *Along This Way*. This song, with words by Cecil Mack (R. C. McPherson) and music by Ford Dabney, was about a man nicknamed Shine who was with George Walker when they were badly beaten during the riot of 1900, according to blues composer Perry Bradford. Shiny of *The Autobiography of an Ex-Colored Man* is class valedictorian of a school that permits the attendance of black students; he is an exemplary leader, an electric speaker, an unlikely but brave opponent, "waging with puny, black arms so unequal a battle" against his white audience's predisposition toward black speaking subjects, "Anglo-Saxon love of fair play" notwithstanding (*AECM*, 29). Johnson repeats and elaborates on the context to the riot and "That's Why They Call Me Shine" in his 1930 work, *Black Manhattan*: "The cry went out to get Williams and Walker."[52]

The idea of sound and its performance, where one voice is superimposed on another in an effort either to control one's sonic environment or to force recognition of its multiplicity, is also found in Johnson's referencing of Gounod's wildly popular opera *Faust*.[53] While there is a good possibility that Johnson saw a performance of Gounod's opera when the Cole and Johnson Brothers trio traveled to France in 1905, Gounod's *Faust* was not simply the version performed in France but the Theodore Drury production in the Lexington Opera House and the performance in the Metropolitan Opera House, where Johnson followed the entire 1902–3 season (*ATW*, 174, 192). Johnson refers to baritone Theodore Drury's "enterprise which annually, for four or five years, gave Negro New York a one-night season of grand opera . . . in the Lexington Opera House for Drury's productions of Verdi, Wagner, Gounod, and Bizet," starting a few years after the turn of the twentieth century (*ATW*, 174). (A decade after the publication of *The Autobiography of an Ex-Colored Man*, Black Swan Records, for which Johnson's father-in-law, John B. Nail, was a board member, would record many of these arias for its label.)

Since Mendelssohn was Bert Williams and George Walker's and Gounod was Theodore Drury's, Chopin, also wildly popular and frequently played in the parlor, registered something more in Johnson's work than a simple marking of the classical as European and of the popular as classical. One would do well to remember the observation made by Ralph Ellison that Duke Ellington's "Black and Tan Fantasy" has "mocking interpolations from Chopin's B-flat minor piano concerto, to which . . . it was once popular to sing the gallows-humored words: Where shall we all / be / a hundred years / from now?"[54] Johnson's use of Frédéric Chopin's thirteenth nocturne (op. 48, no. 1 in C minor) as the courtship song of the narrator and his amour (*AECM*, 123–24) marks the long history of this tradition of interpolation, with the narrator's alteration of the nocturne's concluding chord from a minor to a "major triad" (*AECM*, 124) tracing one of Rosamond's distinct compositional practices of altering phrases from minor to major and ending lines on a triad—here combined into a single action in Johnson's novel. The song in a minor key that seems to be represented by the narrator's sonic experience in the novel—both his fondness for "the black keys" (*AECM*, 6) and the predominating key of C minor present in the pieces the narrator performs and/or hears: Beethoven's "Pathétique" piano sonata, Gounod's aria "Avant de quitter ces lieux," and Chopin's nocturne—is altered as he composes a new resolution in a major key.

In these complex, layered borrowings of music described in the novel, Johnson references the specialized lexicon of the composer, who must know the significance of any musical sequence in order to successfully alter it. Indeed, this is the function of the interlocutor. Johnson extends this function by referencing popular culture's interpolations of these texts, as in the case of Chopin. Composing thus becomes a collective, mutual act of borrowing shaped by all who care to listen. Johnson showcases his brother's signature musical voice, effectively producing a biography of the composer by interpolating Rosamond's voice into his text.

Within the novel's soundtrack, Chopin's nocturne becomes a central feature, informed by all the compositions that have preceded it. Johnson saw it embodying opportunities for multivocality, for new interpretations of difference, and he chose it as a model for an artistic and rhetorical purpose—to show his audience new versions of blackness and black artistic contributions, engaging them in a dialogue evolving about art at a time when there was growing awareness—and in many quarters, fear and xenophobia—about the growing cultural diversity in America. Johnson draws attention to the generation of the musical form of the piano nocturne, which borrows and interpolates to produce its structure. The structure of the nocturne influenced the idea of a soundscape presented through the novel. The piano nocturne is a musical form with no text, one that borrows heavily from a tradition of Parisian vocal nocturnes but builds its structure from contrasting musical styles—torrential, romantic expression and march and hymn, for example. Chopin's piano nocturnes aptly demonstrate this borrowing, in which two voices or more, rather than one, defined the structure, with one of the voices designated as a woman's.[55] In Chopin's nocturnes, as in Johnson's novel, "opposites are allowed to alternate, to oscillate, to resonate, and thus to come into contact. The aspect of reconciliation is never quite achieved."[56] Chopin's thirteenth nocturne is an excellent example of these contrasts, alternating between C minor and E major. As it shifts from minor to major, the nocturne becomes a hymn. The presence of the "hymn passage" in this nocturne "intrudes on music of a more lyrical and passionate nature—music that seems more appropriate for a love song." Without a text (such as the vocal nocturne possesses), the piano nocturne tends to play "episodic construction[s]" against each other; Chopin's nocturnes in particular "play . . . one against the other by embedding a hymn passage that is itself entirely calm . . . within a song of passion."[57] Johnson's *Autobiography of an Ex-Colored Man* similarly does this: hymns, spirituals, and "black keys" are placed in contrast and in concert almost from the outset of the novel.

Johnson's use of Chopin's thirteenth nocturne as well as the "Chopinesque" compositions his narrator authors during his courtship of a woman, sometimes in collaboration with her, underscores the continual referencing and reperformance of music as the ultimate source of its meaning.[58] As Chopin scholar Marianne Kielian-Gilbert writes, "Music can internalize and reference other musics. Compositions can include other music in direct quotation, stylistic evocation or assimilation, thematic and intertextual reference, and juxtaposition. These inclusions also vary in the degree or the relationship of their 'reception' ('appropriation') and integration in the broader compositional context."[59] Thus music's continual reperformance can alter its composition, such that the idea of an original musical truth or an original composition matters less than the expressive practices that direct it, its interpolation.

Johnson's emerging idea of a sound-based aesthetic is seen in this concept of continuous, even simultaneous, reperformance. There is at once the musical impact of the nocturne and the impact of music on the body. As Johnson references both the physically rooted materiality and the bodily transcendent of sonic experience through the body and performance, he moves away from the visually oriented reception of black culture. In doing so, he rejects a legacy of debasing stereotypes rooted in visual difference, a legacy of images popularized by the nineteenth-century minstrel show that were so pervasive that they easily translated from representations in print to film, for example, in D. W. Griffith's *Birth of a Nation* (1915)—based on Thomas Dixon's *The Clansman*—three years after the publication of *The Autobiography of an Ex-Colored Man*. Unlike visual orientation, sound cannot be shut out, nor can its multiple, dissonant strains be singled out. Johnson references the physical experience of listening in this way. Sound is inherently participatory, performer and listener inseparable. In this interracial model of culture, performance is emphasized through the black body without its reduction to deforming stereotype or erasure.

In the novel, the narrator meets his seemingly white companion, later to be his wife, through sound: he hears her before he sees her, and he wonders that "tones of such passionate color" could come from so "fragile" a body. Their passion is characterized by their mutual composition of "Chopinesque" songs for each other as well as their dual performances of such works in voice and piano. The narrator's choice of Chopin as the basis of his shared compositions doesn't represent his conversion to being or playing white, as it has often been taken to mean. Instead, this use of Chopin's music represents a defiance of the idea of original and copy in American music, relating also to American debates about racial and cultural purity. In Johnson's novel, four hands play an interpolated Chopin, representing a physically and psychically transcendent interracialism in sound performance. Johnson's model of Chopin's interlocution allows for an interracialism that doesn't absorb black culture completely, however: black music has a distinct voice within the composition. The narrator's compositions with his companion are placed in contrast with "the truth" he must tell her, that he is black. He must express "in what words I do not know" (*AECM*, 121) this truth, for which there are no words. No words adequately express racial difference while conveying humanity, as demonstrated by the narrator's intense gaze upon himself after disclosing the truth to her. Suddenly he becomes concerned with his visual presentation, and what began as a sound composition is diminished to a visually degrading portrait of a brute: he believes that before her he has become "thick-featured and crimp haired" (*AECM*, 121) with his disclosure.

From the moment of Johnson's relation of his near lynching to Rosamond, the brothers, who were already close, shared a pact. Johnson's suppression of this event, followed by his entrance into musical comedy with his brother, defines the pact. While Johnson would distance himself from his career as a lyricist, even to the extent that he remained silent about major productions such as *The Evolution of Rag-Time*, he was a deep participant, closely affiliated with and loyal to the world of musical theater. Johnson followed this world through his brother, who remained committed to musical theater his entire life.[60] Johnson incorporates and distances his experiences and those of Rosie's in the novel. In *The Autobiography of an Ex-Colored Man*, Johnson understands this story of music to reach beyond the conclusion of this work through the biography of his brother. This story takes Rosie from the Carnegie Hall performance of the spirituals that his narrator witnesses in the conclusion of the novel to the ceaseless sonic environment beyond its pages. The scope includes the Great War and composer James Reese Europe's Fifteenth Regiment through the 1930s break into George Gershwin's smash Broadway hit, adapted to film, in which Rosamond starred as the lawyer: *Porgy and Bess*.

Rosamond's travels and development as a composer carried forth the idea of sound expressed in Johnson's novel, and Johnson began to form ideas of extending the novel's scope. "I have sometimes thought that I might bring [*The Autobiography of an Ex-Colored Man*] down through the Great War and try for another publication of it," Johnson wrote *New York Tribune* drama critic and war journalist Heywood Broun in 1924.[61] For Johnson to "bring it down through the Great War" is to bring the novel down through his brother Rosamond's experience. Johnson wished to extend his novel by continuing its practice of interpolation, of singing in the voice of someone else.

Rather than functioning as a means of characterization in Johnson's novel, music instead provides a ragtime-oriented "lead sheet" directing its listeners toward the life and sounds beyond its pages. On May 2, 1912, after partner Bob Cole's death, Rosie performed as a pianist in Carnegie Hall's "A Concert of Negro Music," an important moment in cultural history marking the widespread American recognition of the spirituals as a musical form. The conclusion to Johnson's *Autobiography of an Ex-Colored Man*, this concert marks for the narrator the error of his ways in abandoning his dreams of becoming "a great colored man," a composer of "classic" black music. Rosamond is on the stage that the narrator has chosen not to enter, indicating Johnson's rejection of sound as a means of merely characterizing his narrator for his more complex referencing of sound composition and performance in the novel. Reaching beyond its pages, Rosie's musical career after the novel's publication was in ascendance. He received an appointment by Oscar Hammerstein to his London-based Grand Opera House in 1912, holding this position for three years, at which time World War I curtailed the opera house's activities. After leaving this post, Rosamond was commissioned as a second lieutenant in the Fifteenth Regiment under the direction of James Reese Europe. When he returned from abroad, he continued to author original compositions and diligently worked to collect and arrange hundreds of spirituals, resulting in the two-volume collaboration with his brother, *The Book of American Negro Spirituals* (1925) and *The Second Book of American Negro Spirituals* (1926). Rosamond's work spurred a performance tour with Taylor Gordon in 1925–26, including a Carnegie Hall performance and a London tour.

The brothers' work on the spirituals in their two-volume collection revived their musical collaboration during the first decade of the new century. Their work on these volumes is representative of some of their original compositional practices as the Johnson Brothers. While there had been other collections of spirituals, the first *Book of American Negro Spirituals* was a best seller, partly because of the work's emphasis on the performance of these songs by its purchasers and partly because of the brothers' signature marks on the collection through their arrangements and prefaces. In this two-volume collection, published over a span of a year, the brothers left their mark on hundreds of spirituals through Rosamond's distinct arrangements and Johnson's prefaces to the books, disrupting the idea of an original spiritual, isolated in a historical past no longer relevant. These songs were made to be adapted and were variable to context, including the present, and Johnson emphasizes as much in his prefaces to these volumes. Rosamond's profound mark on this collection has been neglected as a result of the isolation of music from literary-critical discussion—the perceived separation of text and arrangement, Johnson's preface and the notes on the page as mere songs. The brothers' collaboration in these volumes reflects their shared secret, their pact, twenty-four years after Johnson's near lynching: sound creates a distinct narrative of black modernity and must be altered continuously, even simultaneously, by its reperformance.

Their practice of anthologizing in these works also becomes a biographical act, in which the two composers transform the spirituals by inserting their signatory biographies, Johnson's through words, Rosamond's through music, and the two in collaboration with each other. *The Autobiography of an Ex-Colored Man* introduces this simultaneous and varied narrative of sound and composition involving both Johnsons. James Weldon Johnson's subsequent works continue to develop these ideas, emerging from an acute awareness of the contingency and interdependence of black and white cultures in the Americas. The "secret" of Johnson's authorship of *The Autobiography of an Ex-Colored Man*, it seems, has less to do with Johnson defined in relation to the narrator himself than with the sonic culture the work sounds, the old southern songs (spirituals), and the "cries and groans" that emanate from its pages.

2 Cultures of Talk
Diplomacy, Nation, and Race in *The Autobiography of an Ex-Colored Man*

Obviously, an Afro-American spokesperson who wished to engage in a masterful and empowering play within the minstrel spirit house needed the uncanny ability to manipulate bizarre phonic legacies. For he or she had the task of transforming the mask and its sounds into negotiable discursive currency. In effect, the task was the production of a manual of black speaking, a book of speaking *back and black*.
—Houston Baker Jr., *Modernism and the Harlem Renaissance*

The much-neglected work *The Evolution of Rag-Time* was a precursor to Johnson's sound-based experimentation in *The Autobiography of an Ex-Colored Man*. This early piece demonstrates more clearly the emerging aesthetic—based on black expressive practices at the margins of the nation—that Johnson's novel initiates, developed through his subsequent writings and their referencing of this first book-length, nationally distributed work. *The Autobiography of an Ex-Colored Man* values linguistic heterogeneity: not perfect translation, but the inflection of one culture with another's, transformative encounters of speech and sound that, while based on national identity, encourage transnationalism through the learning of languages, cultural travel, and broader dialogue and exposure.[1] Mikhail Bakhtin's concept of heteroglossia—varied and conflicting discourses shaping a field of linguistic production, whether it is a single literary work with multiple voices or the uses of American language by its many practitioners—provides an opportunity to read Johnson's novel through its many evocations of language and sound, from Spanish to American English, in the cigar factory and the pool hall.[2] *The Evolution of Rag-Time* initiated this practice of articulating a heterogeneous modern black identity through multiple discourses and locations.

In 1903 Cole and Johnson Brothers composed and copyrighted *The Evolution of Rag-Time: A Musical Suite*, described by ethnomusicologist Edward A. Berlin as "a tripartite effort of popular theater music, cultural anthropology, and artistic development of vernacular materials" and "a clear response to cultural and artistic needs customarily expressed separately but here brought together in a unified work."[3] In this work, Cole and Johnson Brothers presented a thematic chronology of interwoven compositions from "Voice of the Savage. (Zulu Dance)" to "Sounds of the Times. Lindy." James W. Johnson wrote "introductory poems" and authored the lyrics to five of the six songs, one in collaboration with Bob Cole; Rosamond wrote four of the six songs, one in collaboration with Bob Cole. The suite was produced by Klaw and Erlanger in a lavish production as part of *Mother Goose*. The *New York Times* reviewed the production, with special praise reserved for the suite by Cole and Johnson Brothers: it "presented several pleasing novelties. The first is a singing and dancing specialty arrangement by Cole and Johnson and designed to represent the 'Evolution of Ragtime.' It served to introduce several picturesquely costumed groups, and ended with a dance led by a dozen or more girls garbed in silk gowns of brown and gold, in which the limits of extravagance seemed to have been reached."[4] Berlin describes the suite as "more than a mere grouping of popular songs. . . . [I]t contains references to earlier styles and period pieces that its public could be expected to recognize."[5]

The suite's final song, "Sounds of the Times. Lindy," "was the high point of the theatrical production, presented with the most lavish costumes and the grand cakewalk finale" and "was also the musical climax," since "the final song is built on motives introduced in the preceding songs and brings these motives to fullest fruition."[6] Moreover, this final song had a compelling, atypical structure: "After reprises of verse and chorus, the formal extensions begin, first with a variant of the chorus, now in a new key and with a habanera-like accompaniment. . . . This accompaniment is retained for a 16-measure modulatory 'development' of the chorus . . . leading finally to a 'recapitulation' of the original chorus, in the original key, and an 8-measure coda."[7] As Berlin notes, the use of "a Hispanic rhythm" interwoven with the syncopation of ragtime made the composition distinct: while the song's referentiality points to its development in the theatrical culmination of the suite, it also indicates the culmination and seriousness of the suite's compositional development and gesture toward the idea of ragtime's "evolution": "Perhaps [the introduction of Hispanic rhythm] . . . was their prediction for a future evolution of ragtime."[8]

Certainly this work by the trio is reflective of their combined outlook on ragtime's expressive possibilities. The work contains the dispositions of all three composers on the role of history and diaspora in the formation of modern black culture in the Americas. Ragtime's "evolution" is not so much a linear progression in time and place as a dispersal and fusion, sometimes occurring simultaneously. The very practice of ragtime, inflected with black cultures not limited by national boundaries, fosters its multiplicity, whether through Latin American rhythmic fusion or African American cakewalk. Indeed, Johnson will further experiment with and develop the idea of ragtime's performance at the margins of nations and cultures in his subsequent writings. He continues these pluralities by composing intentional digressions from an exclusively national context for black art both in *The Autobiography of an Ex-Colored Man* (1912) and his preface to *The Book of American Negro Poetry* (1922).[9]

Berlin's work on this early Cole and Johnson composition assigns to the composing trio the dilemma of "vernacular" versus "art music," in which the black composers must choose and yet cannot. Because their work is both and draws on both, Berlin reads their multiple presence as contradiction—as "ambivalence" and an "inconsistency." Instead, however, we might read their simultaneous presence as a *productive* contradiction privileging Cole and Johnson Brothers as moderns: self-conscious, experimental, and self-commodifying. The presence of vernacular and art songs demonstrates the way in which Cole and Johnson Brothers' composition attempts to control and direct the turn of the century's chaotic, sometimes hostile soundscape. While Cole and Johnson Brothers are characterized by Berlin as representing (and replicating) a middle-class ambivalence about whether or not to acknowledge folk forms of culture, their use of spirituals in many of their works—held at arm's length by most middle-class blacks at the turn of the century—demonstrates a greater self-consciousness and sophistication than the composer's "dilemma" that Berlin characterizes can allow for. The contradiction represents the productive differences of the three members of the trio: Cole's vision of Spanish fusion with black culture of the United States, Johnson's privileging of interpolation, and Rosie's preference for art song.[10]

In the world of music, Johnson encountered acoustic and compositional environments resounding with change, especially complex cultural transferences and appropriations from popular and classic, black and white, American and Latin American. In the world of diplomacy, Johnson encountered an arresting new context to these transferences based on a talk-centered, male-oriented black internationalism. These wide-ranging experiences provided him with the material for his own evolution as a writer. Johnson's participation in and appreciation of the local cultures of New York and Puerto Cabello, Venezuela, made possible the important cultural performance of heterogeneity in *The Autobiography of an Ex-Colored Man*.

In this novel, Johnson interpolated his cultural experience of Venezuela, where he found black Venezuelans unable to distinguish or voice their distinct contributions to the nation and yet where he also discovered a vital culture of talk similar to what he had participated in at the Marshall Hotel and in the clubs of Black Bohemia. He encountered the perplexing paradox of black assimilation as a composer not only in America but also in Venezuela, where black contributors apparently were left without a cultural voice of their own, apart from the nation.

Johnson described his experience of Venezuelan culture in detailed, rich letters written to Booker Taliaferro Washington, the single most powerful black leader in American race politics and an influential patron of Johnson for a brief period that included his appointment to the Venezuelan consulate. Observing, on the one hand, the absence of race prejudice such as blacks experienced in America, Johnson also noted the absence of their distinction through acknowledgment of their cultural contributions: "The pure Negro plays but a small part in life in this country, and there are 'very few of him.'" He continued:

> It seems that his chief work has been to lend a little color to the scene. I judge that soon there will be "none of him." In the course of years the Venezuelans will become a homogeneous race of a Spanish type, in color somewhere between a light brown and a yellow. So, the Negro, in spite of the fact that he has not the great obstacle of prejudice to overcome will make no name in Venezuela as a Negro—But the "in spite of" is the very reason; he will make no name here because he has no obstacle. And I believe that should the same conditions obtain in the United States he would make no name there, but as a racial entity would become lost as he has in Venezuela. . . . He has been shut out from historical greatness of even a race so dark and Negroid as the ancient Egyptians, a people who probably when they built the Sphinx were more Negro than anything else.[11]

As American consul to Venezuela and Nicaragua, Johnson gained a comparative perspective on black cultural identity and racial attitudes in the Americas. Indeed, he wrote George Towns, his friend and classmate from Atlanta University, that by traveling to Venezuela he had "obtained [his] first perspective view of life."[12] Johnson noted in particular the different attitudes toward complexion in the diverse black population and the difference between American and Venezuelan attitudes about racial and cultural assimilation. He used these observations about the cultural distinctiveness of black culture versus the merits of its assimilation into a national identity in *The Autobiography of an Ex-Colored Man*, the bulk of which was composed during his time in Venezuela.[13] Johnson noted the "really excellent" National Band of Venezuela "and was much interested to note that fully a third of the fifty odd members were colored." He was elated with the presidential procession he witnessed in Caracas, where "colored colonels, and generals, and major-generals, clad in crimson and gold, with gold handled swords clinking at their sides, and silver spurs clinking at their heels," were part of the president's suite in attendance at the opera. He confided in Washington, "You know in Europe we are not shut out, but everything we see is white, and we can't feel, somehow, that we are part of the procession; but I felt that night that I, too, was in it."[14] Having come to Venezuela with the project of finishing *The Autobiography of an Ex-Colored Man*, of which he had composed only two chapters before assuming his post, Johnson found more than just time to write—he found a wealth of material on race and nation with unanticipated connections to his "biography of the race." So, inspired by what he had seen in Caracas, the nation's capital, he began forming an idea of "an article, or a pamphlet, or something of that sort on the 'black freedman of North and South America.'"[15] He read international law and found the diplomatic correspondence from the period of the Civil War "an extremely interesting form of history." He had also brought "about fifty books" and subscribed to the *New York Herald*, the *Independent*, *Current Literature*, the *New York Age*, and the *Colored American Magazine*. From this broad background of literary and diplomatic culture, Johnson devoted much of his midday hours, during which no business was done, to "do some work on one of the several literary projects I have in mind," including his poem "O Black and Unknown Bards" and his novel.[16]

These explorations figure centrally in his "biography of the race," *The*

Autobiography of an Ex-Colored Man. In this work, the billiards and club are of New York's Tenderloin and of Puerto Cabello, Venezuela, and the novel's culture of talk is informed by both locations. Between these cultures and nations, talk plays a vital role as a mode of communication constantly expressed but not contained, emphasizing its continual transference and transformation.

Discovering talk emerging as a key aspect in his first book-length work, Johnson identified it as a technique that could also function vitally in his compositional strategy as an author through the practice of simultaneity. As Johnson worked on *The Autobiography of an Ex-Colored Man* in Venezuela, he also wrote "O Black and Unknown Bards" (1908), a poem that wonders about "that subtle undertone, / That note in music heard not with the ears" in the spirituals that also stir the narrator of Johnson's novel. The resonances from one work to the other—from "O Black and Unknown Bards" to *The Autobiography of an Ex-Colored Man*—were extended by Johnson to his other, subsequent works as a formal practice of simultaneity, one that tends to blur the boundaries of the works as independent, discrete entities. This practice would have profound consequences for Johnson's art of diplomacy in his international negotiations, which included not only the American consulate but also his writing.

In *The Autobiography of an Ex-Colored Man*, Johnson linked white America's "Negro question" to the discussion of American culture's distinctiveness.[17] Adhering to the commonplace that a civilization is not great until it has a great literature, Johnson showed how black expressive culture catapulted America to the ranks of the great civilizations of modern Europe and ancient Rome and Greece. Black expressive culture, as Johnson represented it, demonstrated America's cultural legacy and its potential to be a great civilization. All of the distinctive aspects of American culture—dance (the cakewalk), folklore (the Uncle Remus stories), the spirituals (the "jubilee songs"), and ragtime—rested on the foundation of black culture, as his narrator observes:

> The colored people of this country have done four things which refute the oft-advanced theory that they are an absolutely inferior race, which demonstrate that they have originality and artistic conception; and, what is more, the power of creating that which can influence and appeal universally. The first two of these are the Uncle Remus stories, collected by Joel Chandler Harris, and the Jubilee songs, to

> which the Fisk singers made the public and the skilled musicians of both American and Europe listen. The other two are ragtime music and the cake-walk. No one who has traveled can question the world-conquering influence of ragtime; and I do not think it would be an exaggeration to say that in Europe the United States is popularly known better by ragtime than by anything else it has produced in a generation. In Paris they call it American music. (*AECM*, 54)

While this could be taken as an assimilationist argument—black culture was American culture, American culture was black culture—Johnson wished for some of the distinction to remain. He observed that the full assimilation of black culture in the Venezuelan social fabric represented a loss, that the Negro in Venezuela "would make no name for himself as a Negro," and thus, although contributing to historical greatness, he would be "shut out."[18] Johnson emphasized, rather, the imperative of recognizing—hearing—the specific cultural contributions of blacks to the American nation. Johnson's poem "O Black and Unknown Bards" stated the importance of this cultural contribution, and its recognition. The poem's speaker asks, "Heart of what slave poured out such melody / As 'Steal Away to Jesus'?" and declares:

> Not that great German master in his dream
> Of harmonies that thundered amongst the stars
> At the creation, ever heard a theme
> Nobler than "Go Down, Moses." (*AECM*, 134)

Figuring the recognition as hearing enabled Johnson to sidestep the question of black culture's visual presence, substituting a more positive valuation of its expressive presence, commonly shared by all Americans through its sound-based transference.

Historian Christine Stansell reminds us that modernism emerged from civic life, formed from local manifestations that became national phenomena, as in the outgrowth of American Bohemianism from New York City's Greenwich Village and the Lower East Side.[19] Such a reminder emphasizes the politically oriented nature and multiplicity of local cultures that developed into what we now recognize as the national culture of American modernism. John B. Nail, Johnson's father-in-law, was a regular attendee of the New York Society for Ethical Culture's weekly Sunday meetings, and Grace and James Weldon Johnson were also members, indicating their active participation in local New

York culture, which has often been overlooked in studies of Johnson. The Johnsons frequently invited out-of-town visitors to attend the meetings with them, such as Bostonian William Stanley Braithwaite. In addition to these local cultures that are presumed to be circumscribed by national boundaries by Stansell, James Weldon Johnson participated in and drew from his international experience of local culture in Puerto Cabello, Venezuela, to form his distinct modernism, based on a black internationalism that was given voice and significance through Spanish.

Johnson emphasized this international transference, from Black Bohemia to Venezuela and from Venezuela to Cuba and beyond, by using New World Spanish-speaking culture in *The Autobiography of an Ex-Colored Man* to reach beyond national boundaries. The revolutionary Cuban culture referenced in the novel is made to be inclusive of all Spanish-speaking Latin American nations, including Venezuela and Nicaragua. This wide-ranging inclusion of New World Spanish cultures draws attention to their nascent revolutions, which were also a rejection of American occupation in this era of active American expansion.

Johnson staged sonic performances at the margins of culture and nation in *The Autobiography of an Ex-Colored Man*. This performance at the margins, achieved through sound, its transference, and its absence, played out ideas of marginality in order to emphasize the perceived paradox of black citizenship in America as well as to draw attention to the potentially constructive, fruitful relationship between black expressive culture and American citizenship. Johnson's intentional digressions, which are often interpolations between cultures and nations, demonstrate the developing idea in his writing of a modern black culture extending beyond the boundaries of the nation. The presence of Cuban culture in the novel is at once an intentional digression from the American context and a pointed reference to America's expansionist project in Latin America. Diplomacy shows itself in Johnson's writing to be interpolation, a key role that the author assumes in his position as American consul.

The Autobiography of an Ex-Colored Man can be read as a series of digressions from the location of the nation, its histories, literatures, music, and languages. While seemingly improvisatory, the technique creates an emphasis on the comprehension and interpolation of these expressive modes by both the narrator and others. The narrator's exotic encounter of Spanish-speaking Cuban culture in Jacksonville demonstrates how the seemingly trivial conversation—"purely ordinary affairs" and "mere trifles" (*AECM*, 43)—is interwoven with the profoundly political subjects "nearest . . . [the] heart," "the independence of Cuba" (*AECM*, 45) through the practice of conversation: "spirited chatter" (*AECM*, 43) becomes "positively eloquent" (*AECM*, 45) when politicized. The narrator becomes a participant in this practice, discovering that he has "a talent for languages as well as for music" (*AECM*, 45) and assuming the role of interlocutor to his reader by assuming the role of "reader" in the factory where he began work in a relatively unskilled aspect of cigar making. He explains the significance of the position to which he has risen:

> The "reader" is quite an institution in all cigar factories which employ Spanish-speaking workmen. He sits in the center of the large room in which the cigar makers work and reads to them for a certain number of hours each day all the important news from the papers and whatever else he may consider would be interesting. He often selects a novel, and reads it in daily installments. He must, of course, have a good voice, but he must also have a reputation among the men for intelligence, for being well posted and having in his head a stock of varied information. He is generally the final authority on all arguments which arise; and, in a cigar factory, these arguments are many and frequent. (*AECM*, 46)

The process of selection, relation, and interpretation of important news and cultural works distinguishes the "reader" as a composer of sorts who, by his presentation, orchestrates verbal responses that cannot be fully anticipated. Facilitating the transference or translation of culture and nations, at home and abroad, the "reader" serves as a diplomat who makes possible this talk, serving as an interlocutor of sorts, presenting material from newspapers, novels, and a variety of sources for discussion, where talk is made audible and voluble and becomes politicized, becoming dynamic through the voices of the men by eliciting their vocal responses.

The conversational drift of the narrator in the company of his landlord, "a *regalía* workman"—a worker with special privileges who makes the highest quality product—in the cigar factory (*AECM*, 44), ambiguously wanders between Spanish- and English-speaking cultures, ultimately resulting in the narrator's acquisition of the Spanish language, which he relates to his musical ability. The narrator explains his landlord's position: "He was in exile from the island [of Cuba], and a prominent member of the Jacksonville *Junta*. Every week sums of money were collected from *juntas* all over the country. This money went to buy arms and ammunition for the insurgents" (*AECM*, 45). He told the narrator "of the Gomezes, both the white one and the black one, of Maceo and Bandera," and "grew positively eloquent" (*AECM*, 45). Much like the culturally authoritative status of the "reader" that the narrator will later achieve in the Spanish language, this Cuban exile "also showed . . . that he was a man of considerable education and reading. He spoke English excellently, and frequently surprised . . . [the narrator] by using words one would hardly expect from a foreigner. The first one of this class of words he employed almost shocked me, and I never forgot it, 'twas 'ramify.' We sat on the piazza until ten o'clock" (*AECM*, 45).

The narrator's companion in conversation shares his eloquence with the literary and ideological voice of the Cuban revolution, José Martí. Indeed, Martí had moved to the Tampa area of Florida in 1881 and from there organized support of Cuba's exiles while working for Cuba's independence from Spain and from American imperial interest. Martí's eloquence was easily contrasted with state-sponsored newspaper organizations' "perfervid" praise for dictators of the type that Johnson recalled in great detail of his experience while serving as consul in Venezuela. In his autobiography, he recounted the efforts of Gumersindo Rivas, who, as the editor of Venezuelan dictator Cipriano Castro's "personal organ, *El Constitucional*," "strained even the grandiloquence of the Spanish language" (*ATW*, 247). Johnson, who read *El Constitucional* every day, including Rivas's lead editorial, noted that "frequently Rivas listed in an ascending scale the names and deeds of the world's great heroes, sages and saints, including the name of Jesus, and rose to a climax with the name and deeds of Cipriano Castro," quoting an article that ended: "As Christ rose to save the world, so has Castro risen to save Venezuela" (*ATW*, 247). It is clear that for Johnson, the "talk" of many, embodied by dynamic, politicized language, directly opposes the uniformity of efflorescent, distorted propaganda such as Rivas's.

As a Caribbean island, Cuba's struggle for independence represented an entire region's efforts to obtain self-government, resisting dictatorship, colonialism, and expansionism. The "small wars" or "little wars" of Cuba and the Philippines, later Puerto Rico, the Dominican Republic (1914), and Haiti (1915), among others, were the testing ground for the recently expanded power of the American navy, which was intended to rival England's Royal Navy and secure the United States' "national interests." As a result, American "intervention" in Latin American and Caribbean nations, while justified by the quest for political and economic security, also involved its belief in American moral superiority relative to the populations it occupied by force or treaty, whether Theodore Roosevelt's zealous belief in Manifest Destiny and westward expansionism or Woodrow Wilson's belief in "moral force" and "moral rights" (a prior century's term for what we now call human rights), often enforced militarily. Spain's brutal reaction to the nascent Cuban rebellion, which included the forced relocation of approximately 400,000 Cubans to concentration camps, reported in the *New York Journal* and other newspapers, earned the outrage of Americans. But while Cuba's rebellion was characterized in the press and by the American government as a struggle for freedom, McKinley and his cabinet did not intend to grant the island independence or to annex it; they wanted to control its future. Cuba had long been viewed as a key strategic point for control of the entire Caribbean. The Monroe Doctrine, which had provided a hemispheric protection of American interests in the Americas from European presence, was complemented in 1901 by the Platt Amendment, which gave the United States the right to intervene in those same places.

Johnson found himself at the center of this morally murky moment in American history, a representative of his government as its diplomat, on the one hand, and, on the other, a skeptic of its practices, which he viewed as economically motivated and exploitative first and foremost. Early in his diplomatic post to Nicaragua, Johnson submitted a report to the State Department in triplicate, "Style of Business Correspondence," in which Johnson observed:

> One of the things which deserves more attention than is, perhaps, given to it by American exporters is the style of their business correspondence. There is current in the United States among many business men a style of correspondence which is brief and, at times, abbreviated; which uses the simplest and the most direct language, cuts out all unnecessary words, does away with all superfluous expressions and economizes time to the fullest extent. Letters written in such a style are, perhaps, indicative of modern and energetic methods on the part of the firm using it, but to foreigners and especially Latin-Americans such letters appear curt and often convey an

> impression of rudeness. The merchant of Spanish America, in accordance with the genius of his native language, couches even his business letters in courteous terms, and this he expects from others; the effect can be imagined of receiving a letter in which the writer has not even taken the time to put in the personal pronouns.
>
> It is noticeable that European manufacturers generally in writing to merchants here take the time to send out carefully and politely worded letters: it is certain that American exporters should not use less care or go to less trouble.[20]

While American businessmen would do away with pronouns—including the people involved in transactions—in a model of modern efficiency, Johnson emphasizes the "genius" of diplomacy located in language practices. This seemingly minor subject had far greater implications, Johnson believed. Only upon leaving the consulate in 1912 did Johnson feel free to voice his observations fully, in a 1913 address delivered in New York just a few weeks after resigning from the consulate, "Why Latin-America Dislikes the United States."[21]

Directing attention to the fact that among Latin Americans "there exists . . . a smouldering dislike for the United States," which "stands lower in the affections of the Latin-American people than Spain, France, Italy, Germany or England," Johnson provocatively argued that "the deep-seated cause of this feeling of hostility does not spring from the actions of Americans who go to Latin-America but from the treatment accorded to Latin-Americans who come to the United States. In truth, the whole question is involved in our own national and local Negro problem." Between travel to Europe and the United States, Latin Americans, who, "by an overwhelming majority, are not white people," noted their treatment "like 'niggers'" in the United States. Moreover, according to Johnson, "these travelers have returned home and facts concerning the treatment accorded in the United States to a dark skin have been disseminated with something of a masonic secrecy"—"whatever the Latin-American has suffered at the hands of Americans on account of race discrimination he neither discusses or even openly admits." Johnson explains: because Latin Americans are "citizens of sovereign and independent nations," they are reluctant to associate themselves directly with the experience of "the Negro in the United States" and, by association, be attached to "the stigma of inferiority" of its second-class citizens.[22] However, Johnson found that the similarity of circumstance was addressed in the Latin American newspapers:

> Any observation of the newspapers of the capitals of Central and South America will show that these publications make a point of giving space and prominence to lynchings and other outrages perpetrated against Negroes in the United States, even though these outrages may be committed in most obscure communities; and this is often done to the exclusion of other and more important world news. It appears that they cull the American newspapers for these items; the writer [Johnson himself] has seen as many as three in a single issue of a Latin-American paper. No comment on them is ever published, but they always carry a silent warning.[23]

The "masonic secrecy" to which Johnson refers in the matter of American race prejudice against African Americans and Latin Americans alike on the United States' own soil was taken up by *The Autobiography of an Ex-Colored Man*, published just a year prior to this address. Referencing the "one phase of . . . [the colored man] which is disclosed only in the freemasonry of his own race," the narrator observes that "it is a difficult thing for a white man to learn what a colored man really thinks; because, generally, with the latter an additional and different light must be brought to bear on what he thinks; and his thoughts are often influenced by considerations so delicate and subtle that it would be impossible for him to confess or explain them to one of the opposite race" (*AECM*, 14). This difficulty has an impact on the matter of citizenship and national loyalty, which are placed in tension with individual honor. Race discrimination in the United States encourages African Americans to sympathize with and protect "their worst criminals" (*AECM*, 111), understandable to the narrator in the minutes after he has witnessed a brutal lynching. Justifying his decision to "neither disclaim the black race nor claim the white race," the narrator explains his logic: "To forsake one's race to better one's condition was no less worthy an action than to forsake one's country for the same purpose" (*AECM*, 112–13). His choice is brought on by waves of shame that "I belonged to a race that could be so dealt with; and shame for my country . . . the great example of democracy to the world . . . [and] the only civilized, if not the only state on earth, where a human being would be burned alive" (*AECM*, 111). He chooses to stay in the United States, a loyal citizen of his nation, which commits the distinct and unforgivable act of lynching, while attempting to preserve his individual sense of self-respect.

In "Why Latin-America Dislikes the United States," Johnson observes that "in a choice between the loss of national sovereignty and the loss of his individual honor, self-respect and his status as a man he would undoubtedly accept the former; and any affront to the latter is something he will not forgive." The "freemasonry," then, of African American experience translates outward to the Latin American context. Whether or not Johnson was aware of the Cuban Freemasonry that propelled Cuban rebellion against Spain or that the Maceo of his narrator's conversation—Antonio Maceo Grajales—was an active member of the Cuban Freemasonry movement, he recognized the potency of a model of black identity that stretched across national boundaries. In this model, man-to-man recognition of individual honor could transcend racial division and form a better, purer form of nationhood through fraternity. The Gomezes, black and white, were allied in their effort to throw off Spanish rule, undeterred by brutal attempts to put down the rebellion. The narrator, rendering plural "the Gomezes," emphasizes their connection, despite the apparent difference of their complexions. According to Johnson, "The fear that lies closest to . . . [the Latin American's] heart is not that southern republics will lose their independence to the United States, but that they will fall under the bane of American prejudice, a process which he has without doubt, observed going on slowly but surely in Cuba, Puerto Rico and Panama."[24]

Johnson was prepared to make such observations about the United States' imperialist ethic based not only on what he had seen during his diplomatic posts to Venezuela and Nicaragua but also on his prior experience writing the comic opera *Toloso* with his brother, Rosamond, in 1898, which, Johnson observed, was most likely not produced because of its critique of American expansionism. Reading the script of this comedy, set on a fictional island closely resembling the Philippines, one wonders whether Johnson would have been appointed American consul at all if the opera had been produced in its entirety.

When in Venezuela—in fact, shortly after his arrival there—Johnson directed an important letter to a New York company: "The Recreo Club of this city wishes to get a set of corners to convert a pool table into a billiard table, and they have asked me, the American consul at this place, to send for them."[25] Shortly after, Johnson wrote to say that the club "decided . . . that it will purchase a new billiard table." In December 1906 Johnson wrote to say:

> The billiard table and fixtures which we ordered some months ago for the club "Recreo" have arrived, and I am glad to say that all who have seen the outfit and used it, are highly pleased and satisfied. The only thing which went wrong in filling the order was my private cue. You will remember I sent my personal check of $3.75 for a cue and cue-case; both were sent, but the cue instead of being jointed, is all in one piece; so the case is worthless to me. . . . The mistake, aside from inconveniencing me, has afforded the members of the club considerable laughter at the expense of both myself and your firm, and added to a rather general impression in this country that American firms are careless in filling orders.

This correspondence indicates that Johnson, while drawing from his experiences in the clubs of New York's Black Bohemia to depict *The Autobiography of an Ex-Colored Man*'s pool-playing and gambling underworld to which his narrator falls prey, also used his immediate environment of the "Recreo" club in Venezuela, although this club was almost certainly an elite, rather than seedy, cultural locus. Moreover, and as Johnson indicated in a letter to Booker T. Washington, while in Venezuela he had regular interactions with diplomats from other Spanish-speaking countries, including Cuba: "My evenings I generally spend at the club; there I meet all of the other Consuls, and the leading business and professional men of the city."[26] Among these, Johnson warmly and respectfully welcomed Cuba's diplomat to Venezuela in early November 1906. These transferences from place to place, culture to culture, enriched Johnson's developing compositional practice of interpolation by placing it in the crucial context of diplomacy. In this new context, interpolation is an act of diplomacy. Referencing both the "badinage" of the billiards club in Venezuela and the "talk" in the rooms at the Marshall Hotel, Johnson's *Autobiography of an Ex-Colored Man* juxtaposed one culture to the other, playing cultural differences such as language and nation against the counterpoint of shared practices, such as talk and music. Much as Chopin's nocturnes were also Duke Ellington's, Gounod's *Faust* Theodore Drury's, the local culture of Venezuela transferred to the Cuban cigar factory as well as the clubs of Black Bohemia, at once a dispersal and a fusion of Latin American and black American cultures.

The key function of diplomacy in the "reader"—formerly the composer—extends to Johnson's writing. In Johnson's novel and subsequent works, talk and civic-minded culture are local and international at once, questioning the usual assumptions of difference based on nationhood, people, and language. After thinking about the role of black culture in Venezuela, Johnson concluded that culture's persistent transference and alteration might not be so detrimental because it could be directed at mainstream attitudes through its interpolation. Venezuela's male-centered culture and the Marshall Hotel's were connected in Johnson's mind in this way. By digressing from mainstream conversations about culture and inserting other linguistic registers in translation, Johnson amplified the crucial role of interpolation as diplomacy and put it to work in his writing.

Indeed, Johnson's later investigative reporting for the NAACP in US-occupied Haiti in 1920 confirms the politicized, grave nature of Johnson's diplomatic technique. Selected over W. E. B. Du Bois for his diplomatic experience in Latin American nations, Johnson, accompanied by NAACP board member Herbert Seligman, led the investigation in 1920, but in less than a week Seligman had contracted an illness that sent him home to New York.[27] Johnson continued the investigation alone; since the charges of misconduct that had reached the NAACP office were of racial wrongdoings on the part of the US occupation forces, his situation without Seligman was difficult. His position was a carefully measured one. In his personal notes for the investigation, he wrote: "April 8th. It is curious to see how my compatriots have thawed out in the past week. I am now a hail fellow, well met with them all. A regular American fellow. I have simply maintained an attitude of natural reserve, yet with courtesy. I have never offered more than was given."[28]

The result of Johnson's investigation, a four-part series published in the *Nation*, exposed to the public the American military's conduct in Haiti. Censorship of the Haitian press accompanied the American occupation. According to Johnson, Haitian newspapers received orders not to print criticism of the occupation, and, he emphasized, "*the same order carried the injunction not to print the order*." This occupation "has enforced by the bayonet a covenant whose secret has been well guarded by a rigid censorship from the American nation, and kept a people enslaved by the military tyranny which it was his avowed purpose to destroy throughout the world" in World War I.[29] Johnson relied on local informants to provide him with reports of the occupation forces' activities throughout the districts and was also able to secure back issues of the Haitian newspaper *Le Matin* to keep abreast of events. He also secured copies of the Haitian-American Convention and the new constitution of Haiti, which had been written by the American military occupation and passed through the Haitian legislature in 1918.

The news was sobering. Johnson observed that "marines talk freely of what they 'did' to some Haitians in the outlying districts," stories Johnson frequently learned "from the lips of the American marines themselves." It was an atmosphere of terror and brutality, one in which a child, for stealing sugar, had his brains battered out; women were raped; able-bodied men were forced into work camps, where they were beaten. The major factor of this imperialist environment was down-home American racism, Johnson believed. The type of soldier who found himself in Haiti at this time was one who had been passed over for service in World War I and who had since remained in Haiti. Johnson observed that, officered "entirely by marines," "many of these men are rough, uncouth, and uneducated, and a great number from the South, are violently steeped in color prejudice. . . . [I]t falls to them, ignorant of the Haitian ways and language, to enforce every minor police regulation." Therefore, he wrote, "brutalities and atrocities on the part of American marines have occurred with sufficient frequency to be the source of deep resentment and terror."[30] Johnson presented himself as a more effective American representative in his report, as one who did understand "the Haitian ways and language" and yet who clearly inhabited a position outside the American nation through his alliance with the Haitians against their shared experience of subjugation.

In *The Autobiography of an Ex-Colored Man*, Johnson's narrator, observing the European embrace of ragtime and the cakewalk, draws attention to the author's strategy of placing black performance at the margin in a sonic performance of differences made to provoke and decenter stable notions of racial and national identity. The outcome, neither assimilationist nor racialist in outlook, instead preserves the instability of modern black expression and identity in a move similar to, but more developed than, Du Bois's concept of double-consciousness, where "Negro" and "American" exist in uneasy but productive tension with one another.[31]

Oddly, in *The Autobiography of an Ex-Colored Man*, Johnson references the talk of the Cuban, Spanish-speaking culture of Jacksonville,

Florida, as "badinage"—a *French* word for gallant, sophisticated banter. This is an intentional transference on the part of Johnson, making the term in this new context a coinage of Johnson's. His term significantly lends this practice of talk more gravity, inflecting "talk" with cultural and political referents both outside and within the nation and using the margins to articulate what could not be said about the "Negro question" in America—the question of equal access to citizenship and the rights and speech entailed by this status. The cultural practice of "badinage" allows Johnson to explore the idea of a black internationalism that reaches beyond national or linguistic boundaries. Connecting the "Negro question" to black internationalism also allowed Johnson to draw on his prior conversations about and compositions in music, particularly ragtime. Making these connections enabled Johnson to incorporate and propel black cultures toward an artistically and politically productive modernism formed from linguistic and national transferences.

In Johnson's works, black culture's "evolution" is not so much a linear progression in time and place as a dispersal and fusion, sometimes occurring simultaneously. The very practice of ragtime, inflected with black cultures not limited by national boundaries, fosters its multiplicity, whether through Latin American rhythmic fusion or African American cakewalk. Indeed, Johnson will further experiment with and develop through ragtime the idea of black culture's performance at the margins of nations and cultures in his writings published after *The Autobiography of an Ex-Colored Man*. He continues this process of dispersal from this 1912 work, which composes intentional digressions from an exclusively national context for black art, to other, subsequent works that have already been recognized as defiantly digressive, such as the author's preface to *The Book of American Negro Poetry* (1922), as Brent Edwards has shown.[32] The linguistic heterogeneity of Johnson's works tests the boundaries of the American nation while creating shifting registers for the articulation of modern black culture within and outside of it.

3 The Interpolated Body
Passing, Same-Sex Talk, and Discursive Formations in *The Autobiography of an Ex-Colored Man*

Though there are clearly good historical reasons for keeping "race" and "sexuality" and "sexual difference" as separate analytic spheres, there are also quite pressing and significant historical reasons for asking how and where we might read not only their convergence, but the sites at which one cannot be constituted save through the other.
—Judith Butler, *Bodies That Matter*

Grace Nail and James Weldon Johnson's active civic participation demonstrated their commitment to local culture and politics as well as their value of "talk" in such forums as the Civic Club, the New York Society for Ethical Culture, and the James Weldon Johnson Literary Guild. In spaces such as the male-oriented Venezuelan pool hall and the feminist club of New York's "white" Bohemia—Greenwich Village—the Johnsons engaged in "passing" through the potentially unstable concepts of race and gender, using interpolation as a means of achieving the physical alteration of their surroundings.[1] Same-sex talk enabled conversation about the discursive formation of modern identity through concepts of racialized and gendered bodies while at the same time encouraging resistance to them by testing their boundaries. Interpolation—the act of inserting foreign matter or new material into existing material so as to alter, enlarge, or adulterate it—is often applied to text and music, but it is also an important agent of performance. This chapter discusses the performative interpolations at work in Johnson's modern milieu—evidenced by his actions and those of two of his male friends—that the author uses in *The Autobiography of an Ex-Colored Man* as well as in his orchestration of the Silent Protest Parade. This modern environment was a ground for experimentation in articulations of black masculinity, including the expression of a sexuality that was neither the hypersexualized, greedy, miscegenating, and rapacious portrait of Jack Johnson that was created by a white majority nor the repressed, asexual, physically inexpressive portrait enforced by the black church. Both hyperbolic attitudes can be seen as opposing responses to the pressing concern of social change—the "uplift" of a recently emancipated black population—in the modern century. That this fear or repression was located in black male bodies demonstrates the intense focus placed upon men like James Weldon Johnson as perceived agents or symbols of this change.

Recognizing this close physical scrutiny, Johnson chose to direct his works through interpolation, continually transforming and modifying his works by incorporating sound, effectively voicing his works through the bodies of others. Johnson's representation of the interpolated body and interpolated compositions through sound emphasizes its physical significance, as sound enters *into* its listener. As we saw in chapter 1, *The Autobiography of an Ex-Colored Man* demonstrates that auditory exposure necessitates the alteration of its listener. There is a gendered as well as a racial significance to this experience of sound. In this 1912 work, Johnson's interpolated body—the text itself—performs racial *and* gendered passing.[2] As Philip Brian Harper has effectively shown, "Conceptual limits . . . govern the novel of racial 'passing' such that it seems inevitably to support a conservative gender politics wherein black masculinity itself is conceived of as fundamentally problematic."[3] For Harper, the "feminized orientation" of the Ex-Colored Man indicates the extent to which the "literary mulatto" has been figured through "mixed race identity" almost exclusively in relation to femininity, indicating the "perennially problematic" category of black masculinity.[4] The Ex-Colored Man's racial ambiguity is articulated through "a gender identity that is anything but properly masculine, and verging dangerously on a sexual identity that is anything but hetero."[5] The narrator's relationship with his "millionaire friend" underscores the masculine anxiety made apparent by the narrator's racial ambiguity: their domestic relationship is interrupted by the Ex-Colored Man's choice to accept his black identity by leaving his patron/partner. The novel's performance of this relationship, which the narrator describes as his most intimate besides that which he shared with his mother, indicates the difficulty of assuming a "normative masculinity" through these set categories of African American identity.[6] It's arguable that there was no discursive representation of "normative masculinity" for black men in the first decade of the twentieth century, although the male-centered New Negro era at its height in the mid-1920s would change this.

Johnson's acute awareness of his role in Venezuela as a diplomat, a foreigner, and a man developed his perception that the body's exposure to sound was an opportunity to enact and inhere difference. He wrote in *Along This Way* of his observation that Venezuelan society was a male-centered culture, a structure that provided relational limitations for men as well as for women: "I think that I have indicated that the little city of Puerto Cabello constituted a man's world. The women of Puerto Cabello had very little part in that world, and where they did touch it they did so mainly through contact with men of their immediate families. Business, politics, community activities, were wholly and exclusively masculine provinces. Even social life was preponderantly the affair of men; directly opposite of what it is in the United States, where 'society' is run and ruled by women" (*ATW*, 242).

And from his post Johnson wrote Booker T. Washington:

> The true gauge of equality between man and man is a woman. If a man introduces you to his women folks you are safer in assuming that he takes you as an equal than were he to declare that he fought, bled and died for you in the Civil War; so I was interested when the president of the club said to me a few nights ago, "Mr. Johnson, you ought to marry one of our Venezuelan ladies, and settle here." I was glad to hear him say it . . . because his remark indicated a lack of prejudice that was refreshing.

Johnson also acknowledged that he had not "gone into any of the homes . . . [for] two main reasons: first, I am a foreigner, and the people here are very exclusive . . . secondly, and the stronger reason, I am single; and, here, the single young man must seek his way into the home where there are young ladies . . . [with] but one object—matrimony . . . a father . . . cannot invite a young man into his home without some embarrassment."[7]

Certainly these were gendered and spatial limitations. Yet Johnson appreciated the same-sex spaces of Venezuela and their facilitation of a black internationalism based on male culture because he realized, from his experience with the Jacksonville militia onward, that heterosexual relations shaped much of the discursive formations of racial, gendered, and sexual identity in America, particularly through the white phobia of heterosexual "interracialism." Only in the body could those differences of gender, race, and nation be expressed, and yet the body could also transform those categories. Johnson represented modern experience inclusive of these restrictive terms as passing *through* the body, where the transference of sound and culture might alter these categories through the body's exposure to sound.

As Johnson was well aware, and about which he lectured and wrote in the teens, interracialism uniquely propelled American social relations. The spectacle of black masculinity, generated from white fear and its imminent and eruptive violence, was shaped in relation to white femininity and the threat of heterosexual interracial relations. Many of the massacres of black citizens in cities across the United States from 1900 on had gained fuel from rumors of heterosexual interracialism of black men and white women—the rumor of talk suggestive of an even greater sexual intimacy. Jack Johnson had merely brought this fixation to prominence as a celebrity and emblem of social upheaval in the second decade of the twentieth century. James Weldon Johnson had experienced it when he was beaten and threatened by the militia in Jacksonville at the turn of the century. Reflecting on that experience in 1933, Johnson wrote: "At the heart of the American race problem the sex factor is rooted; rooted so deeply that it is not always recognized when it shows at the surface. . . . [I]t is strong and bitter. . . . [I]ts strength and bitterness are magnified and intensified by the white man's perception, more or less, of the Negro complex of sexual superiority" (*ATW*, 170). Although Johnson's language seems ambiguous—"perception" and "complex" seeming to weigh equally on the "problem"—it's hard to miss the implication that this "sex factor" is merely a perception of "the white man." Johnson sought same-sex forums through which to speak of the "forbidden" topic of sexuality surrounding racialized bodies, and he sought to articulate black masculinity through silent protest, achieved through physical transit—the interpolation of bodies and of sound.

Johnson was deeply influenced by his same-sex relationships with two men from his years as a young man in Jacksonville and Atlanta, men who, through their conversation with Johnson and their actions, demonstrated the importance of the body to modern formations of the self. The narrator of *The Autobiography of an Ex-Colored Man* was inspired by personal friends from the Jacksonville of Johnson's young adulthood who led unusual, impulsive lives, attempts at escaping the deadening restrictions of racial, religious, and other social affiliations that tended to dictate individual potential and everyday conduct, including physical movement.[8] Johnson's good friend Judson Douglas Wetmore, a light-skinned black man and a fellow student at Atlanta University who was able to "pass" as white and with whom Johnson would go into law practice, provided the basis for the narrator.[9] (Johnson himself could not pass as white.) "Speaking of his face as pale," wrote Johnson, "does not convey the full truth; for neither in color, features, nor hair could one detect that he had a single drop of Negro blood" (*ATW*, 76). According to Johnson, Wetmore passed as white as a law school student at the University of Michigan by not correcting the school's administration, which had placed him in white campus housing. Wetmore was bold, rash, and a gambler with his fate; Johnson found his defiance of convention compelling, if not advisable. The narrator's "millionaire friend" (*ATW*, 76), a "peculiar and striking character" (*ATW*, 88) who wants to dispose of time through the "escape" of world travel and music (*ATW*, 86), mirrors T. Osgood Summers, widely regarded as "the outstanding surgeon in Florida" (*ATW*, 93), a well-traveled and cultured man of Jacksonville to whom Johnson attributed the origin of his ambition to write. "Dr. Summers began the liberation of my mind," Johnson wrote, underlining "liberation" twice.[10] To Johnson, Summers was "visionary and impractical," lacking in common sense, but this was the very reason for his influence on Johnson, over and above Summers's encouragement of Johnson's pursuit of a career in law, which resulted in Johnson becoming the first black man to pass and be admitted to the Florida bar by open examination in a state court. Both Wetmore and Summers were fascinating to Johnson because of their refusal to be governed by public convention in their personal lives; he admired the risks they took to secure this personal freedom, yet suspected there were dangers attached to securing it at the expense of social responsibility and a public identity. Of Wetmore ("D——"), Johnson wrote: "He caused me to laugh heartily over some of his most dire situations. I knew that he had acted recklessly, but I admired, perhaps envied, the way in which he could challenge life" (*ATW*, 138).

Summers may have been a "cosmopolite" to Johnson—a term indicating his high opinion of Summers, formed from his worldly knowledge and refusal to adopt the distinct, nationally bounded racism of the United States—but Wetmore and Johnson represented a younger generation of black American moderns. The young men had attitudes toward the body as key to the formation of modern identity, with its bodily functions, including sex and sexuality, as well as the performative aspects of race and gender. Moreover, their experiences of race as black men (even with Wetmore's ability to pass) created a shared understanding of the physical and psychic challenges they faced in their ambitious pursuit of individuality. Their emphasis on the body as an instrument and receptor of performance indicated a significant departure from Christian attitudes toward the individual self and its relation to the world. Wetmore in particular was virulently opposed to racially inflected, socially and politically conservative Christian doctrine, which he found oppressive and antithetical not only to racial uplift but especially to modern, progressive ideas of individual identity beyond racial loyalty—ideas that permitted the formerly unthinkable, including racial passing and interracial relations.

Wetmore engaged in the spectacle of modern black masculinity by throwing himself into the world of jockeys and gamblers. In 1894 Wetmore successfully sued his father for an inheritance and spent the money on fine clothing, excellent dining, and travel outside the South, primarily in New England, where, running in the sporting world, he became known as the "black Napoleon." Returning to Florida penniless, he was offered a post at Johnson's daily black newspaper enterprise, the *Daily American*, which Johnson had founded in 1895. The paper failed after eight months, at which time Wetmore again found himself penniless, while Johnson "went broke and in debt" (*ATW*, 144). While Wetmore found a patron to pay for a year of law school at the University of Michigan, Johnson studied law using "the then most approved method in the Old South; that is, by reading law in a lawyer's office" (*ATW*, 141). After a grueling, extensive state court examination at which, upon entering the courtroom, Johnson was greeted with the realization that "my examination had taken on the aspect of a spectacle" (*ATW*, 142)—again confirming the distancing, objectifying regard of black male bodies in American visual culture—he became the first black man to pass the Florida bar, in 1898.

Wetmore, upon returning to Jacksonville, studied with Johnson for several months and underwent the same examination, with the difference that it "was not so well attended as mine; I judge the first novelty had worn off." "Immediately," Johnson continued, "he and I formed a partnership" (*ATW*, 145). The partnership did not last long because of Johnson's divided attentions between his position as principal of Stanton School, which he intended to convert to a high school, one of three all-black high schools in the South; his endeavors in musical compositions authored with his brother, Rosamond, which drew him on trips to New York City; and his law practice with Wetmore, which came last in priority. Johnson's permanent move to New York City in 1901, on the heels of Jacksonville's Great Fire and Johnson's scare with the bloodthirsty militia, finalized the break in partnership.

Wetmore desperately wished to join in the modern experiments in which he saw Johnson and his brother participating in New York City. Wetmore followed Johnson, moving permanently to New York City in 1904. Johnson writes: "As D—— had disapproved of my moving to New York, so I had disapproved of his. . . . [T]he personal element could hardly be absent from the advice he had given me: unwillingness to have our companionship and partnership broken, and dislike of my living in the great metropolis and his remaining in the small city" (*ATW*, 222). In 1903, just two years after Johnson's permanent move and resignation from Stanton School, Wetmore named Johnson executor of his estate in his will. The will demanded the continuation of this bond, a kind of pact between two moderns. Indeed, Johnson described their bond as one of "intimacy" (*ATW*, 391). Johnson provided Wetmore with a photograph of himself, taken by E. M. Battey, a major New York photographer of the time, inscribed, "To my life long friend JDW. Jas. W. Johnson" (see figure 2).[11] (Sadly, this photograph was returned to Johnson as the recipient of Wetmore's personal effects after his suicide in 1930.)

Wetmore's will makes clear his attitude toward Christianity in the modern world and his idea of racial progress through professional advancement. It declared: "Having full faith and confidence in my friend, James W. Johnson, I hereby nominate, constitute and appoint him, the said James W. Johnson, executor of my estate, and direct that he serve without surities [*sic*] or compensation." Wetmore directed his executor to pay $5,000 to erect the "Wetmore Hospital for Colored Citizens of Duval County, Florida" and

> to pay the remaining or additional $5,000 to the Regents of the University of Michigan, of Ann Arbor, Michigan, to be invested by them for the purpose of creating a scholarship for colored youths in any of the professional departments of said University; but it is especially directed that no one shall be eligible to said scholarship unless he has resided in Duval County, Florida, for at least six years, (but temporary absences for pleasure, or for the purpose of attending institutions of learning shall not be taken into account); and he must be between the ages of eighteen and twenty-five years, and the scholarship

will be awarded every three years; and the income from said $5,000 to be given to the one awarded the scholarship for three years. And it is further especially directed that no one shall be awarded the scholarship who seeks or intends to enter the Christian Ministry, as I believe that one of the greatest curses of the Negro Race today is that they are burdened with too many Negro ministers.

Wetmore continued: "It is my wish that my body be cremated, and my ashes be given to my friend, James W. Johnson; and I earnestly request that no religious services, according to that of Christian Creeds, be held over my body, and that if there is any sermon pronounced over my remains, if there is no Unitarian minister in the City to conduct said services, my friend James W. Johnson shall make the last remarks in my memory."[12]

For Wetmore, the institution of Christianity and its ministry were one thing, a sermon was another, reflecting a secular spirit that he shared with Johnson and that he hoped to secure in the pact of his will. Wetmore gave Johnson and "his heirs and assigns forever" "all of my real property," also bequeathing "to James W. Johnson of New York City" $1,000. Wetmore willed money to Johnson's siblings, Agnes Edwards—an adoptive sister—and Rosamond, intended to "buy a trinket of some kind in memory of me."

Certainly, Wetmore's will exposes his egotistical nature by revealing his desire to create a legacy through objects of remembrance—one suspects, to counter his father's claim that he would never amount to anything. But this document attests to the modern spirit of its author, a trained lawyer who, like Johnson, also had a flair for self-authoring and seized any opportunity to irreverently declaim southern religious practices, black and white, that prevented modern expression—for example, through dancing—and advancement—for example, through interracial socializing. Indeed, in his autobiography Johnson describes the ire he raised as principal by organizing a graduation performance by Stanton's grade school children that included dancing. As we will see in the afterword of this work, Johnson's instructions for the dressing and disposal of his body after death indicate his preference, like Wetmore's, for self-mythologizing and his privileging of secular rituals of black expressive practice such as song and dance over the stifling dictates of institutionalized religion.

One of the most profound suppressions came from the black church's forbiddance of explicit talk pertaining to the body and to sex. Either Johnson or Wetmore had in his possession a book of erotica, *School Life in Paris*, a limited edition, privately printed book of 1897.[13] I believe that Johnson, who had read broadly partly as a result of his office work for Dr. Summers, may have been given this book by the older man. If not Summers, then Wetmore, whose amorous exploits were shocking to Johnson and were inevitably exposed to him in what Johnson found to be an unbecoming way—for example, in reading a woman's love letters to him—may have had the book in his possession, and it may have ended up in Johnson's library after Wetmore's death. I think the former explanation is more likely, partly because I believe that Johnson shared this book with his wife when they were newly married. (Grace writes to Johnson at his post in Nicaragua about reading "naughty" material with which Johnson, it is implied, was familiar.) Well before Grace's presence, Johnson had read the book thoroughly. Presenting a wide variety of heterosexual and lesbian acts as well as pedophiliac ones, the work represents a fairly well established genre of writing made available at least since the publication of the *Memoirs of a Woman of Pleasure* (*Fanny Hill*) in 1748–49. The book's pretext is the letters of a British girl, sent to school in Paris, to her friend in England. The young woman lives in a French boardinghouse, where her stern schoolmistress provides a rather different instruction to the girls, which includes a lesbian rite of initiation.

Despite its fictitiousness, such a book might have provided access to a "realistic discussion of sex," which was absent from Atlanta University, where "a boy could see a girl upon a written application with the girl's name filled in, signed by himself, and, if granted, signed by the president or dean" (*ATW*, 68). Johnson bristled at these "repressive regulations," which merely generated idealized, "expurgated," and "emasculated" talk from which sexuality was absent (*ATW*, 68). Johnson devoted lots of time to readings in science, physiology, and the emerging field of psychology and devised a diet and calisthenics routine that he adhered to for most of his adult life. Johnson's possession of such a book as *School Life in Paris* indicates his modern attitude toward the body as the locus of experience, but one that, while providing the opportunity for its physical expression, could not contain it.

One of his most distinct articulations of the transit of sound through bodies, the Silent Protest Parade of July 28, 1917, organized by Johnson, performed the work of bringing the world of black citizens into the minds of all New Yorkers by presenting visual and sound cultures in an arresting composition. Women and children led the parade; men brought up the rear guard. The usual clamor of a parade was muffled to a soft bass drum's slow, continuous pulse, funerary; the sound was paired with the vision of white-clad children and women, followed by men in black suits. The Silent Protest Parade was a breathtaking performance of unexpected and discordant juxtapositions, with New York City's Fifth Avenue the stage upon which this conspicuous theater was enacted.[14] The children held placards that read, "Mother, Do Lynchers Go to Heaven?"; the women, Mosaic commandments such as "Thou Shalt Not Kill"; the men, the citizen's demands, "President Wilson, Make Our Country Safe for Democracy" and "Treat Us That We May Love Our Country." At the rear of the parade, immediately preceding the American flag, stretched a banner from one side of the street to the other: "Your Hands Are Full of Blood." Between eight and ten thousand people marched from Harlem downtown to the bottom of Manhattan, in silent protest of the horrific events of East Saint Louis on July 2, 1917, in which two hundred blacks were killed and six thousand displaced from their homes by arson. The *New York Age* reported that the parade's participants "marched without uttering one word or making a single gesticulation and protested in respectful silence."[15]

For blacks in the early days of World War I, the East Saint Louis riots were emblematic of the modern black experience of brutality in northern and midwestern cities, where tensions over an increased black population and competing workforce frequently led to violent reactions. Indeed, the East Saint Louis riots, unspeakably brutal, would be followed by other incidents across the nation that rivaled that event's savagery: shortly afterward by the Houston Affair of August 1917 and nearly two years later through the "Red Summer" of 1919, so called by James Weldon Johnson to call attention to the mass bloodshed incurred in a mere three months of a single year. In this summer alone, sweeping racial violence was directed at African Americans in over twenty-three cities across the United States following the signing of the Armistice and the return home of American troops.

James Weldon Johnson authored and carefully and precisely implemented the Silent Protest Parade in concert with his good friend, the Reverend Frederick Asbury Cullen, both of whom marched in the parade alongside W. E. B. Du Bois and other race leaders. The parade was backed by the NAACP, whose ranks Johnson joined in 1916 as the organization's first field secretary. The Silent Protest Parade galvanized recognition of this modern condition of terror for blacks while also defiantly demonstrating organized mass resistance to the hatred directed at them. The muteness of the parade's participants, yet their clearly communicated message, underscored both the visual presence and imposed silence of African Americans in their nation.

Building upon his discovery in Venezuela of the potential of linguistic heterogeneity to enact cultural transferences and appropriations through talk-centered culture, Johnson now found that the body could carry these transferences through its complex relationship to sound. Even before he had traveled to the Latin American nations of Venezuela and Nicaragua, Johnson had used Spanish as a means of racial passing in Jim Crow circumstances—a strategy he mentions using, sometimes unintentionally, several times in his autobiography, *Along This Way*. In the instance where it is first mentioned, it was the Spanish language—"¿qué dice?"—that made Johnson's presence in a first-class train car acceptable; in the second instance, it was Johnson's hat from Panama that made his presence in the smoker car acceptable; in the third instance, it was Johnson's copy of *Don Quixote* in Spanish that prompted the "clean bill" from the county superintendent of the rural Georgia school where Johnson taught. "In such situations," he writes, "any kind of Negro will do; provided he is not one who is an American citizen" (*ATW*, 65, 89, 112). The Spanish language in all of these examples preempts the visual marking of inferiority.

Johnson's orchestration of the Silent Protest Parade would not have been possible without his developing understanding of modern experience as located in the physical experience of sound. In the Silent Protest Parade, he inverted the visual and aural cultural condition of blacks in Venezuela, using the observations he had made there to help him understand and articulate the relation of black culture to American culture. The gendered aspect of this experience, collectively shared, placed black men at the rear of the parade to make their claims emphatic and to place them in relation to the claims of the women and children—divided into groups by their gendered experiences of this racial atmosphere, perhaps, but also connected by their experience as muted citizens who were denied heterosexual expression. Johnson drew attention to the visual presence and imposed silence of black Americans to convey black culture's paradoxical status as seen, not heard, by the American nation. Yet this was not an objectifying presentation of black culture, because Johnson used sound—or "silence"—to show its expression of a modern condition whereby distinctions and differences such as those of race or gender could be dissolved by inhering experiences of the world "out there" in the body of the listener—in this case, the parade's spectators, who were white and black, women and men. As David Suisman writes, "More broadly, sound is a means by which the world enters the body. In contrast to the eye, which emphasizes the distinction between the self and the world, the ear brings the self and the world together. Through the eye, you see the world *out there*; you observe it as separate from yourself, perceive yourself in relation to it. Through the ear, you hear the world in your head, it enters *inside you*; you perceive the world from the inside out, as it were."[16]

Johnson understood the key distinction of sound, which significantly related to the practices of bodily interpolation and crossover that he had performed, observed in others, and written about. For the author, the body was the source of modern experience, conveying meaning not through the visual but rather through the internal experience of the body—especially through sound, which, by emphasizing its transference, inhered difference. Both talk-based, same-sex forums and the aural presentation of "silent protest" provided the opportunity for this internal transference of experience. Much as *The Autobiography of an Ex-Colored Man* enacted this sound transfer in its performance or sounding out of its content (as well as in its dissemination and its elicited reinterpretation by others), Johnson's composition of the Silent Protest Parade recalled for him the urgency of keeping alive his anonymously published work, deepening his aesthetic of extension, continuity, and alteration, so that this work could be taken up and claimed by others.

As if in response to Wetmore's request that only he speak a sermon over his body, Johnson's autobiography *Along This Way* registers his pleasure of appropriating the role of "minister," playfully referring to miscomprehension and the resulting opportunities for passing and transgression in his description of the midwestern trips he took in his newly assumed position as field secretary for the NAACP beginning in 1916, "speaking and organizing" (*ATW*, 330). Johnson writes that he was often subject to a "double confusion" of being taken as a clergyman, based on his introduction to the audience as "ex-Minister to Venezuela and Nicaragua": "To many people, 'preacher' comes up spontaneously as the synonym for 'minister'" (*ATW*, 331). Added to this confusion was the perception of these gatherings as something akin to a camp meeting. Johnson recalls: "My meetings quite commonly served a double purpose; an occasion for me to make a speech on the work of the Association and to organize a branch or add to membership; and an opportunity for local talent, especially musical talent, to display itself. Good music helped a meeting, if it was not too good, and there was not too much of it. . . . I preferred spirited singing by the audience to solos by individual artists" (*ATW*, 331).

In his description of the meetings that would result in the genesis of *God's Trombones*, his most beloved work, Johnson blends minister and preacher, speech and music, performer and audience, capitalizing on the ambiguity that can be derived from such presumptions of their distinction and difference. Through *God's Trombones*, Johnson will develop these acts of bodily interpolation and the incorporation of fugitive sounds into his poetics. As we will see, Johnson sought this work's as well as *The Autobiography of an Ex-Colored Man*'s performance and reperformance, actively seeking their translation, transposition, adaptation, and alteration—acts of bodily interpolation—in an effort to mutually alter themselves and their audiences.

4 Cosmopolitan Travels

Diplomacy, Translation, and Performance in *The Autobiography of an Ex-Colored Man (Der weisse Neger,* 1928) and *God's Trombones*

> The jazz that has been brought over to Europe stands in the same relationship to real Negro music as, for example, the jargon of a Polish Jew who has spent but a few years in America and passes himself off as being a hundred per cent American stands to pure English.
> —Frederick Delius, foreword, *Der weisse Neger*

In *Along This Way*, Johnson describes his composition of "Lift Ev'ry Voice and Sing," a commemoration of Emancipation that began modestly, on the Johnson family home's front porch in Jacksonville, and grew to national prominence through its rehearsal by the voices of Jacksonville children emanating outward, as a process that occurs through the body. He emphasizes his customary practice of walking it out—using the rhythm of his body to inspire and fill the lines of his lyric. There is a second part to the lyric's completion through the body: of the hundreds of children and students who "kept singing" the song, it is also "fervently sung" (*ATW*, 156) by some whites, confirming its physical transference through the bodies of its listeners and performers and therefore confirming their alteration through the interracial transfer of song—"*every* voice." The "immanence" of the American Negro, it seems, is expressed through whites and blacks; their voices "lift" and "carry" their listeners to this fact through song:

> I got my first line:—Lift ev'ry voice and sing. Not a startling line; but I worked along grinding out the next five. When, near the end of the first stanza, there came to me the lines:
>
> Sing a song full of the faith that the dark past has taught us.
> Sing a song full of the hope that the present has brought us.
>
> the spirit of the poem had taken hold of me. I finished the stanza and turned it over to Rosamond.

In composing the other two stanzas I did not use pen and paper. While my brother worked at his musical setting I paced back and forth on the front porch, repeating the lines over and over to myself, going through all the agony and ecstasy of creating. As I worked through the opening and middle lines of the last stanza:

God of our weary years,
God of our silent tears,
Thou who hast brought us thus far on our way,
Thou who hast by Thy might
Let us into the light,
Keep us forever in the path, we pray;
Lest our feet stray from the places, our God, where we met Thee,
Lest, our hearts drunk with the wine of the world, we forget
  Thee . . .

I could not keep back the tears, and made no effort to do so. I was experiencing the transports of the poet's ecstasy. Feverish ecstasy was followed by that contentment—that sense of serene joy—which makes artistic creation the most complete of all human experiences.

When I had put the last stanza down on paper I at once recognized the Kiplingesque touch in the two longer lines quoted above; but I knew that in the stanza the American Negro was, historically and spiritually, immanent; and I decided to let it stand as it was written. (*ATW*, 154–55)

While staging the content of his works on culturally unstable or ambiguous boundaries such as that of black internationalism, Johnson reached for connections through the travel, reinterpretation, and collaboration demanded by his works, developing his reach into a major technique as interpolation. His practice was significant in its innovation because of the limited perception of black culture's role in America, divided into two contrasting but complementary attitudes. On the one hand, liberal-minded whites were eager to recognize "Africanness" in black artists and acknowledge their own "white inferiority complex" in relation to this perception of black cultural authenticity.[1] On the other, white supremacists declared the fundamental, always discernible, difference of white and black. Responding to both of these stances, many black writers felt that working-class cultural forms should be left behind in favor of prior "American" traditions.

Johnson wanted to convey something more complex about the relationship between black culture and American culture than these contrasting and yet complementary stances and black writers' responses to them allowed. In order to accomplish this, he incorporated his writing into other critical conversations about culture occurring in a variety of cultural discourses, especially musical studies. He recognized that culture-, citizen-, and civilization-making claims to an American tradition could be altered by shifting their frameworks to discuss major cultural forms such as the spirituals, ragtime, folklore, and dance.

Music was an important area making a transformation through new cultures that were artistic, certainly, but also fueled by new social networks for its production. It is no surprise, then, that music was at the center of cultural discussions and/or contestations over nationhood occurring in the period of Johnson's greatest productivity as a writer, 1901–35. Johnson placed music—not literature or an explicit focus on citizenship and rights—at the center of *The Autobiography of an Ex-Colored Man* for this very reason. Perhaps more importantly, he developed a concept for the dissemination, development, adaptation, and translation of his work from the compositional practices he employed in the writing of it. In this act, music was more broadly construed through the environment of sound, playing out the "new century's" dynamic interrelation of music as both a direct commodity for its consumers and a supplementary commodity for other productions—for example, as an ancillary but essential supplement to advertising, theater, cabarets, and more.[2] Put another way, music was not simply music; it was a dynamic concept with broadly reverberating effects. As I showed in chapter 1, Johnson located music in his writing through its dynamic interrelation with other cultures and commodities, its ability to perform in the margins of difference and in doing so alter its listeners. Music, then, inhabits a broader environment of sound, an aural environment containing noise, silence, and cultures of talk as well as music. Ethnomusicologist David Suisman emphasizes this point: "Music was not like other commodities in every way, however, for its essence was aural experience, a fact that was integral to the commercialization of musical life. In one form or another, sound was the commodity the music industry trafficked in, and as a consequence auditory exposure was inseparable from promotion. . . . [E]xploitation of the aural environment was a fundamental strategy of the industry."[3]

Therefore, music's distinctive feature as a commodity was the way in which it registered in the experiential landscape of modern American culture. The "soundscape" exploits the unavoidable exposure of the ear to sounds. Music becomes located in this broader environment, mattering more because of this new context of relevance and power in American culture at large. This environment is present-based and potentially cacophonous rather than progressively oriented to African American "uplift" and/or American "civilization" through the narratives of cultural foundation popular at the time of *The Autobiography of an Ex-Colored Man*'s writing. Although Johnson customarily is associated with such nation-building narratives—versions of which can be found in his critical prefaces to *The Book of American Negro Poetry*, *The Book of American Negro Spirituals*, and *The Second Book of American Negro Spirituals*—he was in fact more concerned with the dynamic interrelation of new musical culture, a present-tense orientation.

Although *The Autobiography of an Ex-Colored Man* has been read as the first such text by Johnson to assert the cultural "foundation" narrative of black culture in American civilization, the novel offers up a more complex biography of interrelated musical cultures in the contemporary world of the novel's publishing. The narrator's observation of "the Negro in his relatively primitive state" (*AECM*, 102) and his pronouncement of black expressive forms that "these are lower forms of art" (*AECM*, 54) have been taken as indicative of Johnson's personal attitude toward black people and cultures as inferior and underdeveloped, possessing merely raw material with the potential to be great someday. Johnson, however, emphasizes the present experience of music's integral parts, the interrelation and dynamism of new musical culture, not "progress" to civilization.

For example, in *The Autobiography of an Ex-Colored Man*, Johnson took up Sir Harry H. Johnston's *Negro in the New World* (1910), especially the author's use of the term "Aframerican" to reference Americans of African descent in North and South America. (The Aframerican is in the company of the "Amerindian" and the "Euramerican," too.) In this lengthy work, the British Johnston gazes upon what he calls "the negro and the negroid" in the Americas. Addressing the long road to uplift for African Americans, Johnston turns to music as holding a possible solution to what he calls "the Negro-culture problem":

> One dimly perceives a musical solution . . . a possibility that in music the Aframerican—perhaps even the Negro of Africa—may achieve

triumphs not yet attained by the White men. This race is sensitive to rhythm and melody to an extraordinary degree; it almost seems as though they were, or could be, ruled by music. . . . In this undenominated chapel-theatre of Hampton [University] . . . it is a wonderful experience to hear the singing of the Negro students and teachers, both in a mass and in solo parts. They really constitute an already made opera troupe; indeed the singing was more perfect in tune and time than one has heard in many an opera-house. There are Negro tenors at Hampton and Tuskegee that, were it not for the prejudice of colour, would be in immediate request by some impresario.[4]

Johnston's observations reflect the worldwide attention directed at the United States' "Negro problem"—the question of access to the rights and responsibilities of citizenship in the nation when African Americans were perceived by white power holders to be unqualified, unready for it. The hyphenated identity of "Negro-American" in particular was perceived to be an anomaly. That Johnston turns his attention to music demonstrates the intense focus that was placed on this site of cultural expression to express the different, contending positions on the value of black culture as part of the American legacy.

James Weldon Johnson capitalized on this focus, redirecting Johnston's proposed resolution by emphasizing mutually appropriative compositional practices in *The Autobiography of an Ex-Colored Man* and proving his novel's relevance by carrying it into conversation with Johnston's, along the way appropriating "Aframerican" for his own purposes—a term to which he would return in his groundbreaking, scholarly preface to *The Book of American Negro Poetry* (1922).

As Johnson was completing the novel for publication, he found himself in the midst of an international situation that underscored his life-threatening, paradoxical status as an American diplomat and an inferior within his nation. In his autobiography, Johnson described his crucial actions as American diplomat to Nicaragua through the technique of musical comedy, indicating that its strategy had consequences that were more serious than they first appeared. Assuming his post in 1909, Johnson walked into a near crisis situation in which the opposing forces of the Nicaraguan revolution—President Adolfo Díaz (represented by Dr. Toribio Tijerino as delegate of the Conservadores) and Gen. Luis Mena (representing the Liberales)—were poised to battle each other. Had they done so, Johnson's position as American consul would have been rendered ineffective, his life would have been in danger, and the American presence in Nicaragua would have been significantly weakened. According to Johnson, drawing from the orchestrations of musical comedy, he bargained for time and then called a last-minute nighttime meeting between the two parties. An American lieutenant, "a very zealous young man . . . but not an exceptionally brilliant one," proposed "a bit of strategy that gave all of us a laugh for many a day thereafter" (*ATW*, 284)—a strategy that Johnson as consul approved and put into action. Using the scant naval officers he had on hand, Johnson situated them along each block on the way to his consular offices, with orders to stop and question all who traveled that path. By the time the two parties reached Johnson's office under the escort of Lieutenant Lewis, they believed that there was a far more significant presence of naval officers than they had previously thought because they had been stopped so many times.[5] Johnson describes Lieutenant Lewis's ploy in his autobiography with significant reserve, emphasizing the white soldier's appropriation of musical comedy techniques and Johnson's position relative to this as one of authority. But this reserve implies much more. Johnson's signed and sealed oath of office as consul at Corinto, an acknowledgment required by the US government to assume any consular post, demanded his loyalty to the United States. Nevertheless, his ensign's comical deployment of US soldiers underscored Johnson's dual position as a high-ranking representative of the United States and a second-class citizen within the United States—a contradictory and precarious position. Put another way, the white soldier's charade was Johnson's grave reality.

As Johnson would learn upon his return to Jacksonville in 1913, a song like "Lift Ev'ry Voice and Sing" could perform a physical transfer, so that whites and blacks sang of the history and hopes of a people, creating a shared humanity. Musical comedy, by contrast, employed visual tropes, exploiting commonly held ideas of difference by using stereotypes of physical presence and cultural distancing. That the simple lieutenant could employ musical comedy's conventions with such facility must have underscored for Johnson the serious consequences of the comedy this man employed to preserve difference. This event not only underscored Johnson's paradoxical status as an American citizen whose racial status made him "inferior," in the words of his novel's Ex-Colored Man, but also anticipated Johnson's denial for advancement in the consulate, which was also based on his racial status.

For a brief period following his service to the American consulate as diplomat to Venezuela and Nicaragua, Johnson sought to reenter the world of musical comedy. He had left that world behind, he explained in his autobiography, *Along This Way*, for the "more serious work" of writing *The Autobiography of an Ex-Colored Man* and his first diplomatic post, to Venezuela. Yet in 1912 he found himself unable to advance within the consulate because of a new presidential administration (Woodrow Wilson's) whose political cronyism exclusively supported "deserving Democrats" and the imposition of a color line for diplomatic posts. William Jennings Bryan, Wilson's secretary of state, made clear that under this presidential administration black diplomats could only serve in black nations and indeed should consider themselves lucky to hold those positions. Having advanced from his relatively remote post in Venezuela—where he had waited out an outbreak of the bubonic plague—Johnson had served with distinction in Nicaragua on behalf of the United States and now sought a merit-based promotion, as was his due, to a more stable and developed nation, such as Switzerland.[6] He pleaded his case to the State Department in early 1911:

> I have the honor to respectfully make application to the department for a change from Corinto. I desire very earnestly to be sent to a post not in the tropics; this I desire on account of the impaired state of my wife's health, and because five years of continuous service in the low, malarial coast lands of the tropics has had a deleterious effect upon my own health.
>
> Should this application receive the favorable consideration of the department, I would respectfully submit the following named posts in either of which I feel that I could render efficient and acceptable service: Rheims, Geneva, Prague, Fiume, Nantes, Seville, Trieste. I have the honor to be Sir, Your obedient servant, James W. Johnson American Consul.[7]

Johnson's request was not granted. Johnson pressed his case for appointment to the Azores. When William Jennings Bryan received him in his Washington office, Johnson realized with clarity that "I was up against politics plus race prejudice; I might be allowed to remain at my present post; if so, I should be there for another four years at least, perhaps eight. . . . I wrote out my resignation" (*ATW*, 293). The realization was profound: despite his extraordinary achievement in Nicaragua as a diplomat for his American nation, Johnson's status and affiliation were viewed no differently from the actions of that nation's "worst criminals" whose only crime might be simply being black (*AECM*, 111). Indeed, critic Jacqueline Goldsby refers to the event of Johnson's denial of advancement in the consulate as his second near lynching.[8]

Having been forced out of the consulate, Johnson cast about for a clear career path. Relocated to the small-town Jacksonville of his youth after holding national-scale diplomatic posts, Johnson felt discouraged, unsure, and directionless. He wrote some "potboilers," songs for Broadway, and entered a few short stories in a *Life Magazine* contest.[9] Grace Nail Johnson, who joined her husband in Florida, encouraged him to return to a career in musical comedy and to consider opportunities in the more broadly construed field of entertainment.[10] He explored her suggestion, even coauthoring several film scripts with her, although they contain only versions of Johnson's name. The results were the various "Darkey Comedies": "Aunt Mandy's Chicken Dinner," "The Black Billionaire," "Do You Believe in Ghosts?," and "Why Don't You Get a Lady of Your Own?"[11]

While scholars have attempted to date the production of these works to 1894 in order to follow the tidy sequence of careers that Johnson offers in his autobiography, *Along This Way*, they were written after Johnson left the consulate, between 1912 and 1914, and delivered to the Philadelphia-based motion picture film producer Siegmund Lubin, who in 1912 had opened a studio in Jacksonville.[12] These film scripts provide various pseudonyms in substitution for Johnson's full name, James Weldon Johnson, which he had adopted in early 1913, following the publication of *The Autobiography of an Ex-Colored Man* and his departure from the consulate. These authorial personae (Weldon Johnson, Johnson James, and more), while perhaps demonstrating Johnson's discomfort with the association with film comedy, almost certainly indicate, through their close resemblance to his name, his sound-based experimentation with the names of the interpolators who will carry his compositions. These versions of the author's self were matched by the personae that Johnson began to invent to carry his compositions, including the Mose Jenkins of "The Black Billionaire" and the Reverend Jasper Johns of what eventually would be published as *God's Trombones* (1927) and one of its planned dramatic adaptations, "A Plantation Sunday."[13]

Johnson's failed attempt with the "Darkey Comedies"—film scripts, not drama—of 1912–14 led the author back to musical composition of the kind he had achieved in "Lift Ev'ry Voice and Sing." There he had presented sound's interpolation between himself and his coauthor, Rosamond, who set it to music, and between the work itself and its listeners and performers. Now, in 1914, Johnson once again sought this more supple act of sound as he began work on new compositions and adaptations of already existing ones, especially *The Autobiography of an Ex-Colored Man*. What wasn't accomplished in Johnson's projects to reinvent this work was directed at his transpositions of *God's Trombones* for reading, performance, translation, and broadcast. These acts of interpolation were political—one might say diplomatic—as well as aesthetic, facilitating the creation of interracial and continuously altered compositions owned by those who sang them.

Johnson's sense that his novel was unfinished increased as the years following its publication grew. While he arranged for the serialized reissue of the novel in the Chicago *Defender*, one of the nation's most influential black newspapers by the outbreak of World War I, in 1919—during the nation's "Red Summer"—he considered the necessity of acknowledging some of the major experiences encountered and accomplishments made since the book's publication.[14] Johnson first wrote to William Stanley Braithwaite to encourage the poetry reviewer's interest in the anonymously published work and later, once Johnson had revealed his authorship to Braithwaite, to ask him to collect copies of the work in Boston bookstores. He asked him to "make some inquiries around bookshops or old book stands in Boston and see if you can pick up two or three copies of 'The Autobiography of an Ex-Colored Man.' . . . If you can get them, just let me know what the cost is."[15] He wrote Henry Louis Mencken, his literary mentor of the early 1920s, that "as soon as I can get to it, I am going to rewrite 'The Autobiography of an Ex-Colored Man.'"[16] To Heywood Broun he wrote that he had considered "bring[ing] [*The Autobiography of an Ex-Colored Man*] down through the Great War . . . to try for another publication of it."[17]

No biography is ever finished; the story had continued past the work's 1912 publication. Seeking its extension almost immediately after its publication in 1912, Johnson looked for ways to broaden not just the work but consideration of it by attempting its insertion into different discourses and media. In this effort, Johnson drew from his novel's emphasis on music and mutually appropriative compositions, which extend beyond text and beyond the works themselves. In an example of such appropriation, Johnson was quite pleased to have been "introduced to . . . one man who tacitly admitted to those present that he was the author of the book" (*ATW*, 238–39).

Johnson's technique for extending his works included presenting them to potential readers. From the late teens through the mid-1920s, Johnson actively solicited the responses of influential readers whom he had carefully targeted, all of them literary critics/reviewers, none of whom he knew personally, three of whom would prove to be decisive promoters of the author's career as well as his friends. While Broun kept Johnson's personal copy of *The Autobiography of an Ex-Colored Man* for nearly one year and never provided a response to the author's solicitation, Carl Van Vechten, Mencken, and Braithwaite would become lifelong friends.[18] Here we see Johnson's strategy of initiating connection to others through his works themselves: successfully delivered to the hands of personally chosen readers, Johnson's works became acts of diplomacy, and he regarded them as such. Building critical reception of his work, Johnson's technique of solicitation was also a form of local community building through different critics and their journals, different intellectual circles and reading communities: Van Vechten at *Vanity Fair* and Alfred A. Knopf, Inc.; Mencken of the *Smart Set* and later the *American Mercury*; and Braithwaite of Boston's *Evening Transcript* and *Annual Poetry Review*. As a form of "talk," this solicitation also was a form more serious than it first appeared: it demanded response, directed its selected readers to choose to participate in the contract proposed by the work and its author.

"Someone else is very anxious to see the book," Johnson wrote to Broun, pleading that he immediately return the copy of *The Autobiography of an Ex-Colored Man* that Johnson had lent him.[19] That someone else was none other than Carl Van Vechten, whom Johnson had met through Walter White sometime in 1924. White, who had replaced Johnson as field secretary of the NAACP, had also met Van Vechten that year, shortly after the publication of his first novel, *The Fire in the Flint*, through his publisher, Alfred A. Knopf. Nathan Huggins writes that White took Van Vechten "everywhere—parties, lunches, dinners—introducing him to everyone who mattered in Harlem."[20] In a March 23, 1925, letter, Van Vechten told "Mr. Johnson" that he had read through the *Autobiography* "at one sitting."[21] By June of the same year, the two were on a first-name basis; they fostered a friendship that Van Vechten counted as one of his "closest and most-lasting" with an African American. Between 1925 and May 1926, Van Vechten, acting in an informal capacity as an agent for Alfred A. Knopf, successfully recommended that the publisher reissue Johnson's 1912 work. Van Vechten would present Johnson's work to the reading public by authoring its new introduction. "Dear James," Van Vechten wrote Johnson in May 1926, "I have talked to Blanche [Knopf] about the *Autobiography* and it is officially arranged that I shall do the introduction."[22] Van Vechten's introduction helped to re-present Johnson's work as a 1927 creation, responding to Johnson's wish for its extension and/or reinvention.

Van Vechten had criticisms to offer of the work, though. While he admired "the gentle irony which informs the pages from beginning to end," he also thought that "the book lacks . . . sufficient narrative interest; the hero might have had more personal experiences, but after all you were chiefly concerned with presenting the facts about Negro life in an agreeable form, through the eyes of a witness with no reason personally to be particularly disturbed."[23] Johnson responded defensively to Van Vechten's charge, stating that he had not meant to write "a piece of fiction."[24]

"It is surprising how little the book has dated in fifteen years," Van Vechten wrote in his introduction. "Very little that Mr. Johnson wrote then is not equally valid today. . . . On the other hand it is cheering to discover how much has been accomplished by the race in New York alone since the book was originally published." "Mr. Johnson . . . chose an all-embracing scheme," Van Vechten declared. "His young hero, the ostensible author, either discusses (or lives) pretty nearly every phase of Negro life. . . . Jim Crow cars, crap-shooting, and the cakewalk are inimitably described. Colour snobbery within the race is freely spoken of, together with the economic pressure from without which creates this false condition. There is a fine passage devoted to the celebration of the Negro Spirituals and there is an excellent account of a Southern camp-meeting, together with a transcript of a typical oldtime Negro sermon. There is even a lynching."[25]

Van Vechten stirred up "narrative interest" by rendering *The Autobiography of an Ex-Colored Man* as a cultural "transcript" of authentic black experience replete with high and low folk and violence. Van Vechten suggested that his personal knowledge of Johnson, whose name was newly revealed as the work's author in this edition, gave him a privileged interpretation of *The Autobiography of an Ex-Colored Man*, and he presented guidelines for reading the work based on this. He even went so far as to wed Johnson's work to his own novel, *Nigger*

Heaven (1926), proclaiming *The Autobiography of an Ex-Colored Man* a "source-book of the Negro": "When I was writing *Nigger Heaven* I discovered the Autobiography to be an invaluable source-book for the study of Negro psychology. I believe it will be a long time before anybody can write about the Negro without consulting Mr. Johnson's pages to advantage."[26] The introduction echoed the contradictory themes of Van Vechten's controversial novel: that Harlem represented the sophisticated, urban variety of black identities but that black people and their culture were natural and real in a way that white people and their culture were not. Huggins writes that Van Vechten's "two points" in *Nigger Heaven* were that Harlem "was a social microcosm of New York City. The reader had to reject definitions of the Negro as a type," yet also, "at the same time, the reader was expected to accept the Negro as a natural primitive."[27] I suspect Van Vechten knew that his introduction confirmed cultural attitudes about black culture as either noble and primitive or violent and inferior, and he intended to exploit those interests. Johnson, having written the purported "publisher's preface" to his work in 1912—a provocative and sensationalistic addition to the novel that shifted its framework from story to sociology—was almost certainly supportive of Van Vechten's introduction, even if he was not aware of what, exactly, Van Vechten would write. The very fact of the novel's reissue, its extension through an introduction in addition to Johnson's still anonymously authored preface to the work, and its new cultural milieu of 1927 New York provided a satisfactory succession of frameworks that kept the novel alive by carrying it through these new contexts and voices.

In a significant development of the diplomacy he expected his works to perform in print, Johnson sought the extension of his works into music. This transposition to sound and performance allowed Johnson to develop the ideas that had emerged in the soundtrack of *The Autobiography of an Ex-Colored Man* and the compositional practices he employed in writing it that drew from the Cole and Johnson Brothers trio. Transposing his works to sound and performance significantly heightened attention to the cultural contestations played out in this forum over nationhood, specifically the identification and legitimization of only certain of its population as citizens. Not only Johnson's reperformance of his works but others' translations, transcriptions, and transpositions make clear his effort to draw this attention.

Composers, translators, visual artists, poets, and others responded to this call, as the travels, transcriptions, and adaptations of works from *God's Trombones* and the piece in its entirety make clear. Like "Lift Ev'ry Voice and Sing," publishers may attempt to claim and control Johnson's works as text, but the people disseminate those works beyond any such exclusive ownership, whether by text or copyright. The voices that carried "Lift Ev'ry Voice and Sing" beyond any such ownership similarly drew out the compositions comprising Johnson's collection of poetic sermons, *God's Trombones*, largely through Johnson's facilitation of this extension.

One of the earliest such extensions of Johnson's composition was a jazz-infused chamber music piece for high voice and eight instruments by Louis Gruenberg titled *The Creation*. The poetic sermon by Johnson with this title was published in 1918 and served as inspiration to the composer before the collection that would be called *God's Trombones* would be published. Since the collection's publication, the works within its pages have been set to music many times. Johnson was excited by Gruenberg's work and shared the score with Blanche Knopf, who, as the author's editor and agent at Alfred A. Knopf, had recently arranged for the reissue of *The Autobiography of an Ex-Coloured Man*, timed to be released with Johnson's *God's Trombones* from Viking Press.[28]

In an April 1926 letter from Johnson to Blanche Knopf discussing the reissue of *The Autobiography of an Ex-Coloured Man*, he also mentions: "I am sending you at the same time the musical setting of one of my poems called 'The Creation.' I thought you might be interested in seeing it. The score is by Louis Gruenberg. Perhaps you know him. It was published in Vienna."[29] Gruenberg's composition, brought out in 1924 by G. Schirmer musical publishers, was a "jazz-influenced chamber work" that, together with a musical score for Vachel Lindsay's poem "The Daniel Jazz," published the previous year, brought widespread attention to the composer as a proponent of the "new music." Gruenberg, trained as a pianist, had studied at New York's National Conservatory from 1892, at which time it was headed by Antonín Dvořák. He wrote the score for *The Creation* while he was studying at the Vienna Conservatory with Ferruccio Busoni, who, like Dvořák, was known for using folk music in his compositions.[30] A handful of composers who were Johnson's contemporaries—including, but not limited to, Dvořák, Busoni, Dmitry Shostakovich, and Frederick Delius—had identified the value of folk song to national art. Such compositions embraced the influential "nation-building" narrative popularized by the late nineteenth-century

French critic Hippolyte Taine: natural environs create a mood, which creates a people who exhibit that mood, a language representative of that place and people, a folk culture that carries these traits, and, at last, the development of that culture into a national culture that is representative of civilization. The ascension of folk culture to civilization marks the birth of a national culture.

The nation-building narrative could either romanticize or dismiss working-class culture, for this is the culture of the "folk." In the hands of everyday, working-class people, the ostensible folk artist is something other than a crude building block—the artist is a moving, human category. While the nation-building narrative emphasized historical progress and transformation, the folk artist as cultural agent emphasized the imperative of present-tense adaptation. Johnson's plans to extend his work on the "old-time Negro preacher" through musical and dramatic scores indicate his desire to enact the role of the folk artist in multiple, moving contexts.

Johnson planned to extend the works comprising *God's Trombones* in a form similar to Gruenberg's score for *The Creation*. Using one of the influential members of his solicited audience for the work, Rebecca West, Johnson sought an introduction to the composer and musicologist Leonard Constant Lambert. He hoped that Lambert would provide a symphonic score of *God's Trombones* in its entirety, while Johnson would write the libretto. Rebecca West wrote Johnson that she would "write about the matter to [Leonard Constant] Lambert, because I think it is an inspired choice. I wish I could send the poems to him straight away, but maybe he had better wait for your libretto."[31] No collaboration occurred, but Johnson's attempt to coordinate such an endeavor indicates his desire to transform and extend his poetic sermons beyond the page, his strategic targeting of readers and composers of his work, and his effort to create an interracial conversation through music. At the time of Johnson's writing to West, Lambert was working on *Music Ho! A Study of Music in Decline*, published by Scribner's in 1934 and depicting the rise of the new music and the tensions between "revolutionary" and "conservative" trends in modern music.[32] Lambert acknowledges the innovations of Johnson both as a poet and as a composer in his distinctively American milieu.

Johnson also attempted the dramatization of *God's Trombones* as "A Plantation Sunday," the working title for his play, looking to his brother for orchestration and to Millard Thomas to design the set. He had in mind the tremendous success of Paul Green's *In Abraham's Bosom* (1926) and Marc Connelly's *The Green Pastures* (1929), both of which won Pulitzers in the years of their production.

Johnson also traveled nationwide to perform and promote his works in new contexts, significantly linked to his political work for the NAACP, not only giving lectures on behalf of the NAACP but also giving readings of the sermons in *God's Trombones*, effectively using the text in performance as an act of diplomacy. He carefully noted such pacing and pitch in his personal copy of the book. For example, notes for the performance of "Go Down, Death" emphasize the rising intensity, slowed to rise once more. The second stanza contains Johnson's marks, "even—with slightly increased intensity—diminishing in last two lines." The third stanza sustains and raises that, with "increased intensity" underlined and "Call me Death!" triple underlined: "Call Death!—Call Death!" The poetic sermon's fifth stanza slows the pace and lowers the pitch, as Johnson adds "pause" to the lines "And she's tired— / And she's weary—." The sixth stanza increases the pace once more, as Johnson indicates "acceleration"; the seventh stanza emphatically underscores that Sister Caroline, facing death, saw what the living "couldn't" see: "Old Death." The pitch lowers, as "Death took her up like a baby," in a "pitch low with slight acceleration with heightening effect in voice." The concluding lines of the second-to-last stanza slow to near silence with the insertion of a "double pause" between the repeated invocation, "Take your rest [double pause], take your rest."[33]

Johnson's voice conveyed the meaning, delivering the pacing, rhythm, and pauses that he emphasized as crucial beyond the words themselves; forty years of smoking Benson & Hedges cigarettes gave his voice a distinct, complex sonority. As the popularity of the book grew, Johnson increasingly gave broadcasts of his readings, accompanied by nationally recognized choruses such as the Fisk Jubilee Singers, whose major repertoire consisted of the spirituals. Writing to his editor at Viking, Johnson informed Marshall Best of his Sunday, April 12, 1936, NBC broadcast to London at 1:15 EST: "The broadcast will emanate from the Fisk University Chapel. The Jubilee Singers will sing, and I shall read The Creation."[34]

Eventually, these performances by Johnson were taken into the hands of community performers, as a 1938 letter from poet and Federal Arts Project coordinator Gwendolyn Bennett indicates. She mentions to Johnson the Harlem choir that performs his sermons: "The Negro

Melody Singers, a Federal Music Project group, do arrangements of your sermons beautifully. Would you consider taking part in a program during which they would sing them and you would speak at the Harlem Community Art Center?"[35] Such performances, which feature Johnson's and others' voices as well as musical and dramatic arrangements, indicate Johnson's desire to continually adapt his works in order to voice them through others.

Johnson's effort was confirmed through many examples of his work's performances, including their translation to other languages, not simply because of the shift of languages but because of their cultural resituation, extending the issue of translation and also of the kind of modernisms that existed in Johnson's era as contexts to his works. One of the most poignant examples of this has remained unknown or unacknowledged by scholars of his works.[36] Following the 1927 reissue of *The Autobiography of an Ex-Coloured Man,* a publisher in Frankfurt, Germany, successfully acquired the translation rights from Knopf. The German edition, *Der weisse Neger: Ein Leben zwischen den Rassen* ("The white Negro: A life between the races), appeared in 1928, with a brief foreword from the German-born British composer Frederick Delius. Delius's foreword amounts to a biographical intervention in Johnson's work. There is no evidence that Delius and Johnson met, but Delius lived in Solano Grove, just south of Jacksonville, in 1884 and 1885, when Johnson was thirteen to fourteen years old. Sent by his father to manage a family orange plantation, Delius found himself "in the greatest solitude, surrounded almost only by Negroes." Delius credited the surroundings of Florida and, in particular, "hearing" African Americans singing spirituals and work songs in harmony with these natural surroundings with the beginning of his efforts to compose: "I would sit out on my verandah in the darkness of evening, and would hear from afar the singing of the Negroes. It seemed to harmonize wonderfully with the glorious natural surroundings." "Florida's natural scenery and its Negro music gave the strongest impulse to my musical creativity," he continued. In fact, "a whole new world now opened up to me," Delius declared: "I felt this Negro music to be utterly new. It was natural and at the same time deeply felt. For me the Negroes were far more musical than any other people I had until then encountered. Their music emerged as unaffected and instinctive, the expression of the soul of a people that had undergone much suffering. It was almost always sorrowful, almost always religious, and yet always imbued with personal experience and human warmth." Such authentic emotion was explicitly contrasted with its inauthentic forms: "The so-called 'Cake-Walk' which a few years ago was being performed on all the variety stages of Europe was nothing more than a wretched caricature of the true and dignified Cake-Walk that was still being danced at the time in the south of the United States." Delius also defended a purer form of jazz that was southern: "The jazz being written by American composers and so popular in all the European dance-halls and nightclubs is in my opinion simply a travesty. It is overlaid with too much Yankee vulgarity. The Negro of the southern states was never vulgar in my time. Primitive and childlike, yes, but never vulgar." Delius found the jazz imported to Europe to be imposture and a false, unlearned language like "the jargon of a Polish Jew who has spent but a few years in America and passes himself off as being a hundred per cent American stands to English." And, of Johnson's book, Delius wrote finally in his foreword's last paragraph: "I have read James Weldon Johnson's book with the greatest of interest and find it to be an absolutely true and moving description of the conditions there. I believe that if America is one day to give the world a great composer, he will have coloured blood in his veins."[37]

The results of Delius's exotic experience of African American culture, which marked the beginning of his long career as a composer, included the *Florida Suite* (1887), the tone poem *Appalachia* (1896), a portion of which Delius called "Variations of an Old Slave Song with Final Chorus," and the opera *Koanga* (1895–97), based on George Washington Cable's *The Grandissimes*. While Delius's ultimate pronouncement might sound like a reiteration of Johnson's, the former's disposition toward African American culture is clearly nostalgic and romantic, with the customary diminishment of African American expression to a "natural" state of being typical of a child or primitive. Delius's stance is not much different from the white Americans who saw either cultural superiority or inferiority in African American expression. His starkly drawn boundaries between the pure and impure, the authentic and inauthentic, between immigrant and native indicate the extremity of his attitude toward African American culture, which, however, was widely shared by all who perceived there to be a profound difference between themselves and these "others."

These larger cultural debates about the merit and originality of black culture found expression in discussions not simply of musical composition but, more specifically, of the harmonics within them. Composer

Leonard Constant Lambert had a different view of African American expressive culture and harmonics not as distinct from European forms but as "relying on European harmonic forms," making Johnson and Ellington have more in common with Europeans than with Africans.[38] Lambert went so far as to argue that jazz was "the whole movement roughly designated as such, and not merely that section of it known as Afro-American, or more familiarly as 'Harlem.' . . . Even the Harlem section of jazz is by no means so African as might be supposed."[39] Lambert elaborated: "The harmonic element in Afro-American music is an acquired element mainly due to the religious music of the Anglo-Saxon" and the "'juicy' harmony" of early English composers of hymns, such that "the modern English composer brought up in their tradition often hits on exactly the same type of variant of their harmonic style as does the negro composer—possibly Delius, who has been equally subjected to the influence of Anglo-Saxon church music and its negro variants, provides the link."[40] Dismissing the jazz compositions of Tin Pan Alley as "a commercialized Wailing Wall" because of the prevalence of Jewish composers whose emotional characteristic of "masochistic melancholy" inappropriately voices jazz's "sophistication," Lambert finds that "the only jazz music of technical importance is that small section of it that is genuinely negroid."[41] A further, crucial distinction must be made, Lambert declares, between a "genuine composer," like Ellington, and a "player," like Armstrong, calling it "the greatest mistake" to class these two men together "as similar exponents of negro music." Lambert acknowledges that it is difficult to "estimate the contribution of the negro to jazz"; "more often than not it is the work of three composers and three arrangers plus a number of frills that are put on by the players. . . . [O]f this synod only one member may be colored."[42]

Harmonics and composition therefore become contentious when discussing the location and significance of African American expressive culture: whether in the past or present, located in nature or the city, barbaric or sophisticated, American or African. Johnson's disposition on harmonics as a composer therefore entered into these discussions with Delius and Lambert, both of whom invoked Johnson's writing, drawn to engage with it. In his preface to *The Book of American Negro Spirituals* (1925) Johnson argued that harmonics distinguished the spirituals from other folk songs: "I have long thought that the harmonization of the Spirituals by the folk group in singing them was distinctive of them among the folksongs of the world. . . . The voices of Negroes . . . are *never discordant.* In harmony they take on an orchestra-like timbre." Johnson continued: "When the folks at the 'big house' sat on the verandah and heard the singing floating up through the summer night from the 'quarters' they were enchanted; and it is likely they did not realize that the enchantment was wrought chiefly through the effect produced by harmonizing and not by the voices as voices."[43]

Johnson uses this distinction to underscore the historical miscomprehension of these songs and their larger significance, even while privileging the "effect" over the "voices." It is possible to see his practice of seeking his works' extension through others' reading, performance, and/or adaptation of them as a compositional practice similar to "harmonizing": it is a collective effort, whether recognized as such or not, whether delivered in "unison harmony" or "part harmony," whether simply "transcribed" or, more appropriately, "felt." (Johnson emphasizes "feeling" above transcription, asserting that "I think white singers, concert singers, *can* sing Spirituals—if they *feel* them.")[44]

Even if the two composers, Delius and Johnson, diverged on the matter of harmonics, Johnson owned a copy of the German translation with Delius's foreword and was clearly proud of it as tangible proof of the diplomacy enacted by its translation and adaptation through the added biography and musical conversation—harmony—of Delius.[45] The sound of *The Autobiography of an Ex-Colored Man* and its German travels as *Der weisse Neger* confirmed the process Johnson favored by which auditory exposure necessitates the alteration of its listener in an act of bodily interpolation.

Jennifer L. Schulz has shown how Johnson engages racial justice in his works through "the racial contract," directing attention to "the participants' consensual subjectivity, that is, the ways in which African Americans themselves become signatories of the racial contract, a dynamic that was one of Johnson's own productive interests throughout his career as a political and cultural writer" and that "enables an examination of the ways that 'nonideal' contracts involving race, sex, and class both reiterate and repudiate the ideal social contract in its perpetual reconstitution."[46] The two models of citizenship that have defined the modern nation-state, ascriptive versus consensual, although traditionally seen in contrast and competition with one another, appear in Johnson's writings as "juridical and political frameworks [that] set the two models of citizenship . . . in correlation with one another and in so doing can legislate the fragile balance (or maintain the semblance of a balance) between the symbology and the practice of American democracy." Johnson's strategy, then, is that he "refuses to choose—or more specifically, refuses to enter into contracts in which he is set up to 'lose in the change.'"[47] Johnson's narrator's choice to "neither disclaim the black race nor claim the white race" (*AECM*, 113) more properly reflects this strategy of refusal to enter into contracts of loss. Schulz's discussion of the "racial contract" can be fruitful in a discussion of Johnson's emerging aesthetic of sound, inclusive of his compositions in musical comedy and his actions in diplomacy as American consulate, writings and experiences that shaped his subsequent works. Not only his autobiography, *Along This Way*, "functions to re-see, although not to remove or discount, the limitations and fictions embedded in the American social contract during the early twentieth century, which condition the ex-colored man's experience," but also his poetry, social history (or biography), critical prefaces, and unfinished dramatic and musical compositions rework the social contract through a hearing self.[48] The resounding self of Johnson's writings is constructed to shape social discourse in a particular way, making it more ideal by emphasizing its very process of alteration and dynamic reinterpretation through hearing.

5 Framing Black Expressive Culture

Prefaces to *The Book of American Negro Poetry, The Book of American Negro Spirituals*, and *God's Trombones*

When the Negro musician or dancer swings the blues, he is fulfilling the same fundamental existential requirement that determines the mission of the poet, the priest, and the medicine man. . . . [E]xtemporizing in response to the exigencies of the situation in which he finds himself, he is confronting, acknowledging, and contending with the infernal absurdities and ever-impending frustrations inherent in the nature of all existence *by playing with the possibilities that are also there.*
—Albert Murray, *The Omni-Americans: Black Experience and American Culture*

In the period of Johnson's most vigorous poetic composition, 1917–27, the author, with the support of the black editor and anthologist William Stanley Braithwaite, took on the project of editing and anthologizing black poetry from the modern era, situating its beginning with Paul Laurence Dunbar. Johnson's editorial vision produced the trailblazing *Book of American Negro Poetry*, first published in 1922 by Harcourt Brace with his substantial preface, just shy of fifty pages in length. Added to this editorial work were the two equally groundbreaking volumes, *The Book of American Negro Spirituals* and *The Second Book of American Negro Spirituals*, published by Viking and issued in 1925 and 1926, a collaborative project between Johnson and his brother, John Rosamond Johnson, the first book with a preface by Johnson of forty pages. His anthology of black poetry became a standard and was reissued in 1931 with a revised and expanded preface by Johnson, along with a study guide for the poetry by Sterling Brown. *The Book of American Negro Spirituals*—especially the first volume—was also very well received in a competitive market for anthologies of the increasingly popular spirituals. Johnson placed copies of this latter work in the hands of modernist writers (and anthologizers) such as Louis Untermeyer and Gertrude Stein.

Johnson's anthologizing of black expressive arts in *The Book of American Negro Poetry, The Book of American Negro Spirituals, The Second Book of American Negro Spirituals*, and *God's Trombones* is informed by World War I, the Armistice, and Johnson's personal loss of his mother, who suffered a lingering death from September 1918 to early January 1919. His anthologizing practices overlap with his autobiographical impulses, found interspersed in the prefaces to each of these works, where autobiography simultaneously pays homage to Helen Louise Johnson and locates Johnson in his writing.

In this period of composition and anthologizing, Johnson placed himself in literary apprenticeships to the cultural and literary pundit Henry Louis Mencken and the poetry anthologist William Stanley Braithwaite. Yet Johnson never fully embraced the advice of either man. His writing from this period demonstrates the formation of a distinct poetics of form, a way to talk about the self and collective black expressive practices, such that he dissolved traditional distinctions such as national versus racial identity, oral versus literate culture, and high modern versus low folk/primitive forms.[1] As Brent Edwards has shown, Johnson's poetics hinges upon a theory of transcription. A key issue in African American literary criticism, transcription calls attention to the larger concern of phonography or phonographic voice.[2] Working from the understanding that the traditional formal division of literature and culture between orality and literacy cannot account for black creative expression, phonography calls attention to discrepancies, incongruities, and "telling inarticulacy."[3] Moreover, as Nathaniel Mackey writes, tracing phonographic voice through writers not usually placed next to each other in the long-standing critical rubrics that form and inform our conversations about writing, literature, and difference encourages an appreciation of heterogeneity, "resonances and dissonances, the interstitial play between fit and non-fit, . . . [and] non-totalizing drift."[4]

Johnson uses phonographic voice in the prefaces to all of his anthologies and to *God's Trombones* to free black expressive culture from the binary trap of racial determinism or universalism and offers up instead a notion of "play" and constant motion: a claim to both modernity and modernism, unable to be fully "fixed" or transcribed on the page. This phonography represents a kind of indeterminacy—a resistance to fixity in race or form that links black expressive culture to American modernism without subscribing to its potentially objectifying, freeze-frame vision, its prescriptive primitivism and linguistic minstrelsy, by working through its terms while asserting a broader concept of modernism that encompasses black expressive culture and its transcription.

Johnson's broadened concept of modernism demonstrates how he handled his relationships with his literary mentors: while there is an integrative dialogue of positions that are revealed by Johnson's literary conversations through correspondence with some of the most influential writers and editors of the day—most notably, Mencken and Braithwaite—Johnson does not follow their advice to the letter or subscribe to their values and outlooks on black culture in America. Johnson, it seems, had his own idea of modernism, whose story he wished to tell through his own ideas of form, locality, and social criticism. Through these four works—*The Book of American Negro Poetry*, *The Book of American Negro Spirituals*, *The Second Book of American Negro Spirituals*, and *God's Trombones*—Johnson created his distinct poetics of form, their simultaneous and overlapping generation creating a self-referencing interplay with the result of a defiantly incomplete self, resistant to totality—a modernist collage linked to form and autobiography. As we have seen, Johnson permits, even encourages, his works to mutate and travel through others' performances and recontextualizations of them—for example, the many performances, musical arrangements, and broadcasts of *God's Trombones*. Johnson also repeats and recontextualizes his writing in between separate works—for example, from *The Autobiography of an Ex-Colored Man* to his preface to *The Book of American Negro Poetry* and from the preface of *God's Trombones* to his autobiography, *Along This Way*.

Johnson's poetics situated problems distinct to American culture that were formal, ethical, and ideological. As he continued to write, the intrinsic principles of his writing, his concept of the literary in relation to words, text, and voice, began to emerge, extending his notion of the literary beyond the realm of the textual or even the verbal. As Johnson composed three of his major works of the 1919–27 period, he discovered a language that was made not of words but of tone, rhythm, and affect and a present-based temporality that facilitated his significant concept of the simultaneity and interchangeability of his writings. These innovations may seem to be characteristic of this period in modern American literature, particularly what Michael North calls the "linguistic rebellion" against language's standardization by modernist writers. But Johnson's developing poetics is distinctive for its emphasis on meaning derived from variation and interplay, extending beyond the works themselves by emphasizing their transference through vocality and digression.

Gerald Early observes that Johnson's *Book of American Negro Poetry* "was, in truth, a cultural history and cultural manifesto. One might argue that the poetry that follows serves as nothing more than an excuse for the extraordinary and lengthy essay that functioned as the introduction and seems to be the real reason for the book."[5] The prose of the preface and the poetry of the anthology interrelate in a significant way in that, taken together, they articulate Johnson's poetics. Johnson's poetics hinges on sound and performance and must be linked both to practices of modernism and to critical practices in modernist studies. Johnson's prose presents an important dimension of his poetics that is complementary to his poetry in *God's Trombones*. The preface and collection of poetry of *The Book of American Negro Poetry*, connected to and initiating his other, simultaneous works—*The Book of American Negro Spirituals*, *The Second Book of American Negro Spirituals*, and *God's Trombones*—articulates a modernism participating in broadly defined fields of play that are multigeneric and ethical because they encompass the issues of cultural as well as linguistic translation.[6] In this way it can be argued convincingly that *The Book of American Negro Poetry*, preface and poetry taken together, presents itself as "the work that really kicked off the New Negro Renaissance."[7]

As we have seen, Johnson took part in these conversations through *The Autobiography of an Ex-Colored Man*. What is more, he extended the conversation by repeating verbatim sections of this work in his prefaces to *The Book of American Negro Poetry*, *The Book of American Negro Spirituals*, and *The Second Book of American Negro Spirituals*, no longer desiring to "keep the secret" of his authorship of this prior work. Arrangements had not yet been made for the reissue of *The Autobiography of an Ex-Coloured Man*, but a contract from Knopf followed shortly after the publication of *The Second Book of American Negro Spirituals* in 1926; the reissue was timed for release with Johnson's *God's Trombones* from Viking. Johnson's repetitions create a field of referentiality that significantly alters any understanding of these works as discrete entities, and these repetitions set up his significant practice of digression. Johnson's simultaneity of composition facilitates this practice, which also takes place through the very terms Johnson uses to describe language and form.

Katherine Biers reads Johnson's repetition and recontextualization of his writings, from *The Autobiography of an Ex-Colored Man* to his nonfiction essays and from his preface to *The Book of American Negro Spirituals* back to his novel, using the *Autobiography* as Johnson's foundational text of black modernism from which sound his other writings. While these other writings may at first appear to be "a faithful recording executed in a notebook by ex-colored man or by Johnson himself," Biers alternatively suggests that "Johnson's later essays . . . retroactively mobilize a black phonographic aesthetics from within the earlier 'unreliable' voice" of the narrator in the *Autobiography*: "The *Autobiography*'s limits are porous, open, 'ragged,' archiving black performances in a way that preserves their energy and originality, yet allows their discrepant forms to invade and transform the voice that seeks to contain them."[8] This reading's emphasis on the "porous" limits of Johnson's *Autobiography of an Ex-Colored Man* is fruitful and suggestive but places too much emphasis on this text as foundational to Johnson's subsequent works. The strategy of discrepancy and openness Biers finds originating in *The Autobiography of an Ex-Colored Man*, activated by his subsequent works and their references to it, was in fact propelled by biography and was fully in place without its playback through his subsequent works. Rather than understanding Johnson's works as "inaugurat[ing]" black modernism, operating "retroactive[ly]" to send out black phonographic aesthetics, Johnson's works must be understood in a playback that does not confirm, as Biers's reading does, *The Autobiography of an Ex-Colored Man* as originary, especially because this is a problematic term in discussions of national culture.

In his autobiography, *Along This Way*, Johnson erased the complicated borrowing process between his works as simultaneous compositions that helped to form his poetics. It's as if, as he describes it in his autobiography, he had always had this view of poetics, and it had always existed "out there" in the form of the sermon. In fact, Johnson references the one work to the other, citing his preface to *The Book of American Negro Poetry* in the preface to *God's Trombones* and stating that in writing the poetic sermons he "naturally . . . felt the influence of the Spirituals."[9] This referentiality between works is a key component of Johnson's poetics.

Recalling the genesis of the composition that would become *God's Trombones* in his autobiography, *Along This Way*, Johnson described a process whereby his poetry springs from his poetics, fully formed:

> I had long been planning that at some time I should take the stuff of the old-time Negro sermon and, through art-governed expression, make it into poetry. I felt that this primitive stuff could be used in a way similar to that in which a composer makes use of a folk theme in writing a major composition. I believed that the characteristic qualities: imagery, color, abandon, sonorous diction, syncopated rhythms, and native idioms, could be preserved and, at the same time, the composition as a whole be enlarged beyond the circumference of mere race, and given universality. (*ATW*, 335)

Johnson recalled the potency of an evangelist's sermon on the creation, the Bible "slammed . . . shut" (*ATW*, 335), an abrupt transition from "a formal sermon from a formal text": "There was an instantaneous change in the preacher and in the congregation. He was free, at ease, and the complete master of himself and his listeners. The congregation responded to him as a willow to the winds. He . . . brought into play the full gamut of a voice that excited my envy. . . . The congregation reached a state of ecstasy. . . . [S]omething primordial in me was stirred" (*ATW*, 335–36). At this meeting, sharing the stage with the preacher but sitting behind him, Johnson began the composition of what would become his poetic sermon "The Creation."

The poetics Johnson developed occurred over several years of composition, however. He writes: "Seven years elapsed before I formulated the subject matter and chose the title of the second poem of the group that I wrote—'Go Down, Death'" (*ATW*, 337). In the interim, Johnson wrote his key, critically intervening prefaces to *The Book of American Negro Poetry* and *The Book of American Negro Spirituals*. When he returned to the poetic project of the sermons, he had formed a fuller critical context and formal theory of representation for his work—a poetics. Johnson's distinct black modernist poetics provided a transcription of the black body: the body was not simply performative but, according to Edwards, a means through which to articulate a form not contained in the body itself.

Johnson located the inspiration for the composition of his second poetic sermon, "Go Down, Death," in the "intensity of feeling that came across the footlights from the audience to me" (*ATW*, 337). Johnson continued: "I was lifted up and swept along by that sense of demi-omnipotence which comes to a speaker at those moments when he realizes that by an inflection of the voice or a gesture of the hand, he is able to sway a mass of people. It is a sensation that intoxicates; and it carries within itself all the perils of intoxication. Words surged to be uttered; and uttered, they were effective beyond their weight and meaning" (*ATW*, 337). Johnson describes the "electrical effect" of an aspect of his speech, of "the emotional tension of the audience," which "snapped with an explosion" (*ATW*, 337). Meaning exceeded the words themselves. Reading the words alone of his speech that night, Johnson wrote that he "should doubt that they ever possessed the power to do what they did do." Thus, Johnson's "theory": "The inner secret of sheer oratory is not so much in the what is said as in the combination of the how, when, and where. The how is the most important of these factors, and its chief virtue lies in 'timing'; that is, in the ability of the speaker to set up a series of rhythmic emotional vibrations between himself and his hearers," something that can be achieved using "pure incoherencies"—a feat Johnson claims to have witnessed accomplished by "oldtime Negro preachers" (*ATW*, 338).

Johnson specified this artistic craft as "another language" in his preface to *God's Trombones*: "When [the old-time Negro preachers] preached and warmed to their work they spoke another language, a language far removed from traditional Negro dialect. . . . [T]here may have been, after all, some kinship with the innate grandiloquence of their old African tongues" (*GT*, 9). "The old-time Negro preacher loved the sonorous, mouth-filling, ear-filling phrase because it gratified a highly developed sense of sound and rhythm in himself and his hearers" (*GT*, 9). He also indicated the untranslatable nature of what he recorded merely "after the manner of the primitive sermons" (*GT*, 10), "primitive" here meaning originary, foundational, noting that "there is, of course, no way of recreating the atmosphere—the fervor of the congregation, the amens and hallelujahs, the undertone of singing which was often a soft accompaniment to parts of the sermon; nor the personality of the preacher—his physical magnetism, his gestures and gesticulations, his changes of tempo, his pauses for effect, and, more than all, his tones of voice. These poems would better be intoned than read" (*GT*, 10).

Johnson then indicates that "the most impressive concomitant of the prayer, the chorus of responses which gave it an antiphonal quality, I have not attempted to set down. These preliminary prayers were often products hardly less remarkable than the sermons" (*GT*, 11). For what Johnson did include—the elements he found he could set down on the page—he provided his reader with instructions of how to "listen" for the effects, a scansion that combined the marks on the page with "audible" pauses and the "sensing" of "the reader's ear" (*GT*, 11).

Isolating *The Book of American Negro Spirituals* and *God's Trombones*, just two of Johnson's texts that engage transcription and the body, Edwards suggests that Johnson's critical prefaces to both volumes of *The Book of American Negro Spirituals* initiate and answer the critical question of transcription by using the figure of the body, removed from the figure of music, to capture the elusive nature of musical and aural expression in black culture through the form itself.[10] When one encounters the text, "it is [its] stammer that most closely approximates in literary form the bodily transfer with which swing manifests itself. . . . Swing is above all this physical hesitation, this continuing transfer. The rhythm is never lost, but it is never held or captured in the body either."[11] Thus in Johnson's preface to the spirituals, "we read a text that hesitates and wavers, juggling the momentum of its argument. But this should not be surprising, if we read this juggling as an attempt to register the action of swinging itself. The indecision represents a radical possibility for reconceptualizing agency because it turns (in the sense of 'trope,' of course; it turns a metaphor) not on the foundation of some intentional physical act, or of some communicated black 'essence,' but on the ground of *form itself*."[12]

Outlining what is at stake in Johnson's formulation of this radical practice in his preface, Edwards writes: "In this notion of musical form being situated in a figure of the body, there are birth pangs of a theory of vernacular transcription." Rather than fixing or notating "the performed vernacular into written record," "Johnson transfers instead the figure of an individual/collective body. To put it simply: *Vernacular musical form is transcribed through a figure of the black body*."[13] Edwards finds that, put into practice in *God's Trombones*, "the revolutionary possibility that opens up here is that Johnson could discard the mediating figure of music: he begins to toy with the technique of transferring the swing from the vernacular, performing black body or bodies into the very formal body of the poem; in the manipulations of line, measure, and punctuation, the poem itself begins to be sketched out as a 'breathing,' 'syncopating' body."[14]

Eliminating the "intervening figure" that one finds in Johnson's prefaces to *The Book of American Negro Poetry* and *God's Trombones*, one finds in the latter text that "the figure of music no longer mediates between forms . . . but now simply describes the similarly elusive nature of both forms from the perspective of the listener/viewer or reader."[15] For Johnson, Edwards concludes, "The ethical value of black music is that it transforms belongingness and creative originality into a quality that can never be simply owned or possessed; its roots are swung back and forth in the form itself."[16]

But what more might this theory of vernacular transcription, the performing black body, and the fugitive nature of originality/source mean when we consider that Johnson was working on what would become three separate compositions at once: "The Creation" and *God's Trombones*; his introductory essay to *The Book of American Negro Poetry*; and what later became his preface to *The Book of American Negro Spirituals*? The very idea of simultaneity as a self-conscious choice in Johnson's compositional practice affirms and deepens Edwards's idea of form.[17] Unknown to his readers, Johnson's preface to *The Book of American Negro Poetry* produced the preface to *The Book of American Negro Spirituals* as an offshoot, as evidenced by the critical feedback of Johnson's literary mentor, Henry Louis Mencken, to an early form of the preface. Moreover, the writing of *God's Trombones* occurred alongside the conception and early execution of the preface to *The Book of American Negro Poetry*. (The collection and collation of others' poetry is another dynamic within this pattern of simultaneous and overlapping compositions, as indicated by Johnson's correspondence with a crucial literary mentor of this period, William Stanley Braithwaite.) Each work presents a reverberating continuum between author and artist, art and audience, enhancing Johnson's simultaneous composition practice.

Confirming their interrelation, Johnson describes his work on the spirituals as inspiring him to go back and complete his project of poetic sermons, adding six more to "The Creation":

> The research which I did in collecting the spirituals and gathering the data for my introductory essay had an effect on me similar to what I received from hearing the Negro evangelist preach that Sunday night in Kansas City. This work tempered me to just the right mood to go on with what I had started when I wrote "The Creation." I was in touch with the deepest revelation of the Negro's soul that has yet been made, and I felt myself attuned to it. I made an outline

of the second poem that I wrote of this series. It was to be a "funeral sermon." I decided to call it "Go Down, Death." (*ATW*, 377)

Here Johnson underscores the importance of viewing *The Book of American Negro Spirituals* and *God's Trombones* as synthetic, simultaneous, complementary projects. He makes clear that the works are connected through their "attuning" to each other, much as the author feels attunement to his subject and his role as the temporary medium of their transmission through sound and feeling. Such transcription of feeling may alter but not be contained by the body, emphasizing its continuous and necessary alteration through others.

Mencken's letter to Johnson regarding the preface in draft form confirms this connection of the works through sound and indicates, significantly, that Johnson's effort in writing the preface to *The Book of American Negro Poetry* led to the second project of writing the preface to *The Book of American Negro Spirituals*. Rather than understand this interrelation as a chronological development, it is necessary to recognize Johnson's intentional ambiguities, digressions, and generic porousness as a choice not to choose text over sound. This intentional ambiguity of Johnson was noted by Mencken, who was given an early draft of Johnson's preface. Mencken wrote Johnson:

> I have a feeling that this preface falls between two stools. As a treatise on the negro as artist it is too fragmentary; as an introduction to negro poets it is both inconclusive and over diffuse. My suggest[ion] is that you cut down the front part (on negro music) to a few suggestions, and expand the latter part so as to include some discussion of the chief poets whose poems are printed. The part relating to music is very interesting, and ought to be expanded into a separate article, or even into a book. Why not go into the history of ragtime at length, establishing names and dates accurately? It ought to be done—and the thing would be easy to dispose of. Then you might do similar essays on negro poets and negro painters and sculptors, and so have a sound book on the negro as artist. The stuff, as it stands, is excellent. The fault is not in the matter, but in the design. I think a preface to poetry should stick to poetry pretty closely.
>
> I prefer your alternative reading on page 13. The whole thing interests me immensely—but leaves me curious about some of the poets. In your place, I'd give less space to the older poets, and more

to the new ones. And out of your acquaintance with Dunbar you ought to be able to dredge up more stuff.[18]

This letter from Mencken indicates that Johnson's *Book of American Negro Spirituals* and *Book of American Negro Poetry* were at first conceived of as a single project on poetry that, as Johnson wrote in what he knew would be a groundbreaking preface, had to incorporate music. Significantly, Johnson intentionally had not stuck to poetry as an exclusively literary form or as text at all.

Placed in comparison with Mencken's letter, Johnson's choice not to alter the emphasis on the earlier poets—that history was important—becomes more conspicuous. He would, however, use the opportunity that later presented itself to write the preface to *The Book of American Negro Spirituals*, a second preface to *The Second Book of American Negro Spirituals*, and also *Black Manhattan* (the "separate book" on music that Mencken suggests, although Johnson chose not to focus on ragtime in particular but rather to tell a history of black performance, as we shall see in chapter 7 of this study).

The preface to *The Book of American Negro Poetry* introduces a slippage between vernacular forms of art, which Johnson privileges, and the so-called high modern, text-based poetry his preface supposedly introduces.[19] While revising America's story of origins in expressive culture to be black, Johnson simultaneously confounded the notion of mutually exclusive forms of vernacular and written, low and high, and even black and white (with black culture signing both within and outside of the borders of the nation), such that the idea of the originary ceases to exist. (The term Johnson employs—"Aframerican"—best articulates this contradiction and its rejection of origins.) Referring to Johnson's framing practices in *The Book of American Negro Poetry*, Edwards writes that "the anthology breaks and breaks again. . . . [T]he book splits its own binding."[20]

The simultaneous projects of *The Book of American Negro Poetry*, *The Book of American Negro Spirituals*, *The Second Book of American Negro Spirituals*, and *God's Trombones* are related by what Mark Sanders describes as "an alternative way of conceptualizing the Harlem Renaissance/New Negro Movement as the moment in which black history is invented," in which historicity is emphasized by black writers in order to emphasize their participation in American modernity and modernisms.[21] It is not so much history as historicity that offers the strategic repositioning of black subjectivity and agency: historicity, and the purported "new" of the New Negro, displaced the ahistorical, disembodied, and yet, paradoxically, merely physical presence of blacks in American life. As Sanders puts it, "The New Negro assertion of black historicity" operates as "a pretext for the claim of agency, access, and political participation."[22]

Johnson had been reading Mencken's *Prejudices* and Edna St. Vincent Millay's "Renascence" while authoring the introduction to *The Book of American Negro Poetry*.[23] Johnson also explained the unique project of this book, revealed in letters to his friend Anne Spencer: "I am doing a book on the Aframerican poets, which will, in part, be an anthology."[24] Johnson was thinking about the work that his preface would do to frame the expressive practices of African American culture inclusive of, but not limited to, poetry. He had encouraged Spencer to send all her poems to him; one week later, revealing his plans, he insisted, "Don't say you don't belong—you do."[25] Johnson's collection would bring to light the few familiar names of African American poets like Paul Laurence Dunbar alongside contemporary, understudied ones like Spencer. Johnson intended his anthology to intervene in the collaborative and competitive enterprise of the modern American anthology.

The poetry anthologies of this period (1919–31), edited by Harriet Monroe (Macmillan), William Stanley Braithwaite (Small, Maynard and Company; later B. J. Brimmer Company), and Johnson (Harcourt Brace and Company), presented themselves as the "new" American poetry; inclusion in these volumes was much sought after because it affirmed the importance of the individual poets. The anthologies also helped extend the longevity of a poet's works and reputation, because these anthologies became important teaching tools as the curriculum of universities altered to accommodate American authors and the new form of criticism accompanying modernist writings. The editors of these anthologies, Braithwaite and Monroe in particular, were in competition with each other to a degree that has been brought to light solely through archival research of their private correspondences with closed, intimate literary circles—Monroe with Frost, Pound, and Sandburg; Braithwaite with Johnson, Benjamin Brawley, and others.[26] Both these editors raced to pronounce and define which authors and cultural outlooks represented what was "new" in American poetry, and so it is only appropriate that the initial dispute between Monroe and Braithwaite involved the ownership of the title for a journal called *Poetry*. Although Braithwaite was the first to announce his founding of a journal with this title, Monroe was first to publish her journal, *Poetry: A Magazine of Verse*, in 1913.[27]

Within this editorial competition between Monroe and Braithwaite, black culture had a significant if circumscribed role to play. Braithwaite decisively recognized artistic ingenuity in the works of Johnson and later Countee Cullen, Jessie Fauset, and Langston Hughes, publicizing them in his editorial column in the *Boston Evening Transcript* and in his annual poetry anthologies. But both Monroe's and Braithwaite's editorial visions presented a limited purview of innovative forms of black writing, representing opposing editorial views on black poetry. On the one hand, Monroe recognized the cultural particularism of black culture, which was a raw "source material" for all poets, and embraced imagism as an appropriate articulation of black culture for black poets. On the other hand, Braithwaite insistently argued for the universal claims to beauty and the emotive as the criteria for good poetry and bristled at the idea of judging black poetry as particularist and exceptionalist.

Johnson's editorial and poetic works of this period entered into this conversation about poetics and race and represented a stance different from either Monroe or Braithwaite. Johnson accommodated both viewpoints: in his preface to *The Book of American Negro Poetry* he affirms the importance of a high standard of artistic accomplishment and insists that such a level of accomplishment and originality has been and continues to be a distinct feature of black culture. Johnson extended this formulation to claim that the distinct origins of American culture and literature were derived from black culture. The dictates of what was a legitimate use of black culture in American poetry were significantly altered by the assertion in *The Book of American Negro Poetry* that black culture was crucial to the conversation about distinctly American poetry. Initiating his 1922 preface with the observation that "the public, generally speaking, does not know that there are American Negro poets," Johnson set about demonstrating the "intellectual parity by the Negro."[28] But Johnson made explicit that his subject had "a direct bearing on the most vital of American problems," that of America's greatness: "The final measure of the standard and greatness of all peoples is the amount and standard of the literature and art they have produced.

The world does not know that a people is great until that people produces a great literature."[29] Just in case his reader thought the collection to be a special plea on behalf of the Negro race, one that isolated their example from the greater nation, Johnson made his message about national art clear with this statement: "The Negro has already proved the possession of these powers by being the creator of the only things artistic that have yet sprung from American soil and been universally acknowledged as distinctive American products."[30] Thus the recognition of America's greatness would hinge upon the recognition of black culture's innovative artistic products, apparent in the expressive arts of folklore, spirituals, dance, and ragtime. In these creations, black culture demonstrated the power to originate and create universally appealing and influential works of art.

George Hutchinson has pointed out that black writers like Johnson strove to use locality and ethnicity in their poetry as an appeal to spiritual humanity beyond personal experience. Their modernism embraced the socially oriented work of modernists such as Irish playwright Arthur Synge. As Hutchinson observes, "Collectively, the African American modernists looked more to Shaw, Synge, Stanislavsky, Tolstoy, Sinclair Lewis, Whitman, and Sandburg than to Yeats, Joyce, Meyerhold, Kafka, Stein, or Pound," drawn to the former group of writers' use of the social world as the objective reality or content of their work.[31] Moreover, these writers acquired public power any way they could in a dominant culture, and so "Harlem Renaissance writers depended far more than the high modernists upon realist social discourse because their objective social position vis-à-vis the dominant language differed from the modernists."[32]

Johnson explicitly admired the social realist work of the modernist playwright Synge, stating in his *Book of American Negro Poetry*:

> What the Colored poet in the United States needs to do is something like what Synge did for the Irish; he needs to find a form that will express the racial spirit by symbols from within rather than by symbols from without, such as the mere mutilation of English spelling and pronunciation. He needs a form that is freer and larger than dialect, but which will still hold the racial flavor; a form expressing the imagery, the idioms, the peculiar turns of thought, and the distinctive humor and pathos, too, of the Negro, but which will also

> be capable of voicing the deepest and highest emotions and aspirations, and allow of the widest range of subjects and the widest scope of treatment.[33]

Johnson's discussion of ragtime, "jes' grew" songs, and their appropriation culminates in his introduction of autobiography to the preface, where he links his activities as a composer with his assertion of black culture's expressive capabilities. This reference indicates Johnson's desire to work out a poetics of form that is based on text and sound. He writes: "I was, about that time, writing words to music for the music show stage in New York. I was collaborating with my brother, J. Rosamond Johnson, and the late Bob Cole. I remember that we appropriated about the last one of the old 'jes' grew' songs. It was a song which had been sung for years all throughout the South. The words were unprintable, but the tune was irresistible, and it belonged to nobody."[34] The song's popularity and familiarity are part of its fundamental dynamism, a flexibility that makes possible its appropriation by the Cole and Johnson Brothers trio. This is emphasized by Johnson when he assures his readers that the "jes' grew" songs have not "ceased to grow"; "they are growing all the time," affirming the continued, creative process of their practice by black composers.[35]

Yet the preface to the anthology's poetry rests not so much on a foundation theory of black culture as on a series of gaps or contradictions, such as the reference to the nation's literature and yet the inclusion of the poetry of Cuban writer Plácido in translation. Johnson's project of *God's Trombones*, emerging simultaneously with *The Book of American Negro Poetry* and *The Book of American Negro Spirituals*, helped develop these discrepant concepts into a coherent poetics of discrepancy.

For Johnson, the spirituals entered into the conversation about the "new" poetry and the "American language" because of the way in which they underscored cultural transmission and modes of expression. Individual and communal practices in the creation of the spirituals and the spontaneity, variety, and interchange of their meanings made them emblematic to Johnson of his developing poetics: that is, their meaning is created through their continuous motion and voicing as a cultural practice, much as Johnson shaped his works to be recontextualized, adapted, and revoiced. Johnson used the practice of the spirituals as his own critical practice in writing this preface.

In his preface to *The Book of American Negro Spirituals*, Johnson connected the spirituals and ragtime, underscoring the innovative, fluid character of both expressive forms and emphasizing the spirituals as the "genesis" of fluid, improvisatory meaning in black cultural expression that was distinctly American.[36] "The temptations for these digressions are almost irresistible," Johnson writes after mentioning wide-ranging references to Aubrey Miller and Irving C. Lyles's musical comedy *Runnin' Wild* and the Spanish habanera (*BANS*, 31). Although Johnson takes pains to distinguish the "rhapsodical hand clapping" that propels the singing of the spirituals from "hand clapping to dance-time music" such as the Charleston, he nevertheless juxtaposes them (*BANS*, 31). By linking the spirituals and ragtime as "jes' grew" songs (like Topsy of Harriet Beecher Stowe's *Uncle Tom's Cabin*, who provides this experiential reasoning for how she has come to be, ignoring any biblical explanation), Johnson rehabilitated ragtime from mere automatic, mechanized response to a significant expressive form linked in tradition to the spirituals.

So-called Negro dialect, too, is rehabilitated from fixed stereotype in his preface to the spirituals. Its use in the spirituals and elsewhere is described by Johnson as "variable and fluid" (*BANS*, 43), as he emphasizes its necessary pairing, rather than with "straight English" (*BANS*, 43), with "the poetry of the texts of the spirituals" (*BANS*, 38)—an appropriately layered description referencing the layers of meaning in text and sound in the medium of the spirituals. "Negro dialect," Johnson takes pains to emphasize, is not "uniform and fixed," as it is commonly understood, "nor is the generally spoken Negro dialect the fixed thing it is made to be on the printed page": "Not even in the dialect of any particular section is a given word always pronounced the same. It may vary in the next breath in the mouth of the same speaker. How a word is pronounced is governed by the preceding and following sounds" (*BANS*, 43). The spirituals' musical notation also eludes fixity, and this seems to be the very point. Johnson writes:

> There are the curious turns and twists and quavers and the intentional striking of certain notes just a shade off the key, with which the Negro loves to embellish his songs. These tendencies constitute a handicap that has baffled many of the recorders of this music. I doubt that it is possible with our present system of notation to make a fixed transcription of these peculiarities that would be absolutely

true; for in their very nature they are not susceptible to fixation. Many of the transcriptions that have been made are far from the true manner and spirit of singing the Spirituals. (*BANS*, 30)

It's significant that Johnson refers to the "spirit" not simply of the spirituals but of "singing the Spirituals," the enactment of this dynamic expressive form. Paired with this fluidity of "the 'language' in which these songs were written" are Johnson's many references to the passing and transmission of the spirituals through the bodies of its performers. From the beat that passes "from hand to foot and from foot to hand" in "stop time," or "what the books have no better definition for than 'syncopation'" (*BANS*, 31), to "the swaying of the body" that "marks the regular beat, or, better, surge, for it is something stronger than a beat, and is more or less, not precisely, strict in time" (*BANS*, 29–30), Johnson emphasizes the transfer of sounds that are not contained within the body or indeed within an individual.

Johnson's discussion of the spirituals' elusiveness and fluidity was significant to broader cultural conversations taking place in the American nation. Whites had turned their attention to the spirituals in discussions about the origins of a distinct national culture in folkways, either dismissing the form as imitative or embracing it as culturally and racially distinct. This discussion developed as American modernist innovations took hold because many white writers sought spiritual and artistic regeneration through so-called primitivism, attempting a cultural and moral authenticity in and through their perceived ideas of black culture as simple and pure.

In his preface to *The Book of American Negro Spirituals*, Johnson entered squarely into the debate about the worth and cultural importance and status as original of the spirituals in the debate over the merits of folk cultures as diverse as the spirituals and Romanian folk songs. Johnson was less interested in assigning African or European origins to the spirituals than he was in revealing the presence of black culture as it inheres in American culture. He intentionally connected the spirituals and ragtime to fortify his critique of widespread response to ragtime as vulgar and unworthy of study. Indeed, Johnson's preface to the spirituals gave him the opportunity to address a personal controversy, a debate that raged between noted music critic Henry Edward Krehbiel and Johnson in the pages of the *New York Tribune*. Krehbiel wrote a negative review of Johnson's *Book of American Negro Poetry* that was based upon the critic's objection to Johnson's description of ragtime, specifically, his praise of it as a popular musical idiom of modern America. Johnson wrote a letter of rejoinder titled "The Popular Musical Idiom of America Today" that was published in the April 9, 1922, issue of the *New York Tribune*—an issue that also contained poet and literary critic Louis Untermeyer's glowing review of Johnson's poetry anthology.[37]

In his preface to *The Book of American Negro Spirituals*, Johnson roundly critiqued Krehbiel's prior study of the spirituals, declaring that "spirituals cannot be properly appreciated or understood unless they are clothed in their primitive dignity," emphasizing further the distinction between those who, in the proper spirit, "love" the spirituals and those who "dissect" them (*BANS*, 14).[38] Johnson further specifies that "scientific" or "historical inquiry" indicates that the spirituals are the Negro's "own, original creation," confirming that the proper spirit of appreciation and understanding of them entails an awareness of their "history," "science," and "feeling" (*BANS*, 14). Krehbiel's study, Johnson implies, has it all wrong, because its "dissection" merely conveys a preexisting prejudicial stance of the author toward "a people they [such critics] wish to feel is absolutely inferior" (*BANS*, 14).

Johnson's critique of Krehbiel and others is extended as he discusses the practice of notation of the spirituals in prior studies. Melodic lines have been traced by previous recorders of the spirituals, Johnson acknowledges, but these transcribers have missed the key aspect of the spirituals: their harmony, which distinguishes them from most other folk songs. This harmony conveys the tonal slide, the rhythmic play, the fluid context of these songs—in short, it conveys their spirit or feeling through the act of their transmission, or what Johnson calls "swing." The spirituals' proper transmission hinges on their performance in this spirit, which Johnson contrasts with "play[ing] the notes too correctly" or "not play[ing] what is not written down" (*BANS*, 28). Any performer, black or white, may "flounder . . . either in the 'art' or the 'exhibition' pit" (*BANS*, 29). Johnson assures the reader that in this study, "the only development has been in harmonizations, and these harmonizations have been kept true in character. . . . [T]he songs . . . have not been cut up or 'opera-ated' upon. The arrangers have endeavored above all else to retain their primitive 'swing'" (*BANS*, 50). Acknowledging the work of a handful of whites in helping to bring attention to the spirituals as an important cultural form, Johnson makes clear that *The Book of American Negro Poetry*'s dedication is reserved for those "through whose efforts these songs have been collected, preserved, and given to the world" not through notation but through enactment. Like the children in Jacksonville who sang the Johnson brothers' "Lift Ev'ry Voice" into national culture, black composers, musicians, and singers carried the spirituals beyond themselves, singing, in the words of Johnson's poem "O Black and Unknown Bards," which begins his preface, "far better than [they] knew" (*BANS*, 12). Beginning the preface with his poem allows Johnson to reflect on his creative practice in relation to the spirituals.

In his *Slave Religion*, Albert Raboteau notes the improvisatory, fluid, and multiple meanings of the spirituals, contingent as they are upon their performance, noting that "in the creation as well as the performance of the spirituals, spontaneity, variety, and communal interchange were essential characteristics." He continues:

> To fully understand these slave songs . . . the reader of the spirituals must imagine them as performed. . . . [S]pirituals were not only sung in the fields or at prayer and worship services but were shouted—that is, danced in the ring shout—with the result that the lyrics of the songs were acted out or dramatized by the band of shouters. The shout would start with a leader calling out a verse of a spiritual while the shouters responded by walking around in a circle. When the singers who stood outside the ring took up the chorus, the shout proper would begin with the ring band shuffling rapidly to the beat announced by the hand-clapping and foot-tapping of the chorus of singers who were said then to be "basing" the shouters.[39]

Well before jazz, "the flexible, improvisational structure of the spirituals gave them the capacity to fit an individual slave's specific experience into the consciousness of the group . . . through song," as Raboteau notes.[40] Back and forth, "an individual would extemporize the verses, freely interjecting new ones from other spirituals. Frequently, before he was finished, everyone else would be repeating a chorus familiar to all."[41]

Johnson used the centrality of performance in the spirituals to model the meanings he hoped to enact in his prefaces to *The Book of American Negro Poetry*, *The Book of American Negro Spirituals*, and *God's Trombones*. Johnson's own form in these prefaces tunes itself to the black expressive practices he introduces: resistance to notation, digression, playing with the beat, swinging from one body to another, meanings inside and outside the individual, carried by all and yet elusive.

Moreover, Johnson redirects and extends his works through their accumulating recontextualization with each other, much as the spirituals represent porous meaning that alters with performer and setting. Writes Raboteau: "Because the spirituals were open formally and thematically to change, a spiritual in one situation might mean one thing and in another something else, without negating its earlier meaning. A particular verse might have a particular significance for a person at one time and not at another."[42] Thus, *The Book of American Negro Spirituals* confirmed Johnson's developing poetics. Johnson's exploration of the porousness of meaning and form was also an autobiographical inquiry, reflecting on the position of the author in relationship to his subject, as seen not only in his self-referencing through the poem "O Black and Unknown Bards" but also in his location of self in the writing of the preface, naming the place from which he wrote of the spirituals—Great Barrington, Massachusetts.

Johnson's personal experiences of the spirituals, the ring shout, barbershop quartets, and more appear throughout both of his prefaces to the two volumes of the spirituals. The autobiographical element allows Johnson to attest to the originality and "artistic genius" of the authors of the spirituals, certainly, but also to digress from his subject as fixed in either time or location.

The spirituals' interpretation of biblical events blows breath and dynamism into what has been "given in the gospels" through "magical poetic phrase," "piercing lyrical cries," and "the innate expression of his own emotions and experiences" (*BANS*, 41). Johnson too attempts this fusing of personal emotion and experience with what is given in the spirituals, creating a dynamic, interpolated relation of his subject as a continuously altering medium of expression.

In his preface to *The Second Book of American Negro Spirituals* (1926), Johnson emphasized the "unexpected variety" of the spirituals, which, he stressed, were "still in the making."[43] Johnson distinguished between collectors of the spirituals—oftentimes white northerners—and their creators, stating that it is left to "the Negro to establish his title as their sole creator" (*SBANS*, 16). Again invoking "further digression" (*SBANS*, 17), Johnson conveys his mistrust of early notations of ragtime and the spirituals, stating that "the first of the so-called Ragtime songs to be published were actually Negro secular folk-songs that were set down by white men, who affixed their own names as the composers. In fact, before the Negro succeeded fully in establishing his title as creator of his secular music the form was taken away from him and made national instead of racial" (*SBANS*, 16).

Continuing his metaphor of the body in relationship to expressive culture, Johnson draws attention to the widespread miscomprehension of "the Negro, intellectually and morally empty, . . . here to be filled, filled with education, filled with religion, filled with morality, filled with culture, in a word, to be made into what is considered a civilized human being" (*SBANS*, 18–19). He declares that "spirituals . . . have been . . . the main force in breaking down the immemorial stereotype that the Negro in America is nothing more than a beggar at the gate of the nation, waiting to be thrown the crumbs of civilization; that he is here only to receive; to be shaped into something new and unquestionably better" (*SBANS*, 18). The current reassessment of the spirituals has provided "this awakening to the truth that the Negro is an active and important force in American life; that he is a creator as well as a creature; that he has given as well as received; that he is the potential giver of larger and richer contributions" (*SBANS*, 19). This recognition of the spirituals' merit as art "gave rise to what can be termed The Negro Youth Movement, a movement which embodies self-sufficiency, self-confidence and self-expression, and which is lacking the old group sensitiveness to the approbation or opinion of its white environment" (*SBANS*, 19). Johnson's preface to *The Book of American Negro Spirituals*, to which he refers numerous times in his preface to *The Second Book of American Negro Spirituals*, provides this recognition, creating a conversation between its two volumes while crosscutting between art forms present and past, such as jazz and the spirituals.

Moreover, continuing his practice of sharing his works with others as an act of diplomacy, Johnson forced recognition of his anthology of the spirituals. Johnson sent *The Book of American Negro Spirituals* to poet and influential critic Louis Untermeyer, who was working on an anthology of early American poetry. Based on the information Johnson provided, Untermeyer decided to include spirituals and work songs as an appendix to his collection.[44] Johnson also sent a copy of *The Book of American Negro Spirituals* to Carl Sandburg, who wrote Johnson from the *Chicago Daily News*: "Your foreword covers wide ground, accurately, persuasively,—the best statement and explanation of the singing of the spirituals that I have ever seen. The scores are an advance; they notate elusive approximations of notes; for perfectly successful scoring new devices would have to be invented. When people shall ask me what book to get on the American Negro Spirituals I shall tell them by all means to get this one."[45] Johnson also sent a copy of his collection of the spirituals to Gertrude Stein. All noted white modernist poets, Untermeyer, Sandburg, and Stein were called upon by Johnson to recognize the distinct relevance of the spirituals that Johnson related in his collection.

Anthologizing poetry and spirituals, rehearsing his framing of these works, allowed Johnson to develop his ideas about black expressive culture and its transference, articulate its relevant place in American literary modernism, and generate the author's improvisatory aesthetic of text and sound. His activity as an author of these shifting frameworks informed his focused, simultaneous exploration of language in *God's Trombones*.

6 "The Creation"
God's Trombones and Johnson's Formation of a Black Modernist Poetics

> He strode the pulpit up and down in what was actually a very rhythmic dance, and he brought into play the full gamut of his wonderful voice, a voice—what shall I say?—not of an organ or a trumpet, but rather of a trombone, the instrument possessing above all others the power to express the wide and varied range of emotions encompassed by the human voice—and with greater amplitude. . . . The old-time Negro preacher loved the sonorous, mouth-filling, ear-filling phrase because it gratified a highly developed sense of sound and rhythm in himself and his hearers.
>
> —James Weldon Johnson, preface to *God's Trombones*

In the eleven or so years between 1919 and 1930, poetry became a major platform for advancing broader arguments about a distinctively American form of literature. Within this conversation about culture, art, and nation, black authors created innovative forms of modernism that sometimes went unrecognized by white editors at the "little magazines." Such was Johnson's experience as he sought the publication of his first poem, "The Creation," of what would be issued almost ten years later as *God's Trombones.* In this chapter, I discuss Johnson's modernist poetic project in the postwar period, culminating in the collection published by Viking Press, *God's Trombones: Seven Negro Sermons in Verse* (1927).

As Michael North has shown, the use of idiomatic and so-called dialect-driven speech was a main operative in the poetry of modernism. He describes the issue of the *Oxford English Dictionary*, founded in 1871 and published over the next forty years, as "the most important event in the stabilization of the English language," against which authors such as T. S. Eliot, Ezra Pound, William Carlos Williams, and Gertrude Stein rebelled.[1] North convincingly shows this "linguistic rebellion" to be at odds with the literary modernist projects of Johnson, Zora Neale Hurston, and others while leaving open-ended the pressing issue of language in relationship to performativity and the embodiment of voice in these authors' works. Johnson's poetic sermons, beginning with "The Creation," emerged in this same period of the modernist innovations of Vachel Lindsay, T. S. Eliot, and Carl Sandburg that involve so-called black dialect and folk. The project of *God's Trombones* also worked against the standardization of English emblematized by the *Oxford English Dictionary*'s release, attempting to eliminate the reductive quality of dialect by emphasizing the rhythm, tonality, and poetry of black folk speech as a living, transmitted practice. Not only standardization but also the imposition of text as the form fully representing experience silenced black artists such as preachers and their expressive modes, which were not often noted on the page as text. Indeed, Johnson contrasted the life and spirit of the spirituals with the "books of idiotic anthems" sold for profit by "gospel hymn-book agents" that replaced them for a time in formal Sunday worship (*BANS*, 49). In combination with Johnson's simultaneous project of *The Book of American Negro Spirituals*, *God's Trombones* moreover underscored the resistance of black expressive culture to notation. The sounds it conveys are elusive, in-between, unrecordable except by their transmission through the voices of others, as Johnson emphasized in his preface to the work. Johnson carried his ideas about black expressive culture into his practice as an author, combining and extending his written works—*The Book of American Negro Spirituals* and *God's Trombones*—the one to the other, voice to voice.

The poet, critic, and anthologist Harriet Monroe has been acknowledged widely as a shaper of American modernist poetry through her journal *Poetry*, which published authors as varied as Margaret Mead, Edna St. Vincent Millay, Robert Frost, e. e. cummings, Ford Maddox Ford, and Vachel Lindsay. She has even been credited with the first printed use of the word "Imagiste," which accompanied the publication of H.D.'s poems in her journal in 1913. Such an acknowledgment underscores Monroe's shaping of the "new" American poetry centered on such modernist innovations as imagism.

Less attention has been paid, however, to her editorial view of black authors and the poetics of American culture through the lens of race. Monroe almost exclusively published imagist poems by black authors such as Fenton Johnson and Langston Hughes while promoting white authors' explorations of the exotic, such as Lew Sarrett's "Chippewa Corn Dance" (Monroe described it as an "authentically dramatic" chant of "a Chippewa corn dance in the original to a wild accompaniment of tribal music") and Vachel Lindsay's "The Congo":

> Fat black bucks in a wine-barrel room,
>
> . . . .
>
> Pounded on the table,
>
> . . . .
>
> Hard as they were able,
>
> . . . .
>
> THEN I had religion, THEN I had a vision.
> I could not turn from their revel in derision.[2]

Johnson's "The Creation" did not fit Monroe's criteria for her journal. Its rejection confirmed for Johnson the importance of his project as one of language and register rather than image and propelled him to develop his poetics through both the poetry of *God's Trombones* and the sound-oriented prefaces of *The Book of American Negro Poetry* and *The Book of American Negro Spirituals*.

As Harriet Monroe wrote in her preface to Vachel Lindsay's *The Congo and Other Poems*, "The return to primitive sympathies between artist and audience, which may make possible once more the assertion of primitive creative power, is recognized as the immediate movement in modern art."[3] This "quick response between artist and audience," she continued, could also be found "in a measure . . . in modern vaudeville."[4] "Vaudeville" was a term frequently used in discussing the essential aspect of performance in modern poetry, referencing its appropriate channeling of "primitive" creation and characterization of the immediacy of the art and the demand for an instinctive response to it. It was obviously a problematic, troubling term for modern black poets. Lindsay, Millay, and others made their signature as poets through their performance of their poetry. Sterling Brown, Johnson, and others were wary of the reception of their poetry as pure performance, the response to their use of vernacular culture as mere vaudeville, mere source, mere transcription, not poetry. Monroe recognized the poetic experimentalism and authentic performance of folk culture through the voices of white writers. Yet in her editorial practices, she isolated black writers into performance and imagism as original "sources," not poetic experimenters.

Harriet Monroe's introduction to the first edition of her anthology, *The New Poetry: An Anthology of Twentieth-Century Verse in English* (1917), confirms this relationship between the imagistic and the performative, a vision of what Monroe describes as its "ideal of absolute simplicity and sincerity" which also functioned as the editorial vision of *Poetry: A Magazine of Verse*:

> The new poetry strives for a concrete and immediate realization of life; it would discard the theory, the abstraction, the remoteness, found in all classics not of the first order. It is less vague, less verbose, less eloquent, than most poetry of the Victorian period and much work of earlier periods. It has set before itself an ideal of absolute simplicity and sincerity—an ideal which implies an individual, unstereotyped diction; and an individual, unstereotyped rhythm. Thus inspired, it becomes intensive rather than diffuse. It looks out more eagerly than in; it becomes objective. The term "exteriority" has been applied to it, but this is incomplete. In presenting the concrete object or the concrete environment, whether these be beautiful or ugly, it seeks to give more precisely the emotion arising from them, and thus immeasurably widens the scope of art.[5]

Imagism functioned to strip away unnecessary mediation of the object and the sensory experience it bore through racial images that could facilitate that purification. If imagist poetry functioned almost as an epigram, then racial epigrams projected the self to a primitive state, the state of the "other," a kind of racial posturing that has a long tradition in American literature. Although employed by some black writers, the poetic technique of imagism became a dangerously objectifying form of racial poetics, involving clinical distancing and objectification. While the intent of much imagist poetry was to strip away the mediating voice of the speaker, for which a distilled image would be substituted, such poems were in fact capable of reinforcing the distinction between the poem's subject and the linguistic project of its author. Imagism that represented a racial image could confirm for its reader or author the same boundaries of difference that pluralist writing confirmed. Racial "others" could direct the white self to a place of regeneration while affirming cultural purity and distance between blacks and whites. The minstrelsy of Ezra Pound and T. S. Eliot in their private correspondence, the incorporation of popular black song into their poetry, demonstrate their intentional and willful manipulation of racial personae in the search for the modern, a performative model that reinforced the distinction between white and black.[6]

Against this performance model of black culture as object and other, poet Sterling Brown confided to Johnson his shared interest in the issue of linguistic transcription and his contempt for the reception of his poetry as performance.

Brown characterized Johnson's position on vernacular transcription in *God's Trombones* as a "distinction between traditional and authentic dialect. I am very much interested in that problem," wrote Brown.[7] Offsetting this cultural and politicized project of the two writers, however, was the delicate, complex position Brown found himself in as he publicized and performed his own works. In the hands of his audience, he wrote to Johnson:

> I am being—I would have said lionized—but that would be silly—poodleized (victimized) by literate and semi-illiterate—who have heard through no fault of mine (unless my going up and down in the subway stations with a bell and a sandwich board reading "I have a book coming out") or my book. These hostesses—young no longer, alas, but still dumb—craves to hyeah me recite my worses—If I were to pull out a dialect piece on some of these Boahstonians or the word Nigger they'd swoon . . . "Oh, Mr. Brown, we have heard of Slim Greer. Do let us have his exploits."[8]

Brown's characterization of his poetry's reception through the female gaze enhances his position of entrapment, so that his objectification is sexualized. The gendered reception of "dialect" in his poetry sexualizes and racializes his objectification: a female gaze and reception shape his masculine delivery while diminishing his status to that of a pet. Johnson, too, encountered this objectification as he struggled to make clear his original literary project in *God's Trombones*, composed over the course of about six years, the first poetic sermon of which was "The Creation."

On January 15, 1919, James Weldon Johnson wrote William Stanley Braithwaite a weighty letter describing the lingering death of his mother, who finally passed on January 7, 1919. He wrote:

> I am getting myself together now, and I hope to do some sure enough work. I have finished the "Sermon" and I am sending it to you for

your criticism. I feel quite well satisfied with all of it except the closing lines which tell of the actual making of man. I wrote this part out in two ways; I shall send you both readings, and I wish you would give me your idea as to which is better. I am partly inclined to omit the making of man. As soon as I hear from you, I'll get the poem off. Do you still think I should send it to the Yale Review?

In this same letter, Johnson encouraged Braithwaite to

> get out the little Afro-American anthology which you spoke about. This is something you can do in three days, as a sort of rest from your real work. I believe there is a market for such a book now. I hope we shall be able to arrange to get together for a couple of weeks next summer and get that Negro Literature underway; there is a book that will make money. We can put it in every colored school and college in the country; and I have no doubt that it will have some circulation in white schools.[9]

Days later, presumably after a dismissal by Braithwaite of the project, Johnson assumed the anthology as his own. He wrote to Braithwaite: "I'll tackle the Afro-American anthology," adding, "You did not say what you thought of the 'Sermon On the Creation,' . . . am awaiting your judgment before sending it out."[10]

Through this process of framing black culture and black expressive practices, Johnson was also framing his own literary works and developing a stronger ethical philosophy—a poetics—of his practices. Indeed, the younger poet Sterling Brown wrote Johnson describing *God's Trombones* as "the marriage of music and idea."[11]

Charles Scruggs's *The Sage in Harlem: H. L. Mencken and the Black Writers of the 1920s* (1984) brought to light the overwhelming influence of Mencken's critical perspective on and his mentoring of black writers during the Harlem Renaissance. Mencken's emphasis on the medium of prose and the lens of realism—using skills of observation, writing what you know—influenced Johnson, the irreverent, satirical essayist and novelist George Schuyler, and a host of black writers from the period, shaping widespread black perception of the accomplishments and long road ahead in black letters. As Scruggs shows, Mencken's emancipatory vision for black letters was perhaps too limited by this emphasis on genre and source, and while black writers might not have openly questioned his stance, they certainly did not hold themselves to the guidelines he laid out for "good literature."[12] As much as Johnson admired Mencken's iconoclasm and irreverent treatment of mannered literary convention, he did not hold the same attitudes, and he maintained his own vision of literary and cultural innovation. (Even Johnson's persistence in writing poetry, and sending it to Mencken for publication consideration, could be considered an act of defiance, a plain rejoinder to Mencken's assertion that prose was all that mattered in modern America.) As Johnson's *God's Trombones* and some of the other signal texts of the Harlem Renaissance demonstrated, not just prose but poetry, not just realism but song, broadly construed, could effectively articulate modern black identity in modernist writing.[13] Writing and cultures that were traditionally distinguished from each other had the potential to convey not only the multiplicity of expressive modernist modes but also their asymmetries through social critique. Johnson used the sermonic tradition to enact this complex register. Scruggs suggests that both Johnson and his fellow Floridian Zora Neale Hurston authored portraits of a preacher who was "more complicated than he appears to be."[14] In creating these figures, Johnson and Hurston acknowledged the preacher not just as a moral leader or a wise man but as an artist—a poet, a performer, a musician capable of sounding the multiple registers of black artistic expression as a continuous practice.

Johnson's preface to *God's Trombones*, which asserted that the author had "tried sincerely to fix something of [the old-time Negro preacher]" (*GT*, 11), was presented to its audience as an explicitly modernist project, engaging language and region while accommodating the poet's license in making it his own. Johnson's preface, acknowledging the culture of black preaching as one located in the American South reaching back to early colonialism and slavery, also acknowledged the time and place of Johnson the poet: New York City, 1927, emphasizing both his creation of and distance from his subject. The collection engages the creation of folk image and anthropomorphism—for example, a God who bends over his creation of man "like a mammy bending over her baby." Johnson's poetic sermons draw on the persona of the black preacher and on the multiple registers of meaning in the sermon as well as the range of linguistic features of tonality and vernacular. Upon the recommendation of Henry Louis Mencken, one of Johnson's literary mentors (in addition to William Stanley Braithwaite), he attempted to publish the first sermon he wrote, "The Creation," in the pages of Harriet Monroe's journal, *Poetry*. The remnants of this editorial exchange reveal the challenges that black modernist writers faced as they sought recognition for their own innovative literary projects.

Johnson was working on putting his assertion regarding black expressive practices into practice, forming a more complete poetics based on the contradictions and "breaks" in the composition of the poetic sermons that constitute *God's Trombones*. Mark Sanders cites the "aggressive eclecticism" of *God's Trombones* as it "asserts an indigenous modernism of form."[15] This work's preface asserts that while possessing this "innate power" of "emotional endowment, . . . originality and artistic conception, and . . . the power of creating that which has universal appeal and influence," the "Aframerican" poet must strive to employ "an instrument of greater range than dialect . . . if he is to do more than sound the small notes of sentimentality" (*GT*, 8). And he positions his poetic sermons in the collection as open-ended responses to this imperative: "The form of 'The Creation,' the first poem of this group, was a first experiment by me in this direction" (*GT*, 9). In *God's Trombones*, Johnson attempts to divert the limited reception of African American poetry by reappropriating the phonic range of black expression, locating its voice *in between* his preface to the work and his poems.

On April 29, 1919, Mencken wrote to Johnson encouragingly of his first poetic sermon, "The Creation": "This is not only an interesting experiment; it seems to me a very positive success. I think you are quite right to avoid the usual grotesque dialect. Why not send it up to Miss Harriet Monroe, editor of *Poetry*? Her address is 543 Cass Street, Chicago. Tell her that I suggested it. I'd ask it for The Smart Set at once if it did not fall so far outside our field."[16] Armed with a letter of introduction from Mencken, Johnson presented his work to Monroe.

Partly as a result of Mencken's qualified appreciation of Harriet Monroe's vision of the new poetry, set down in his essay "Prejudices" (1919), Johnson was able to attempt an entrée to *Poetry*'s pages. Mencken praised Monroe as the "mother superior" of the new poetry movement (in contrast to Amy Lowell, "the schoolmarm of the movement, vastly more the pedagogue than the artist").[17] According to Mencken, "Miss Monroe has managed to retain a certain judicial calm in the midst of all the whooping and clapper-clawing, and so she has avoided running amuck, and her magazine has printed the very best of the new poetry and avoided much of the worst." Still, Mencken continued, "the movement shows signs of having spent its strength."[18]

James Weldon Johnson wrote Monroe in 1919, including a letter of introduction from Mencken and enclosing the poem, now known to virtually every reader of American poetry, "The Creation." This poem was the germ of what would be published in 1927 as a signal text of the Harlem Renaissance in letters, *God's Trombones*. Johnson enclosed the poem for her consideration, but Monroe rejected it, writing in her editorial note in the margin of the poem, "The Creation, but 'ironed out.'" In her letter of rejection to Johnson, Monroe referenced a performance of the sermon titled "The Creation," which she had seen a few years earlier: "The enclosed poem is extremely interesting, but it does not seem to me so good a version of this folk-lore subject as one which I heard some years ago, recited by a lady—a southern poet whose name I stupidly forgot—in a program of Negro monologues. I urged her at the time to write out her recitations and print them, but I don't know whether she has done so. THE CREATION, as she gave it, seemed to me really sublime. I regret that we cannot use this version."[19] Evidently Monroe did not recognize Johnson's project of rendering the language of the black folk preacher standard while retaining the rhythm and tonality of the vernacular as sufficiently modernist.

In addition to sending a rejection letter to Johnson, Monroe wrote Mencken:

> Mr. Jas. Weldon Johnson sent me his *Sermon on the Creation*, also your letter to him suggesting that he offer it to me. I thank you for keeping *Poetry* in mind, and enclose a copy of my letter to him, to explain why I am returning the poem.
>
> His version of what is evidently more or less current folk-lore stuff is very much ironed out compared with the one I heard.[20]

Mencken responded:

> I had a notion, too, that Johnson's poem was a bit too suave and sophisticated, but it seemed to me that you ought to see it. He is, by the way, a remarkable man—a good politician as well as a sound writer. The thing, of course, was not for us. We have gone back to short lyrics, and wallow in the high respectability of it. After all, *some* one must do it. You have got all the other magazines imitating your experiments. I never miss reading *Poetry*. It is amazing how you keep up its interest.[21]

On May 9 Monroe wrote Mencken again to clarify her position on Johnson after having read his *Fifty Years and Other Poems* (1917), suggested by Mencken: "That Negro, Mr. J. W. Johnson, just escapes being a poet, I think. His book has good bits in it, but it rambles and dilutes."[22] "That Negro" was a strong indication of Monroe's classification of Johnson's poetic endeavors. Mencken dropped the issue of Johnson's talent but continued the issue of language and "dialect": "I hear that Sandburg has been making some experiments in the vulgar American dialect—the 'I seen your girl' sort. I have not seen the stuff. At the start it will undoubtedly seem grotesque—but let us not forget what Synge and company did with the Irish dialect, once thought only to be fit for low comedy. Surely a speech spoken by 90,000,000 Americans must have some possibilities."[23]

Johnson submitted "The Creation" to Max Eastman's the *Freeman*, in which it was subsequently published in January 1920. Years later, Mencken solicited "Go Down, Death," the second poetic sermon written by Johnson, for the pages of the *American Mercury*, his new literary journal sponsored by Alfred A. Knopf. Johnson made clear that if "Go Down, Death" was to be published in Mencken's journal, it needed to be accompanied by an explanation of the use of language by the author.[24] The poet's interaction with Monroe had made him aware of the necessity of his work's mediation to its audience, not only between his poet and preacher but also between the text and its intonation.

The American fascination with folk speech and its bearing on national identity—also present in discussions of music, as we have seen—made Johnson's poetic sermons more pertinent in the years between his composition of "The Creation" in 1918 and "Go Down, Death" in 1926. Mencken later inquired with enthusiasm whether Johnson had any other "dithyrambs of the sort like 'Go Down, Death' for publication," confirming not simply the editor's high opinion of Johnson's writing but more so his recognition of the power and currency of folk speech in discussions of modern America.

Johnson had the last laugh on Monroe. Her rejection of his work in 1919 was reversed when she solicited for his poem "The Creation" to be included in her 1932 anthology, the third edition of her successful anthology originally published by Macmillan in 1917. Johnson demanded top dollar for his work to be published in its pages, charging fifty dollars—more than Robert Frost would for the inclusion of three of his poems. Protesting heartily over the fee, Monroe yet managed to include the poem.

For many black writers like Johnson and Brown, the project of poetry was defined differently because of their deep and warranted suspicion of their works' reception as performance. The linguistic engagement of their works demanded explanation, translation, so that their audiences were obligated to recognize the explicit connection of these works to ethical and political issues. These writers' projects have often failed to be recognized as properly modernist. It has only been in recent years that the writing of many of the authors of what became known as the Harlem Renaissance—or, more broadly, the New Negro Renaissance—have been reassessed as modernist writings. George Hutchinson writes: "Given all the factors in the dialectical construction of canonical 'modernism' and 'modernist' literary criticism within the academy (overwhelmingly in contradistinction to 'realism' and other qualities embodied in New Negro writing), it should not be surprising that the Harlem Renaissance writers have only recently begun to be considered modernists."[25]

Johnson's works of this period were of necessity more broadly and specifically conceived through language, so that he could address the issue of transcription rather than the unproductive binary of oral versus literate cultures. Hutchinson continues: "Because realism and naturalism together have served as the straw man designating whatever modernism is not in Europe and the United States since the 1930s, the modernism of the Harlem Renaissance has been difficult enough to detect irrespective of the grip of racism on the academy."[26]

The modernist project of black writers entailed garnering public power through the written word in as broadly cast a net as possible. Black writers remained engaged to social responsibility and social context, but this position was not antithetical to modernist writing. As Hutchinson observes, "The very voicing of formerly suppressed speech could be an intervention in the settled language of literature no less 'new' and disruptive than the experiments of the avant-garde."[27] For Johnson, the project became an attempt to voice rather than to record black expressive culture, to convey its practices rather than to reduce or rigidly define them. Such presentation required the mediating voice of his prefaces and the notes of introduction that accompanied the publication of his poetry in literary journals. Yet that mediating voice is elusive and contradictory—using Johnson's words from his introduction to *The Book of American Negro Spirituals*, it is full of "intentional digressions"—rather than proscribed and uniform.

The poetics Johnson formulated through his many overlapping

works of this period needs to be appreciated as part of an ongoing modernist project that was his distinct answer to issues of social asymmetry in relation to the world of American literary modernism. It is equally important to see Johnson's overall endeavor to link literary modernism with social criticism as part of a larger network of practices performing similar work during this period. As Hutchinson points out, many of the little magazines of the late teens such as the *Dial*, the *Freeman*, and the *New Republic* were engaged in a project of modernist writing *with* social criticism, one oftentimes privileging localities not just of place but of ethnicity in an ongoing, transracial national project of creating the "American" language.[28] *God's Trombones* gave Johnson the opportunity to connect a range of popular and elite genres of language as a means of articulating an aesthetic of black expressive culture and its transfer—an aesthetic Johnson would develop subsequently through the locality of *Black Manhattan*.

7 From Noun to Verb
Black Phonographic Voice in *Black Manhattan*

I feel too . . . that the narrative does achieve living continuity; that it moves, and that in parts of it there is dramatic power and even poetry.
—James Weldon Johnson to Edwin R. Embree, on *Black Manhattan*

Black Manhattan (1930), Johnson's social history of black New York and the black theater and arts, functions simultaneously as Johnson's preliminary autobiography, predating the publication of *Along This Way* by just three years. The two works were composed at the same time and subjected to a gradual process of distinguishing the one from the other. One of the most telling indications of this process can be found in Johnson's manuscript notes for *Along This Way*, where Johnson writes: "[Marcus] Garvey—NY or Autobiography?"[1] Garvey would be placed tidily in Johnson's *Black Manhattan*, not in his autobiography, distancing the leader and his persistent criticisms of Johnson and the NAACP from the author's most intimate portrait.

Black Manhattan functions as a monumental history of black culture emanating from New York from the period of Dutch settlement and British imperialism predating the American nation through to the book's post-Harlem Renaissance moment of publication. *Black Manhattan* also locates Johnson's presence within this narrative as a well-known personality who had, in the words of W. E. B. Du Bois, "helped to make [Negro art]" and "was personally acquainted with its chief characters." Johnson, as Du Bois pointed out in his review of the work, "furnished the lyrics to many popular songs and the literary flavor to some of the plays. He was part of that first climax of Negro art in New York."[2] But the author's delivery of this material is oddly distant and ambiguously framed. First, Johnson refers to himself in the third person throughout the text when he mentions his name at all, resulting in what appears to be a kind of disembodiment or even erasure.[3] Second, he employs two different voices: the outside spectator who enunciates a documentary, detached voice, and the participant who is implicated in watching. Third, he goes so far as to use *The Autobiography of an Ex-Colored Man* of 1912—a work that had finally been attributed to him as a novel in 1927, with its reissue—as documentation for his present work, using a novel to document a history.

In recent African American literary scholarship, "phonography" has emerged as a key theoretical term when discussing issues of interpretation in relation to African American literary production. The concept is significant because it rejects the teleological relationship of orality to literacy, one that heralds literacy as the progressive end of orality.[4] Phonography can account for the silences, noise, and inarticulacy that are frequently written onto African American culture but are seldom heard emanating from its authors' works.

What links *The Autobiography of an Ex-Colored Man* and *Black Manhattan* may be Johnson's understanding of his novel as a "biography of the race" that appropriately tells this performance history of blacks in New York. Indeed, the concept of performance in each work refers not just to the agents in the pages but to the works themselves: *Black Manhattan* and *The Autobiography of an Ex-Colored Man* perform to one another, and the play between them is constitutive of a poetics of prose, of autobiographical transcription to the page. Johnson's voice in this 1930 work might appropriately be described as "phonographic": a voice that accommodates not only the aesthetic function of music (and, one might also add, theater) but also the function of silence and speechlessness in the complex cultural construction of both black Manhattan and the text itself—*Black Manhattan*. Therefore, the concept of phonography yields a key interpretation of Johnson's narrative voice—his ambiguities and apparent ambivalences—that is especially instrumental in re-sounding this complex and neglected work.

In Johnson's works, phonography is a broad and multivalent concept encompassing multiple performative registers: the figure of the black performative body in the American theatrical world, and the enunciation and practice of an aesthetic of modern black identity. These multiple registers are delivered through a complicating narrative voice derived from the combined forms of biography and autobiography in the text.

Phonography is, moreover, significant to Johnson's autobiographies in their configuration of the writer in relation to the black diaspora. Nathaniel Mackey's work suggests that phonographic voice need not be limited to a discussion of African American authors in intraracial conversation nor restricted by national borders. The critical practice of phonography, striving to hear, in the words of Mackey, "textual dissonance and disruption," frees writers from the entrenched, possessive loci of national borders, national race culture, and literary periodization.[5] These kinds of dissonances, according to Mackey, help to define writers in a global context in which they are linked by their practices of experimentalism. Johnson strived to work off of the specificity of the nation in his conversations about American culture and civilization, but he also used multiple outside subject positions—"Negro American," "Aframerican," Haitian, and West Indian, among others—to articulate that national identity. In his autobiographies *Black Manhattan* and *Along This Way*, he uses multiple enactments of black diasporic expressive culture that are simultaneously textual and aural, existing not in a historical trajectory but continuously and simultaneously. These subjects, enacted by Johnson, complicate the conventional treatment of the author as a nation builder exclusively devoted to the idea of origins and progress.

In Johnson's works, phonography is not a nationally bounded referent, nor does it operate exclusively through ragtime, as has been suggested by Katherine Biers in her innovative but limited study of Johnson's *Autobiography of an Ex-Colored Man*.[6] Linking Johnson's phonography to his formation of a poetics of form through the transcription of voice, Brent Edwards attributes its enactment to poetry, excluding Johnson's prose works. I suggest that prose and autobiography expand these critical possibilities, developing and extending the idea.[7] Johnson's use of autobiographical form is significantly linked to what Edwards in the context of the lyric calls "radical strategic choices": the autobiographical form, like the lyric, "is not a timeless, universal form; it is marked by history—and its history couches a threat to the enunciation of black subjectivity."[8] In Mackey's words, the lyric form "has legacies of domination and conquest and moral complication that make [its] claims to subjectivity and sublimity hard to countenance"—as does the genre of autobiography to black experience.[9]

Johnson's phonographic practices are linked to his use of the autobiographical form. In *Black Manhattan*, autobiography significantly alters the meaning of what Johnson narrates—black expressive culture—by drawing attention to the processes of self-transcription and embodiment that "move" through and transform the static "record": processes that facilitate articulations of modern black identity and modernist black creativity. Where Edwards assumes that poetry and poetics necessarily provide the window of form to modernist expression, I argue that in *Black Manhattan*, autobiography provides this window and is articulated through phonographic voice. In other words, there is no need to locate black modernist innovation simply within poetry or to presume that this form alone incorporates vernacular, popular, and contemporary forms. Johnson chooses autobiography not to imbue the form with its conservative, traditional meanings of self tied to its teleological progression but rather to articulate and extend the modernist possibilities for black individuation and collectivism. Within this choice of form, Johnson is again antiteleological: his silences, ambiguities, "noise," if you will, are linked to the form itself. Johnson replicates black modern and modernist forms rather than translating them into a kind of empirical project. This replication of form is an aesthetic choice that is necessarily political. Autobiography enables Johnson to address the issues of performativity and embodiment: transcription passes through but is not linked to the body, resulting in an antiessentialist formation of the self. Thus, the subject and form of autobiography are linked such that one cannot be extracted from the other: performativity and embodiment are addressed through the fluid if at times disembodied speaking subject.

Johnson held a prestigious Julius Rosenwald Fund fellowship from 1929 to 1930, which he successfully extended through September 1931 "to complete literary work begun under a grant made June 25, 1929."[10] In his letter of acceptance of the Rosenwald fellowship, Johnson stated that "among the things I wish to do first are" work on "a history of the Negro in New York," "another volume of poems," and "a novel that would be a comprehensive and composite picture of the Negro and his relations to American life" and to "write the text of an oratorio to be set to music" of *God's Trombones*.[11] The fruits of Johnson's initial fellowship period were *Black Manhattan*, *Saint Peter Relates an Incident of the Resurrection Day: Selected Poems by James Weldon Johnson*, published the same year in a small, private edition, and substantial work on the oratorio of *God's Trombones*. The extension of the fellowship allowed Johnson to plan for the initiation or completion of other works, too. Johnson announced his current projects in a letter of thanks to Edwin R. Embree, president of the Rosenwald Fund. He planned to revise and enlarge *The Book of American Negro Poetry* and to complete his oratorio based on *God's Trombones*. He also had other creative works in mind: "I have some unpublished poems, and I want to do more to make another volume. There is a novel of Negro life, such as has not yet been written, that I should like to do. And there is a Negro play rumbling around in my mind. Then there is a book that I feel I must write before very much longer. A book, not precisely an autobiography or the story of my life but an expression of how life, America, and the world have looked to me through my eyes."[12] This latter work would take shape as Johnson's autobiography, *Along This Way*, published in 1933 by Viking Press.

Black Manhattan was an archival project that extended Johnson's 1925 essay, "Harlem: The Culture Capital," which was included in the groundbreaking anthology *The New Negro*, edited by Alain Locke. Johnson's archives were both printed materials and oral and talk-based histories of the race capital, the nation's center of autonomous black thought, politics, and culture. He used extensively Arthur A. Schomburg's personal collection of black culture, which would later form the major repository of papers at the Harlem branch of the New York Public Library. These materials, documenting black American, Latin American, and African history and biography, increasingly became a source for African American scholars beginning in the late 1930s. Johnson's project also drew on oral materials, the "intimate knowledge" and memories of local informants who had lived close to the theater and entertainment worlds of New York, Johnson's subject. While writing *Black Manhattan*, Johnson contacted former publishers and colleagues in music, theater, and the literary world in order to generate lists of performances, performers, and dates. Johnson named and remembered the actors, singers, composers, politicians, and other historical actors, creating a shared history of those who had figured prominently in Harlem. And he used the figure of the theater as a key site through which this history could be narrated, a retrospective history with a working title of "Harlem: A Backward Glance" and a forward-looking study, for, as Johnson asserts in his story, "Harlem is still in the process of making. It is still new and mixed; so mixed that one may get different views—which is all right so long as one view is not taken to be the whole picture" (*BM*, 281).

The figure of the theater was an appropriate choice for Johnson's story because it was the first profession into which black citizens of post-Reconstruction America were permitted to enter. It also referenced the geographic and social setting of Harlem in a segregated nation while inverting the usual notion of black inferiority. Like the racially divided audiences of theatrical performances, Harlem looked down on Manhattan but from the vantage point of understanding both locations and attitudes, black and white; the American nation looked to the ideal society of Harlem. This relationship of gazes was put forth by Johnson as an acknowledgment of the defining presence of American spectatorship in relation to black expressive culture. But the figure of the theater could represent more than the rigid social codes of segregation; it could represent more than the history of exclusion. In fact, it could represent the dynamic responses to those codes that took the form of dialogue and sound-based movement. A unique site of expression, theater represented the rhetorical space where sound could link the said and the unsaid, text and performance, through a broad notion of politicized black expressive culture.

Johnson's work wasn't what his reviewers, publisher, or funding institutions had expected, however. Rosenwald Fund president Edwin Embree expected a vibrant study of various well-known Harlem personalities, from Marcus Garvey to Madam C. J. Walker. The work's publisher, Alfred A. Knopf, somewhat misleadingly publicized the work in this way: "Famous Negro Personalities, the Harlem of the past and of the present, the development of Negro music, art, and literature, are all in this panorama of Negro history in New York. Men like Frederick Douglass and Booker T. Washington share their fame with singers, dancers, jockeys, and pugilists."[13] Johnson's final product was a sober social history that advanced its claims through a written and remembered record of theater and politics rather than an entertaining collection of character sketches. After its publication, Embree wrote Johnson a letter critical of the final product. *Black Manhattan* was not, he implied, what Johnson had been funded to present. He faulted the work for lack of "flair," calling it "not quite up to the high standard that you set in such characteristic specialties as the *Autobiography* and *God's Trombones*": "I have just finished *Black Manhattan*. It is a fine record of an important development. Personally I must confess that I am a little disappointed. I recognize its importance. The book does not have, however, quite the flair that I expected in anything from your pen." Embree continued by suggesting the type of writing that he had had in mind: "Now that the book is out of the way as an important piece of historical record, what would you think of doing a little sheaf of portraits—frank, colorful sketches of a few persons and places: Florence Mills, Charles Gilpin, W. E. B. Du Bois, John Nail and Marshall's Café and one or two other places that give the flavor of Harlem life."[14]

Johnson defended his work, responding to Embree's criticism by pointing out the challenges he was faced with in the writing of it. He acknowledged that Embree "miss[ed] the 'lift'" that he had gotten from "the purely creative work that I have done, the thing you find in *God's Trombones*, *The Autobiography*, or the Preface to the *First Book of Spirituals*." But, Johnson countered:

> Black Manhattan is not in the real sense a piece of creative work. It is a factual book, and it was only here and there that I could allow the creative impulse to take wing, and then only for a short flight. The nature of the book demanded that sort of technique. And may I add, it demanded other things which deaden any desire to undertake another book of the kind—the collecting of masses of data, the laborious wading through, sifting and collocating of that data, the tedious verifications and the seemingly endless revision. It was a job that needed to be done, but at times I had to scourge myself in order to go through with and finish it.
>
> Yet I think it well worth the toil and I am glad I did it. One section alone of it justifies, I think, the whole book—the record of the Negro in the theater. This is the first time that anything approaching a full, consecutive and accurate account of the development of the Negro in American theater has been set down. So I think in this and the kindred fields it will prove a source book, and coming writers will draw upon it. I feel too . . . that the narrative does achieve living continuity; that it moves, and that in parts of it there is dramatic power and even poetry.[15]

While Johnson appears to accommodate Embree's assessment of the work as a merely "important" record, he instead voices his primary approach to his subject and its writing, one that privileges motion and life. While seeming to claim for his work an empirical value as a "source book," Johnson actually means "source" in the sense that his subject matter has "living continuity": it is continually re-sounded by moving *through* those who, as Du Bois noted, "live . . . through" its pages.[16]

Other reviewers noted the unusual presentation of *Black Manhattan* but, unlike Embree, praised its approach. The *New York Times Book Re-*

view, for example, noted *Black Manhattan*'s uncharacteristic praise for the city "in its physical aspects, that have their psychic reverberations, a city of towers of intolerable song," which Johnson alters from "foreboding" to "an opposite emotion." *Black Manhattan* "is at once a history, a series of appreciations of Negro personalities, and a testimonial to a cosmopolis that makes less dubious distinctions than do the more provincial cities of the United States."[17] Harlem as the modern city of America—Harlem, U.S.A., as it was popularly called—was accommodating of variety and contradiction, much as Johnson's story of it reflected this dynamism.

Du Bois, Johnson's long-time colleague at the NAACP, reviewed *Black Manhattan* for the *New York Evening Post*. He described Johnson's work as "a three-part essay, of which the second part, the story of how Negro art forced itself up from the New York Tenderloin, is the most gripping. There are few more fascinating stories," Du Bois wrote.[18] Through Johnson's technique of addressing each of the well-known personalities of "Negro New York," "one lives . . . through the careers of Will Marion Cook, Abby Mitchell, the 'Black Patti,' Jesse Shipp, Alexander Rogers, Ada Overton Walker. The story is brought down to our own day with references to Harry Burleigh, Jim Europe and W. C. Handy, the 'father of the blues.'" Johnson treated this artistic climax through a series of portraits, and he included himself both as one of its artists—a character in the cast—and as a documenter of the scene.

Carl Van Vechten, Johnson's friend and informal literary agent for Knopf, responded to the complexity of Johnson's narrative with his characteristic enthusiasm and appreciation of his friend's writing style: "I must say that I enjoyed the second reading even more than the first. There are chapters of your irony that do not always pierce the ears on the first jab of the needle! I love the parts about the churches & Garvey & the classes in Harlem & I adored the Garland Anderson story. . . . [O]f course it will be a great source but for a long time to come as was The Autobiography & no one—absolutely no one, except Defoe, can write like you."[19] Van Vechten's remarks draw attention to Johnson's understatement, finding the "flair" that Embree thought was lacking. The "chapters" in which it was delivered undercut any expectation that a study of the black theatrical world would be mere entertainment.

As artist and documenter, Johnson used his *Autobiography of an Ex-Colored Man* as documentation of the artistic era of which he was a part. Doing so might seem contradictory if the project of *Black Man-*

hattan is viewed as historical, but Johnson wanted to write a story of the Negro in New York. Therefore, using his prior work confirmed both as continuous, biographically relevant projects that were concerned with life, motion, and culture "in the making," a phrase that Johnson had applied to the spirituals, ragtime, and Harlem in his writings.

Phonography offers an important way of rereading the crucial issue of voice in African American culture, but it should not be used as yet another replacement for the romantic framework it seeks to critique. That is, although sound offers up a useful critique of the ways in which visual culture has often rendered African American subjects silent, it does not always deconstruct meaning or the narratives of origin and nation formed by the archives. Jacques Derrida's reading of the archives—as manifesting two contradictory claims, of the paternal "commandment" of institutional powers actively imposing value on only certain aspects of material culture and of the maternal "conservation" of nostalgia safekeeping these items—does not adequately describe Johnson's project in *Black Manhattan*.[20] Johnson himself has been widely recognized and described in prior critical studies, with or without this specific terminology, as a "black cultural *archon*" (in the Derridean sense, a collector of sacred texts forming a narrative of origins, of the authentic), but his use of archives, even his making of archives, reflects "the impurities that the keepers of any collection of sacred texts or objects must reject," as Biers has noted.[21]

Johnson's concern in *Black Manhattan* was with sound-based movement, the creation of character through performances, the public, and the nation. Theater, then, was much more than the text of a script or the bare execution of acting technique. The gesture Johnson articulated involved the making of a public record—not just his effort in writing this story but the efforts of all the "outstanding characters" he references in the work's dedication. While he references a visual vocabulary frequently in the work's opening pages, referring to the "backward glance" at Harlem, the effort to "etch in the background of the Negro," and the "cut-back in projecting a picture of Negro Harlem" (*BM*, xix), many of these phrases were added last, before its publication. Johnson's visual references instead operate as elements of public movement, more complex than the spectacle of black culture reduced to mere physical presence. The author's strategy in rendering a complex image of sound and motion was to sidestep the reductive tendencies of American visual culture and instead to offer new terms and values through digression.

Digression from the expected paradigm of the visual actually enables Johnson to accumulate details such that what seems like another subject altogether actually serves as a device of incorporation. Describing the world of Harlem and the theater in this way created a rhetorical space in which one might "see . . . the writer, the reader, and the work in a cultural—and thus a historical, a political, and a social—setting."[22]

A key example of Johnson's creation of complex, sound-based movement is his use of his own novel, *The Autobiography of an Ex-Colored Man*, in describing the world of Black Bohemia of the first decade of the twentieth century. While its subject and the images employed appear to be visual, the layering of Johnson's works and their contexts demonstrates a moving, sound-based framework of record. Johnson's novel becomes an archive of record; Johnson here reveals that the description of a club in its pages was of Ike Hines's notable venue; and he describes, through repetition, the "portrait gallery" of photographs contained there, reasoning that his novel "will furnish, perhaps, a fresher picture of these places and the times than anything I might now write" (*BM*, 75): "The walls were literally covered with photographs or lithographs of every colored man in America who had ever 'done anything.' There were pictures of Frederick Douglass and of Peter Jackson, of all the lesser lights of the prize ring, of all the famous jockeys and the stage celebrities, down to the newest song and dance team" (*BM*, 75; *AECM*, 76).

This passage, its repetition, establishes a complex relationship between the visual and its textual representation through sound, played out on the pages of *Black Manhattan*. While Johnson's prior work appears to be an archive of visual culture, *Black Manhattan* propels that work into motion by focusing attention on those expressive, sound-based transferences that are generated in a creative space such as Hines's club, where "early Negro theatrical talent created for itself a congenial atmosphere, an atmosphere of emulation and guildship" (*BM*, 78). Outlined in this way, with the romantic plot that drives the narrator of *The Autobiography of an Ex-Colored Man* excised, Johnson emphasizes the continuous, moving framework of his writing and of the sounds of others carried through its pages.

Johnson's study was based upon the firsthand recollections of a number of his acquaintances, including his father-in-law, John B. Nail, whose business was located at 461 Sixth Avenue from 1881 to 1909. Nail's nurse, Lucille V. Miller, wrote that he was born in 1853, that he came to New York with fifty-nine cents in his pocket and only the pair of shoes he was wearing, that he saved and continued to support his family in Baltimore, and that he went into business with his brother Edward in New York City's Tenderloin district. "By sheer persistence Mr. Nail soon procured work after coming to New York in one of the old downtown clubs." Her note continues: "Saving[,] he was able to start a business of his own in partnership with his brother. It was not long before the Nail Bros. place of business on 6th Ave., near 28th, became equally as famous as Delmonico's on 5th Ave."[23] Comedian and performer Irving Jones, whose career preceded Johnson's in Black Bohemia, was also a contributor and was thanked in the author's preface for his "intimate knowledge" (*BM*, xix).

Several of the reviewers of *Black Manhattan* noted his creation and use of a historical record. Harry Salpeter of *Book World* observed that *Black Manhattan* "reads like an appendix to the theatrical history of New York," an "impeachment" that Johnson admitted.[24] Another reviewer remarked that *Black Manhattan* was "not a deep or inspired social study, but neither is it exacting in what it demands." This reviewer continued with a remark more incisive than he realized: "You get the impression that Johnson is willing to let the reader's opinion of the Negro rest on the record."[25] Neither simply visible nor reductively physical, the theater was used by Johnson to emphasize that which could be conveyed through or outside of text or speech, inside or outside institutions of knowledge and power such as the archive and its history.

Like Johnson's "real" autobiography of 1933, *Along This Way*, *Black Manhattan* has been neglected by literary criticism or has been used as a "source text" to explain his other writings rather than to account for its interpretative complexities. This simplistic treatment—of his autobiographies and of autobiography in his works in particular—is indicative of a larger, even defining problem having to do with the neglect of form in African American literary criticism, one that Kimberly Benston, Brent Edwards, and others have pointed out: one type of African American literary criticism privileges the universal, the other the contextual, and these divergent treatments, combined with the false binary of form versus content, perpetuate the neglect of form.[26] This binary is a legacy of New Criticism, which, in privileging certain notions of form, sought to make a distinction between originality and mere mimicry—a distinction in which African American authors could never be "real" but simply "imitative," bad copies of the original. (Phillis Wheatley's poetry in heroic couplets is perhaps the most prominent and one of the earliest examples of this dismissive critical treatment.) African American literary criticism has defined its practices as necessitated by a project of voicing and embodying black expressive culture in response to this New Critical legacy and its reflection of the larger institutional oppression and silencing of black cultural practices. Yet this response to the New Critics creates its own bonds: embodiment, a rendering of the physically and temporally permanent, derived from authentic origins, tends to replicate the same silencing and objectifying practices. Some Black Arts criticism, for example, has shown itself to replicate the very same disposition through which Wheatley's work was dismissed as imitative and lacking originality. As Edwards has pointed out, "One way out of this bind [of form versus content] is to think of what is called content as simply the way matter is realized by form. . . . [T]here is no matter without form . . . but form is a principle independent of matter, which can invade or alter the form of that matter—and that effect is content."[27] Johnson himself puts this principle of form into play by using autobiography to "invade" the content of its matter and to narrate himself and others out of its textual, deterministic confines of self.

In *Black Manhattan*, autobiography significantly alters the meaning of what Johnson narrates—black expressive culture—by drawing attention to the processes of self-transcription and embodiment that "move" through and transform the static "record": processes that facilitate articulations of modern black identity and modernist black creativity. In an essay on Johnson's critical preface to *The Book of American Negro Spirituals*, Edwards has argued that Johnson's use of the term *swing* represents a "complex conception of subtly diasporic, individual/collective cultural agency" that ties art to politics: "The notion of artistic creation as a dialogue becomes a principle not simply of individual/community collaboration but also of black diasporic collaboration, and that collaboration is always political."[28] The very choice of form, therefore, is political and resistant to the binary of form versus content. Edwards asserts that "Johnson refuses such a dichotomy between form and content": he "locates the '*ethical* value of the music' precisely in its 'formal qualities'; . . . the ethical value of black music is that it transforms belongingness and creative originality into a quality that can never be simply owned or possessed; its roots are swung back and forth in the form itself."[29]

In *Black Manhattan*'s articulation of the theater and the record, Johnson accomplishes something quite similar, linking autobiography to collective experience and expression, privileging not himself but the *process* of transcribing himself, tracing individual and collective embodiment *through* black expressive culture. Johnson's narrative in *Black Manhattan* discounts its received status as a "source text" in several ways, not the least of which is Johnson's use of his earlier novel *The Autobiography of an Ex-Colored Man* (privileged as a modernist work) as a source text for *Black Manhattan*. Johnson borrows verbatim his description of a club in Black Bohemia from his novel to evoke the atmosphere of New York's prewar African American culture in the Tenderloin district, in which he participated. This reuse of his prose indicates not a tired repetition of the same sound bytes by the author, as some critics have suggested, but Johnson's modernist view of the function of his ideas and text. Here we find the introduction of a poetics of writing: for Johnson, ideas and text itself are not discrete entities; they are open, fluid, and unclosed. Ideas move, offering a modernist interpretation of what Johnson calls in *Along This Way*—written simultaneously to this work—the "freedom in motion" of writing prose. While linked to Whitman's free verse, "freedom in motion" is attached to a modernist idea of form as mutable and to open, not closed, empirical categories of meaning. Defying the form's convention, Johnson uses autobiography as an open-ended, antiteleological form.

Discounting *Black Manhattan*'s function as source text is Johnson's special care to describe it as a "story" and "not . . . in any strict sense a history." Writes Johnson: "I have refrained from repeating expansively matter already easily accessible in published form," underscoring its function as the creative extension of voice and self from this "story" of performance, a story that accommodates the narrating self's subjective interplay with the subject (*BM*, xix). At the center of this narrative, and giving critical force to the whole, was the story of the rise of the black theater—taking up more than half the book in chapters 8 through 22. As Johnson recalls (or perhaps wrote simultaneous to its composition in *Along This Way*), "One of my prime purposes in writing . . . [*Black Manhattan*] was to set down a continuous record of the Negro's progress on the New York theatrical stage." Johnson's comments on this work demonstrate his perception of it not as an originary source text but rather as a modernist, innovative work in which "theater" and "record" extend beyond their literal meanings, facilitated by Johnson's distinct use of autobiographical form. Johnson's description of this rise of black performance overtakes the work as a whole: the theater functions as a complex cultural sign, as does the record. Both theater and record have implications for the process of providing the transcriptions of the self that are demanded by autobiographical form: neither the record nor the theater is static or originary in Johnson's work.

Johnson's description of the 1900 riot in New York, which he witnessed firsthand as a visitor to the city before his permanent move, most aptly illustrates his use of theater and record in this work as a means of connecting popular and elite genres through an improvisatory aesthetics drawn from musical cultures of the time. To theater Johnson links popular black art as the unwitting object of the riot. "During the height of the riot," Johnson wrote thirty years after the event, "the cry went out to 'get Ernest Hogan and Williams and Walker and Cole and Johnson.' These seemed to be the only individual names the crowd was familiar with" (*BM*, 127). In the pages leading up to this description, Johnson had shown how popular lyrics had become "epithets of derision," as in the case of Ernest Hogan's song "All Coons Look Alike to Me" (*BM*, 114). The mob grasped at the names it knew to conduct its "brutish orgy," directing popular lyrics written and performed by black Americans as a justification of the violent pursuit of any African American. Through the riot Johnson traced the manipulation of expression, looking at how an angry mob drew on an emergent, modern black expressive art to mobilize its own violent expression. Theater, it seems, is owned by no one; the originary is constantly reinvented; and African Americans in particular are subjected to dispossession and appropriation. It's noteworthy that Johnson's self, rendered in the third person, is bound up in this example. Here the effect of his phonographic voice serves to emphasize his objectification along with the other artists he mentions.

Narrating the dissonances of black cultural production around the New York riot, from which Barry Carter, Rosamond's friend, never recovers, Johnson also explains the fate of his former musical partner Bob Cole. While Rosie traveled abroad to advance his musical ambitions, composing and conducting the orchestra for the revue *Hello Paris* (1911), Bob Cole remained behind; soon his health had suffered to the extent that he could not perform. Although it was rumored that he had syphilis, James Weldon Johnson described Cole as suffering a nervous breakdown. Johnson strongly implied that Cole's death in 1911 was suicide and that his failing health was linked to the audience reception of his musical comedy as minstrelsy—a prison house for a creative genius such as Cole.

In *Black Manhattan*, theater passes through but is not possessed by its participants in both negative and positive movements. Thus the issue of embodiment in black expressive culture is resolved not by locating the (autobiographical) form within an individual or a collective body but in describing—replicating—theater's movement or passage through the form itself. By treating form as the moving thing, Johnson's narrative practice sounds the issues found in phonography: theater passes on creative originality and belongingness, taking Johnson beyond his individual contributions, by taking his body and individual contributions as such out of the conversation. Theater mediates autobiographical transcription so that it is tied to individual and collective experience and expression. And, as the title itself suggests, the physical and embodied image of a moving "Black Manhattan" demands juxtaposition with and against the rooted, static "white witch" of Johnson's 1917 poem and *The Autobiography of an Ex-Colored Man*: "She sits like a great witch at the gate of the country . . . constantly enticing . . . and tempting. . . . And all . . . become the victims of her caprice" (55).[30]

In his prose writings, Johnson has been pigeonholed as a historicist, as a holdover from the nineteenth-century model of "uplift," as a privileger of the "real" to the extent that the literary-critical conversation about his works has not been trained to listen for or indeed hear the modernist complexities sounding from his work. The concept of phonography demonstrates the multigeneric commitment of James Weldon Johnson as a modernist writer committed to the form of autobiography as antiteleology and antiessentialist. Phonography, combined with a consideration of form, offers an effective example of the expansive, creative possibilities of Johnson's work itself, a text long silent.

The "noise" of Johnson's autobiographical composition in *Black Manhattan*—making use of technologies as various as recordings, print culture, and visual culture; fusing diplomacy and musical comedy, occupations he held simultaneously—offers a distinct view of American culture and African American voice. Indeed, Johnson's multivocal productions across multiple genres of writing, performance, and movement through a range of national and international spaces offer up a moving record through which to rethink the relation between African American cultural production and the broader dynamics of the US sphere in this period.

Edwards has remarked upon how "the extent to which black musical performance continually informs, and even frames, [Johnson's] approach to black modernity has not been fully recognized."[31] He argues that "in Johnson's poetics, there is almost never a description of a direct transmission from the oral to the written: almost always, the figure of music intercedes. Music as a metaphor seems a necessary mediating element in the process of linguistic transcription."[32] Edwards seems to think that Johnson's most radical form of modernism never arrives, but I argue that there is another place—voice and form—through which to look for Johnson's "radical modernism": in his use of and signing on autobiography, which generates in his text a stuttering, swaying discussion of black performance.

In his customary practice of simultaneous compositions, Johnson wrote *Black Manhattan* while taking notes for his autobiography, *Along This Way*, which would be completed and published in 1933. *Black Manhattan* was already a revised idea of what Henry Louis Mencken had suggested as a book on ragtime to be distinguished from Johnson's project of collecting and prefacing the spirituals; the revised edition of *The Book of American Negro Poetry*, issued shortly after *Black Manhattan* in 1931, was Johnson's extended response to his underwriter for the later project, Edwin Embree, president of the Julius Rosenwald Fund.

In his preface to the revised edition of *The Book of American Negro Poetry* (1931), Johnson swung between 1922 and 1931, citing his original framing of the poems that follow in his preface to the first edition, "The Negro's Creative Genius" (1922). Johnson himself drew attention to the fact that his original—and "necessary"—1922 "extended introduction" was "forty-eight pages." In a mere ten years' time, he writes, his focus in that preface, "the main contributions which the Negro had already made to our common cultural store," had now become "historical data," "accepted facts." Moreover, Johnson's statement about "traditional dialect" had become, in his view, "regarded as more or less canonical. It is as sound today as when it was written ten years ago, and its implications are more apparent."[33] "The sketches of the poets included have been made critical as well as biographical, and a list of references for supplementary reading has been added."[34] Johnson was finishing up the 1931 revision of the poetry anthology on the Rosenwald fellowship he held in 1930–31, with the author's fresh awareness of Embree's criticism of *Black Manhattan* for not performing a character sketch of Harlem celebrities. Johnson's revision of *The Book of American Negro Poetry* was informed by Embree's criticism of *Black Manhattan*. Here Johnson provides biographies with criticism, as if to respond to and yet defiantly reject Embree's criticism.

The unwritten "story" Johnson wished to write of Negro life in America that he listed among his prospective projects for the Rosenwald fellowship was articulated, for the time being, through his other works generated in this period. As he worked through the framework of his autobiography, he acknowledged: "For several years the idea has been edging in upon my mind that I should write—no, not the story of my life; that at once falls over into the things not worth while. Perhaps the idea is that I should draw an outline, a sketch, an impression maybe in spots, of what America has looked like to me through the years of my life."[35]

As we shall see in chapter 8, again Johnson invoked the interplay of a shifting framework of record conveyed from body to body and from work to work.

8 Not the Story of My Life

Along This Way

Mr. Erlanger . . . rushed down the aisle shouting, "Rossmore (the name by which he always called my brother), we'll have to take that woman out and get somebody who can sing the part." Rosamond jumped up from the piano and shouted back, "How in the world can you expect her to sing when you keep yelling at her?" A silence . . . fell on the theater. . . . The silence gave Rosamond opportunity to realize the enormity of his act.

—James Weldon Johnson, *Along This Way: The Autobiography of James Weldon Johnson*

Autobiography operates in crucial ways in the period framed by Johnson's *Autobiography of an Ex-Colored Man* (1912) and *Along This Way* (1933), his most productive years of writing. In between Johnson's works, autobiography becomes revolutionized, unanchored from its moorings in convention and chronology, as it swings between biography and the interior self, between a collective people whose name and status are continually altered from within and without, and a defiantly private, persistently individual self. Autobiography is an innovative, sometimes furtive, sometimes outwardly defiant form that facilitates in the figurative use of "swing" or play between these individual and collective forms of expression and ways of knowing. In *Along This Way*, autobiography is the means through which Johnson articulates a black diasporic identity and a poetics of self.[1]

Through his autobiographical intertextuality of selves within and between his works, Johnson narrates modern black expressive culture, drawing attention to the violent history producing it. But this practice does not amount to a nation-building story of origins, as his prose writings have often been interpreted. Criticism has placed emphasis on Johnson's nationalist, assimilationist, and in some views accommodationist investment in a narrative of black cultural origins. These readings obscure his intentional disruptions of that kind of story. Rather than represent himself as a romantic, organically developed hero, Johnson presents a body through which pass the currents of black cultural experience and expression in the Americas.[2] Thus Johnson wrote "not the story of my life" but the story of New World black modernity, its transmissions and repeating frameworks of experience.

The automatic biography of Johnson that rolls out like the music of a player piano is the result of his self-authoring. His inevitable biography in brief, its perpetual repetition, works as a counternarrative, one that competes with Johnson's modernist tensions of self, which he articulated in *Along This Way* through autobiographical reverberation. In text and sound, Johnson selectively positioned, repeated, recontextualized, and revised his autobiography from its prior forms and works. Just beneath the surface of the seemingly automatic, seamless biography of American success lie the intentional ambivalence, complexity, and contradiction of Johnson as author and subject, as both creator and expressive medium. It is the tension between these narratives and the latter, previously obscured narrative of Johnson with which this chapter is concerned.

In his groundbreaking history of Harlem, David Levering Lewis, continuing a tradition of critical reception of Johnson initiated by Black Arts writers such as Amiri Baraka and Jean Wagner, presented Johnson as a member of the black upper class whose position sheltered him from the realities of black existence, belonging to a "lineage" that "placed him among the tiny elite of Afro-Americans whose families had been free, literate, and prosperous before the Civil War."[3] Dismissing the "ambivalences" expressed in Johnson's writing and thought as "uniquely Johnson's own," Lewis explained away his contradictory stances on a range of political and literary issues as emblematic of the limitations of New Negro ideology.[4] Dismissing out of hand critical treatments of Johnson as "'rootless,' 'marginal' (except in a statistical sense), a 'racial hypocrite,' or 'among Negroes . . . the first modern,'" Lewis instead chalks these seeming "ambivalences," contradictions, and "inconsistencies" up to Johnson's "Talented Tenth" class consciousness:

> To fall away from orthodox religion, to mine the black folk tradition for its barely known riches, and to cheer the marines in the Caribbean and the capitalists at home were not aberrations but the reasonable reflections of genuine convictions of upper middle-class status. Yet the class was part of the race, and the generality of the

race was not yet, they conceded, Civic Club material. Hence, the violent tensions in psychology and logic of Johnson and his class as they protested that if they matched the best whites, given the distance travelled and the roadblocks surmounted, it was because they were, in truth, superior human material.[5]

This flattening out of Johnson into a mere class-activated agent whose affiliations would be set by his birth and experience as an elite reflects the entrenched way in which the class background of African American subjects has been treated deterministically, as either engaging or failing to engage and reflect the general population. This reading of Johnson through the lens of class determinism has become so pervasive that Kevin Boyle's recent history of the Sweet case in Detroit, Michigan, in which Johnson and his colleague Walter White at the NAACP were involved directly and influentially, portrays Johnson's early life as "wrapped in a cocoon of middle-class gentility" in "the serenity of the family parlor, with the Bible opened on a marble tabletop, the piano standing majestically in a shaded corner, and his mother by the fireplace, reading *David Copperfield* to her sons."[6]

One of the sources of this condemning portrait is Johnson's own autobiography, *Along This Way*, which his readers have treated as a source text—as the literal life that had somehow eluded readers in Johnson's prior works such as *The Autobiography of an Ex-Colored Man* and *Black Manhattan*—and which would retrospectively provide an explanation for these autobiographical complexities. Blind to, or perhaps deceived by, Johnson's rhetorical strategy in the narrative of presenting a self insulated, apart from, and uninformed by the racist logic that would inevitably be confronted by the author—a well-established convention in black autobiography—some readers have determined Johnson too removed from the representative black experience of his era for him to have been an effective or devoted leader. His racial affiliation, the degree of his conviction, has been measured by his class background, his ability to please influential whites; his autobiography has been called upon to reinforce his removed position and to "other" his exceptionalism as "nonrepresentative"—as if exceptionalism wasn't already part of the practice of autobiography.

To be sure, Johnson begins his autobiography with a grounded self and concludes with a defiant one who defends his "inner life." Somewhere in between these two rhetorical points of the narrative, however,

Johnson describes two, possibly three personal experiences of near lynching.[7] In *Along This Way*, the narrating subject of the autobiography's first and final chapters is placed in relation to the contingencies of external, uncontrollable horror, effectively underscoring Johnson's modernist tensions of self. To describe Johnson's vision in his life and works as "roseate" when juxtaposed with these experiences of racial terror that Johnson presents is to realize, at last, the impact and legacy of Lewis's hyperbolic portrait of the man.[8] This portrait reveals, too, the way in which autobiography by black authors has been taken as the conveyance of an identity so elemental, so essential as to render literary meaning null: it is implied that one should not search further for tropes, rhetorical figures, or figurative language but embrace the literal life to the exclusion of language's inevitable manipulation.

Contrary to this hardened concept of Johnson as a writer deeply invested in the idea of the past as foundational, originary, and reconstitutable—romantic and nostalgic—is the modernist notion of perpetual and varied replay such as one finds in reading for Johnson's autobiography in his works.[9] Johnson's repeated and continuous autobiographical beginnings in his works demonstrate his rejection of the idea of a static and recoverable past. This rejection is a conscious choice with political implications. While it may seem to typify the perpetual beginning of New Negro Renaissance era writings—what cultural critic and historian Gerald Early describes as a series of beginnings without development or coherence—the repeated beginnings of the Renaissance also can be read as symptomatic of, and providing the opportunity for, the rejection of a pure past to which one is tied and the substitution of a new, proliferating, present-minded self.[10] Read as an act of defiance, the rejection of a pure, originary past has broad implications for Johnson's narrative practice—his form—as well as for his emerging poetics. Johnson's repeated, innovative self-referencing articulates this poetics and his distinct modernism, rather than a prescriptive modernism imposed by his contemporaries or a retrospective modernism generated by institutional memory. Johnson privileged black expressive practices in his writings, which were continually animated and revised both in sound and in print. These practices were enhanced by the presence of autobiography in each work, because the autobiographical form is preoccupied with time and the past in "living motion" through the narration of the self by the author's prior selves.

Johnson placed fragments of his own experience from text to text in order to uproot the idea of an isolated, deterministic, unchanging self of the sort that, ironically, readers would ascribe to him after his death. His innovation was to create, through his works, multiple autobiographical personae that initiated dialogues about modern black identity and black modernist practices. This was more than a mere strategy of insertion into a conversation of white American moderns; it was a way of creating his narrative of modernism. Autobiography's function and status as a distinct genre have been questioned, appropriately enough, since it collaborates with multiple discourses.[11] Autobiography is contradictory and problematic—Johnson uses the form for this very reason—for the license it provides in representing the self but also for the fact that it underscores its own contradictions, limitations, and gaps of knowledge. Here, in Johnson's works, we see the initiation of a modernist implementation of autobiography, distinguished from nineteenth-century models of African American autobiographical narrative. Johnson's segmenting/fragmenting of his life story into the multiplicity of his works, his self's incompletion and yet incorporation into his works, competes with his totalizing, summarizing, automatic/scripted biography. Through his use of autobiography, Johnson invites his readers to consider the spatial, temporal, and ethical dimensions of black diaspora emanating from his soundtrack.[12]

While seeming to "document," anthologize, and attest in the service of a moralizing agenda, Johnson instead affirms an ambiguous, elusive mode of representation that supports the multigeneric qualities of the visual, textual, and aural—none reducible to the other and yet collaboratively expressive modes of representation. Johnson's developed poetics emphasizes that although visual, literary, and aural modes of expression are not equivalents, they do not oppose one another. As Paul Gilroy, Brent Edwards, and my work here have shown, oral and written cultural expressions are not in fact in opposition to each other, and critical study of African American cultural forms is severely disabled by such a false binary. One only has to consider the example of the spirituals, elusive in origin, based on biblical text, and transmitted without written notation for two hundred years, to see how complex and intertwined are the modes of text and the aural. Johnson's use of self-reference, fragmentation, multiplicity, and repetition articulates and affirms this cultural complexity by replicating its very process.

Johnson assembles his prose works—his critical prefaces to *The Book of American Negro Poetry* and *The Book of American Negro Spirituals*, as well as *The Autobiography of an Ex-Colored Man*, *Black Manhattan*, and *Along This Way*—in order to animate the idea of their simultaneity by juxtaposing independent modes of expression simultaneously. As Edwards has shown, Johnson's critical preface to *The Book of American Negro Poetry* anthology helps to articulate the problem of time and totality through "collation."[13] I would like to take this further to suggest that Johnson practices a kind of autobiographical sound collage to articulate the tensions of representation in different expressive modes, textual and sound based. In Johnson's works, text and sound are juxtaposed, emerging as a collective practice of black cultural expression that is neither exclusively oral nor textual. This is Johnson's appropriate response to the false distinction drawn between oral and literate cultures, an issue enhanced by the history of African American subjectivity.[14] Infusing his prose with a soundtrack that plays throughout each work, Johnson references the "noise" of American popular culture, in which black subjectivity faced seemingly perpetual eradication—a background noise expressing cultural anxieties of assimilation that occasionally burst forth as violent challenges to the black self.[15] Johnson introduces multiple, simultaneously existing modes of black expressive culture that counter this noise.[16]

In Johnson's writings, autobiography animates the self through encounters that both are and are not located in the body and are perpetually present through intertwined experiences of sound and text. This formation of the self also offers a practical theory of the interpretation of black culture in the Americas. In and between his works, Johnson provided interplay between individual and collective/communal black bodies, both of which have been fragmented and re-formed by history. For example, one finds Johnson separating his autobiography into two works, his history of "Negro New York," *Black Manhattan* (1930), and his autobiography, *Along This Way* (1933), initially a single composition. And yet he referenced the one work to the other, citing *Black Manhattan* verbatim in *Along This Way*. His simultaneous writing of these works emphasizes the space in between them, and the plurality of voice and media, as simultaneity becomes the operative concept. Perpetually incomplete, Johnson's technique of self-referencing enables the repetition and rearticulation of his autobiography in all of his texts, his self-referentiality between them operating as a kind of autobiographical intertextuality. Through this representation, his readers collaborate and are implicated in the act of fragmentation, repetition, and reformation. While readers are drawn in to participate in his textual self's completion, Johnson underscores the continuous (and contingent) process of making meaning and a self.

In his convincing study of the framing work accomplished by Johnson's preface to and anthologizing of "American Negro poetry," Edwards reveals Johnson's strategic positioning of black expressive culture in diaspora. Of this work he writes: "[The preface] digresses precisely in order to contend that Negro expression is both constitutive of the American 'cultural store' and excessive to it—what Paul Gilroy terms a 'counterculture,' but one that simultaneously defines the core of national culture."[17] Edwards underscores Johnson's intentional digressions and slippage in terminology: from high modernism to popular and vernacular culture; from nation-based black poetry of America to culturally, vernacularly, and linguistically diverse black poetry of the Americas; from "Negro" to "Aframerican."

No doubt these slippages were informed by the many factors that made Johnson's life atypical: his identity as an "Aframerican," his mother from the Bahamas; his ability to speak Spanish and therefore "pass" as something other than an American Negro; his mobility in the varied diplomatic careers that took him to Venezuela, Nicaragua, and Haiti. Johnson was born and raised to adulthood, the first thirty years of his life, in the South and was a man who, although a dedicated New Yorker, was also a southern gentleman (in a way that his colleague at the NAACP, W. E. B. Du Bois, could never be). Moreover, the range of his writings could be considered atypical: he had written popular lyrics for the musicals of Broadway and the parlor as well as the magisterial works of critical prefaces and the autobiography for which he is now known. Rather than understanding Johnson as the patient if obdurate uplifter of his race, scholars might more productively examine his intentional engagement of contradictions, silences, and references to sound, features that are readily available in his life and works and that help connect them, sometimes through discrepancy.

Along This Way has been treated simply or reductively by its readers not only through the deterministic lens of class status but also through the way in which institutional knowledge has framed Johnson's significance to an overall narrative of African American history and culture. The very terms and phrases Johnson's critics, historians, and biographers frequently use—notably, a "near lynching," "public speaking," "teaching in the backwoods of Georgia," "admission to the bar," "fame and fortune as a song writer," among others—are derived verbatim from the index to Johnson's autobiography, *Along This Way* (416–17). So when one discusses Johnson, it is as if the terms have already been set and codified. Johnson's story has been treated as one of constant mobility, of aspirations and constraints, a life in motion in defiance of racist, oppressive denials of self, which has inadvertently led to *Along This Way*'s function as the source, the "real," originary truth of Johnson's prior literary works and his life. But this is the simplified version of what Johnson has presented here, for coherence and contingency intermingle uneasily in the events he describes.

In his autobiography, Johnson began not with his birth but with the history of his maternal great-grandmother, a Haitian, and a longer history of black self-determinacy in the context of world imperialism. The history was also interracial, for the father to this great-grandmother's children was a white Frenchman. Filling out the genealogy, Johnson presented his parents, his father from Virginia, his mother from Nassau, the Bahamas, who together represented black cultural experience in the Americas, the New World experience of hyphenated, now dual, African American identity existing across the boundaries of the nation-state. So Johnson began his autobiography by digressing into the multiple registers of an "other" America, one located both within and without the United States.

Johnson forms his narratives by decentering his works as discrete entities, offering instead creative play—an in-betweenness—from one work to the next and also within each work, where one finds generic "play" between time, point of view, vernacular and text, autobiography and biography, and forms and genres themselves. Johnson places parts of himself in all of his writings; he draws attention to the creative tension between ascribed and self-generated identities. This is found in the strategic positioning articulated in all of his works: he uses incompletion and duality—of works and selves—to reveal them as the paradoxical location of his identity. Johnson's multigeneric and modernist use of autobiography to rename and reposition both self and community permits him to trope modern black identity as the crucial act of creation, reappropriate an imposed, fragmentary identity, emphasize its breaks, and rebreak it as an assertion of self-authorship. Moreover, in Johnson's practice, modern black identity joins media such as sound and text when literary studies often have neglected their complex relation.[18] Rather than thinking through such media as sound and text independently, literary critics must strive to discover their interrelation, perhaps following Johnson's "lead sheet."

Johnson's notes for *Black Manhattan* and *Along This Way* had begun as early as 1926, while he was secretary of the NAACP. They were gradually separated into two projects. His manuscript notes from 1926 occasionally bore the title "Autobiography" and were recorded in personal notebooks or on NAACP letterhead. Other notes more strongly indicated the black history of New York, notes that bore the dates of monumental historical markers such as the abolition of the slave trade by different nations.[19]

When *Black Manhattan* was published in July 1930, Johnson concentrated his efforts on this second project. The extension of his Julius Rosenwald Fund fellowship covered a period of time in which Johnson was unsure that he would return to the NAACP. During his year-and-a-half-long absence, Walter White had proven himself poised and capable of assuming Johnson's post, and Johnson had begun to experience with greater frequency the ailments that would plague him for the rest of his life, stomach ailments and "neuritis" in his arms. Through the help of Edwin Embree, the Rosenwald Fund's president, Johnson was appointed to a position at Fisk University that had been created especially for him. (Howard University lost its bid for Johnson to join its faculty.) As Adam K. Spence Professor of Creative Literature, Johnson became the first African American to hold an endowed chair of creative literature at a university, joining the company of Robert Frost at Amherst College and Thornton Wilder at the University of Chicago. As Johnson told his students in his first lecture on creative writing, "Fisk is the first of the Negro Universities to try it."[20]

Beginning in 1931 and until his untimely death in 1938, Johnson taught introductory courses in English and American literature, courses on the Negro in American literature, and creative writing courses. His lecture notes demonstrate his reflection on literary genres and conventions, certainly; they also indicate, sometimes explicitly, Johnson's reflection on his own literary accomplishments. As professor of creative literature Johnson acquired the comparative leisure that allowed him the time to write his autobiography; his teaching of literature at this post facilitated his contemplation of his accomplishments as an author and allowed him to consider reflexively the tradition of autobiography into which his writing would enter.

Johnson's course on contemporary American literature, covering 1890 through 1930, explicitly discussed models of autobiography offered by Walt Whitman, Henry Adams, and W. E. B. Du Bois.[21] Johnson considered only American forms of autobiography in his lectures; he also assigned his own literary works to explore the literary forms he introduced. Using *The Autobiography of an Ex-Colored Man*, *God's Trombones*, and *Black Manhattan* as course materials, Johnson considered his role as a reader and a writer employing different techniques and forms and how he would answer the questions posed by a lecture in the course: How does any generation regard its writers? Will those writers be remembered and taught to future generations?[22]

Johnson taught *The Autobiography of an Ex-Colored Man* in his creative literature and writing course in 1932. His lecture notes indicate his altered relationship to this work at the time of his writing *Along This Way*. By 1932 *The Autobiography of an Ex-Colored Man* had become a moving framework of historical record. The shifting framework that *The Autobiography of an Ex-Colored Man* had come to represent for Johnson as he assesses his literary production in 1932 indicates the powerful way in which it informed Johnson's autobiography. Teaching *The Autobiography of an Ex-Colored Man* while writing *Along This Way* provided Johnson with a perspective on the literary aspects of the latter project. While criticism has addressed the relationship between the two works, the creative genesis of *Along This Way* has been addressed only in a preliminary way and through limited models that favor this work as an explanation for The *Autobiography of an Ex-Colored Man*.

Johnson's *Along This Way* achieves what I call an autobiographical intertextuality through the reappearance of all of Johnson's past works and prior selves, which are brought into play in a wonderfully complex composition. In this new compositional space, his works sound off of one another, and the shifting framework of *The Autobiography of an Ex-Colored Man*, its continual alteration and extension, becomes more apparent through the repetition of this work in all of his subsequent works. Johnson's multiple selves convey a poetics of movement through sound.

Johnson's lecture notes for his literature and creative writing courses from 1931 to 1933 reflected his attitude toward the shifting literary works that he had put into motion. His 1932 creative literature and writing course advised students to "strive for objectivity—honesty—sincerity." "Stand off and look at yourself . . . as though you were writing about another person." But rather than merely channeling a singular, uniform version of the self, Johnson emphasized the complex variety of narrative techniques: "1. Author becomes narrator; 2. Character in story becomes narrator; 3. Author assumes omniscience and omnipresence." Johnson cited *The Autobiography of an Ex-Colored Man* as "the only piece of fiction of Negro life—so far as I know—written according to this [first] method."[23] By this Johnson meant that he had created a first-person point of view of a subject other than himself to narrate the work.

In fact, Johnson assigned his students a similar exercise in which they would make use of their knowledge to tell a story from another person's point of view, specifically, one of the inversion of racial experience: "Assignment: story of a white boy grown up a colored child of Negro couple/contrasting complexions then learns he is really white." What Johnson asserted to his students in *The Autobiography of an Ex-Colored Man* may be applied evocatively to a reading of Johnson's composition of this work in 1912, but these lecture notes and writing assignments more appropriately demonstrate what this 1912 work had come to mean to Johnson by 1932. It was by acknowledging the separation and overlay of his works in relation to autobiography that Johnson brought the selves of his prior works into play.

Joseph Skerrett's "symbolic action" and Valerie Smith's "evasion and privilege" both trace a critical direction that uses *Along This Way* as the "real" autobiography that may illuminate the "simulated" one, *The Autobiography of an Ex-Colored Man*.[24] Skerrett explored the symbolic psychic situation of fear versus confidence in expression and leadership that Johnson's 1912 work explored through its narrator's actions and ideas. He convincingly argues that Johnson explored the psychic relationship of fear and confidence symbolically through the relationship between the author and his good friend Judson Douglas Wetmore. "From the distance of Puerto Cabello," Skerrett wrote, "Johnson symbolically objectified problems he could not confront directly back in New York," problems most clearly defined by Johnson's relationship with Wetmore, which Skerrett characterizes as one of "an individual to an alter ego."[25] Skerrett observes that in *Along This Way*, "Johnson's psychic strategies for dealing with this general challenge of maintaining his identity in the face of constant race-based attacks are basically of two types. One is role-playing . . . [and] one [is] of withdrawal."[26] According to Skerrett, the strategies Johnson describes in his responses to race-based confrontations over the course of his life are also the strategies of Johnson's 1912 narrator: "The narrator of *The Autobiography of an Ex-Colored Man* is a projection of Johnson and of his alter ego, D. [Wetmore]; through the duality of the tragic/ironic narrative, Johnson 'outers' and then exorcises the weakness he saw so clearly in (and shared with) D.—the temptation to desire and seek a less heroic, less painful identity than their blackness imposed on them."[27] Skerrett, while sensitive to the problem of using *Along This Way* as text subsidiary to *The Autobiography of an Ex-Colored Man*, nevertheless uses the autobiography as a source to restructure an understanding of the relation between Johnson and his creation.

Building on Skerrett's exploration of the relationship between Johnson's life and his fictional 1912 work, Smith observes that in *Along This Way*, "Johnson argues that the difficulties he confronted (in his case the consequences of his racial identity) were also the source of his creativity and power."[28] In contrast to this later work, Johnson's "simulated autobiography [*The Autobiography of an Ex-Colored Man*] . . . provided Johnson with an opportunity to explore a path he did not choose in life, but one that fascinated him nonetheless."[29] The relationship between the two texts is characterized, according to Smith, by the impact that having written the 1912 fictive work had on Johnson's real-life decisions: "Insofar as the ex-colored man operates as Johnson's alter-ego, his fate may be seen to justify Johnson's own choices. Whatever discomforts his political work or public service may have caused him, Johnson seems to have believed that they became part of the fabric of his life and provided the source of his musical and literary productions."[30] Smith suggests that the writing of a work in which the narrator provided the consequences of the opposite example (having "sold [his] birthright for a mess of pottage") showed Johnson the importance of choosing the more difficult route of engagement and not evasion and the resulting artistic agency that direct confrontation enabled. Thus Johnson's 1912 work and his 1933 autobiography represent a defining range of thought, from the "evasion and privilege" of the Ex-Colored Man to the confrontation and activism that provided Johnson with creativity and that were the artistic "source" of his works. Again, however, Smith's argument also excludes the 1933 autobiography from consideration as a literary text of equal status with Johnson's *Autobiography of an Ex-Colored Man.*

Productively focusing his attention on the narrative strategy of

Along This Way, Robert Fleming employs the trope of masking to explain Johnson's narrative approach in his autobiography: "Johnson's art masked the naked anger of the early notes he made as he planned his autobiography. Musical comedy had taught him how to use humor; fiction had taught him to dramatize, to show rather than tell, to permit—or even force—the reader to draw conclusions or make generalizations from facts presented without overt judgment."[31] Johnson certainly employed the concept of duality and played with visual troping of the American racial experience in composing *Along This Way*, evidencing the deep influence that the work of his former colleague at the NAACP, Du Bois's *Souls of Black Folk*, had made on him. Yet "masking" doesn't appropriately represent Johnson's narrative practice because it suggests concealment and a merely dualistic representation of the "seeming" mask and the "real" self. Johnson brings his past selves to bear on the autobiography in order to represent rather than to inhibit the creative expression of his works and his experiences.

In his notes for the autobiography, Johnson wrote: "It is not my purpose to make this book the story of my life. My point of view is as I have lived my life as an American and yet not an American thus having the advantages of an inside and an outside view."[32] Addressing the difficulty of conveying his point of view, Johnson took up and improvised upon Du Bois's by now well-known concepts of the "veil" and the "gift" of "second sight" that ambivalently formed African American consciousness, concepts that had deeply influenced Johnson's writing of *The Autobiography of an Ex-Colored Man* twenty years earlier. Johnson later experimented with using the stereoscope as a visual metaphor for his experience of American culture, the technique requiring the superimposition of two slightly different perspectives to form the whole, "true" scene. He used the stereoscope as a repetitive narrative technique to create a reinforced vision of "America as it has looked to me." Johnson also considered many titles for his autobiography, many of which took up this visual trope. Among the possible titles for the work were "As I Remember It," "My World," "My Two Worlds," "Through Colored Glasses," "Two Worlds," "Two American Worlds," "Two Worlds in One," "My Country," "My Country and Me," "As I Remember It," "I Look at Life," "How It Looks to Me," "As I Look at It," "These Two Worlds," "The Worlds within a World," "Between Two Worlds," "The Two American Worlds," "In the Two American Worlds," "This Was the Way," "My Little World," "The World of Weldon Johnson," "Along This Way," "The Bitter with the Sweet," "Through the Veil," "Looking at the World," and "Both Sides of the Line Offside."[33]

Johnson wished to convey the tension between his perceptions and the ways in which he had been viewed in a visual and spatial relationship. But Johnson's main thesis asserted that narrative is predicated on travel and that there can be no story without freedom of movement. Thus the visual that Johnson invoked in his autobiography became something more than itself as he freed it from the reductive, segregated dictates of American visual culture and propelled his story through the multiplicity of his selves, their texts and their sounds, not the duality of a self, and through the simultaneous presence of all of his works as constitutive of but not limited to these selves.

Johnson divided his autobiography into four parts. Each section marked an important transformation in Johnson's personal development and his pursuit of a profession. Part 1 introduces Johnson's family history and concludes with Johnson's graduation from Atlanta University. Part 2 describes Johnson's position as principal of Stanton School and concludes with Johnson's departure for Venezuela and the dissolution of the Cole and Johnson Brothers trio. Part 3 narrates Johnson's experience as consul to Venezuela and Nicaragua and ends with Johnson's resignation from the Foreign Service when he was denied promotion. Part 4 begins with a brief return to Jacksonville before he abandoned it for New York, where he found work as a contributing editor for the *New York Age* and as field secretary for the NAACP. Part 4 is especially immersed in the profoundly worsened civic status of African Americans not only in the South but in America as a whole. Johnson discovered upon his return to Jacksonville that it had become "a one-hundred percent cracker town."

Johnson wrote that when he dropped his letter of resignation from the American consulate in the mailbox, he felt that "the problem was more serious than my resignation from Stanton School; notwithstanding, it caused me only little more hesitation. I dropped the letter in the mail box, and marked another turn on the way along which I have come."[34] Upon returning to Jacksonville, he questioned his decision: "I had burned my bridges, but I could not entirely keep down the question as to the wisdom of my action. I had . . . placed myself where I had to make a new start, without knowing what direction I should take." Johnson describes his attempt to control his advancement, a major theme of his autobiography, but this theme of "the way" offers a rigid and misleading tidiness to his life narrative, for, as in the example of his near lynching in Jacksonville, such control was a mere fiction. There was little or no opportunity for reasoning dialogue in many of the life-threatening situations that Johnson describes.

Psalm 140, a psalm of David, from which Johnson likely derived the spirit of his title, invokes the idea of justness for all righteous men: "Guard me, O LORD, from wicked men; keep me safe from violent men, who plan to thrust me out of the way. Arrogant men set hidden traps for me, rogues spread their nets and lay snares for me along the way." The psalms, songs probably intended to be sung on the pilgrimage to Jerusalem, are altered in Johnson's autobiography, where the pilgrimage is the secular pursuit of justness for all men in the face of the deprivation and savage terror of racist, "wicked," "violent" Americans. No doubt Johnson recalled his terror of the lynch mob composed of National Guardsmen in 1901 as he invoked David's song. The "way," then, of Johnson's autobiography invokes song as a means of invoking protection from the traps and violence of wicked men. By referencing the spirit of song in his autobiography's title, Johnson offered another way of reading *Along This Way* and its visual tropes, particularly through the repetition of certain passages that begin to reverberate with meaning through their very intertwining.

A key example of the author's intertwining of the visual with text, with the effect of creating a portrait of sound, occurs in Johnson's repetition of the "portrait gallery" of *The Autobiography of an Ex-Colored Man* to *Black Manhattan* and to *Along This Way*. Not only does Johnson reference his novel as a source in *Black Manhattan*, as we have seen, but in *Along This Way* he now incorporates elements of both texts. The "Club" of the novel is Ike Hines's in *Black Manhattan*; what is more, in recalling his activities during his early days as a composer in New York's Black Bohemia, Johnson also begins a similar practice of a portrait gallery in his study at Fisk, as evidenced by a letter he wrote to Sterling Brown. In his autobiography Johnson describes the Cole and Johnson Brothers trio's prosperity:

> With prosperity, we added a degree or so of luxury to our mode of living. We bought furniture, books, and "objects of art," and had the set-up supervised by a professional decorator. Across one wall was stretched a seine, to which was attached with clips our collection of autographed photographs. This collection grew to include nearly all

> the important persons connected with musical theater. Our studio now became a center for both Negro and white artists. . . . [O]ur first big party was given for Miss May Irwin and friends she might wish to bring. She brought eight or ten persons; we had invited about an equal number of colored guests. The party was a success.[35]

So it turns out that not only Hines's club but also the young men's studio had walls papered with the autographed portraits of "nearly all the important persons connected with Negro theater." Johnson chose to enact this previous life as well as the world of *The Autobiography of an Ex-Colored Man* by creating a "gallery" of portraits at Fisk that he had begun while writing his autobiography. He requested an autographed portrait from poet and reluctant mentee Sterling Brown: "In my study here at Fisk I have a small and, I might say exclusive gallery of celebrities. Persons who visit us, especially students, are very much interested in these photographs. This little gallery is, I need not say, incomplete without your picture."[36]

While the photographs themselves represent a visual idiom of image making, the repetition of this practice of creating a "gallery" indicates their complex interrelation. The photograph is *constructed* authentication, and Johnson realizes this as he creates a narrative from this visual collage of photographs in a series of "galleries." Their repetition in three texts as well as in private correspondence creates a sound collage of repeated and altered passages describing them as well as the emerging voice of the selves who have placed them together. The repetition, recontextualization, and dialogic reworking of the photographs create a shifting framework of record, one that emphasizes the continuous making of human expressivism through its culture and practices.[37]

Viking Press planned publicity for *Along This Way* that would create broad interest in the work. It arranged for a *New Yorker* profile, only the second ever of an African American since the magazine's founding.[38] (Johnson confided to his friend Anne Spencer that the profile was "New Yorkerish.")[39] The press had considered serializing a portion of his autobiography to raise interest in the book, but Johnson fell behind on the edits that were necessary to reduce the work to one volume, at under 425 pages, and so its partial issue as a serial never materialized.[40]

Substantial portions of Johnson's early life were edited out of the final manuscript. One of these passages describes Johnson's experience as a member of the Atlanta University quartet, a musical group that, because of its popularity, traveled and performed to raise funds for the university. On one such trip, the quartet visited "Echo Lake" with their chaperone, Professor Chase:

> We amused ourselves throwing our voices across the lake and having them come back magnified. Gadsden, Porter and I tarried for two or three last echoes after Mr. Chase and [George] Towns and young Bumstead had started. When we covered the short distance between the lake and the road we found that we were at a fork, and that our three companions were no where in sight. . . . We were at a loss both to know where they had gone and which fork to take. We began calling out, one at a time and all together, "Professor Chase, Towns, Bumstead, which way did you go?" We muttered among ourselves, "they ought not to have gone on knowing there was a fork in the road. If we are late for the event, it will be their fault." I tried once more with all my might, "Professor Chase, Towns, Bumstead, can't you hear us?" Then in . . . irritation I blurted out as loudly as I could "Go to hell! I bet you can hear that." The three of us started down what happened to be the right road. We had gone only a short distance when we became aware that our three companions were not many steps behind us. It became plain to us that the three of them had hid themselves along the side of the road at the fork to enjoy our bewilderment when we reached that point and had, of course, overheard all that we had entered. I didn't look back. I was, to say the least, uneasy. Consigning a venerable professor of Atlanta University to hell was an offense I had never dreamed of committing.[41]

In his description of this incident, one can almost hear the echo of Johnson's voice: "You can go to hell! Go to hell! Go to hell!" The potential outcome of his outburst could have been expulsion, of course, and Johnson describes several incidents in which either he or his friends were faced with this threat in his autobiography. This particular incident was excised from the final manuscript. While it's obvious that this incident fails to show Johnson as an unambiguous exemplar, "Echo Lake" clearly conveys the ineffable nature of sound and speech in relation to black subjectivity. The "for hire" musician on the stage who makes money for his university is not granted the dignity of defending his status as an equal, as one who rejects trickery because he too is a man, not an object of amusement. Johnson directed his reader's ear to the indescribable nature of black experiences in this reverberating framework. And he demanded the audience of significant literary and political leaders to prompt conversation about this "unspeakable" regard for black artists and their work.

In what had become his common practice, Johnson sent copies of his autobiography to well-known literary and political figures—not only Carl Van Doren of the *Nation* and Carl Van Vechten of *Vanity Fair* but also President Franklin Delano Roosevelt—as an act of diplomacy. Johnson suggested as much to his editor at Viking, Marshall Best: "I think it would be a splendid thing to give President Roosevelt a copy of *Along This Way.* Primarily—his reading of the book might have some beneficial effect upon his attitude toward the Negro and his action. Secondarily—he might acknowledge the book in a manner that would make first-class publicity. You remember that we sent President Coolidge an inscribed copy of the First Book of Spirituals, and used his letter of acknowledgment and appreciation very advantageously as publicity."[42] Johnson went so far as to suggest a strategy for getting *Along This Way* directly "into President Roosevelt's hands." By November 24, 1933, Johnson had received word that Mrs. Roosevelt had acknowledged receipt of the book and had stated that she would hand it to the president. *Along This Way*, then, made it into the president's library.

Carl Van Vechten offered a sensitive reading of Johnson's work, calling it, in a letter to his friend, "a great performance, great in its reticence, great in its outpouring." He continued: "To me, who already knew so much of your life, the book is packed with drama. I can imagine that for those who know nothing about you it will come almost as a thunderbolt of excitement. It stands with the GREAT autobiographies. . . . To me, you are one of the masters of English. You write a simple, sonorous English which is both highsounding and unaffected. You have to go to Defoe for a comparison."[43] Van Vechten's references to *Along This Way*'s "performance," "drama," and "sonorous" language appropriately reference Johnson's emphatic use of expressive modes that are not limited to the page or to the text. Nor would Johnson's life be limited by a single representation, instead offering continuous and shifting frameworks of expression and record.

Afterword
Remembering James Weldon Johnson

Up the golden street Death galloped,
And the hoofs of his horse struck fire from the gold,
But they didn't make no sound.
—James Weldon Johnson, "Go Down, Death"

In 1938, the year of the Depression's second dip, Johnson was still riding high, enjoying the success of his national and local reputation as literary man and literary counsel—"father confessor," as Gwendolyn Bennett praised him in January 1938.[1] In February 1938 Viking laid plans for the simultaneous reprint of all three of Johnson's publications with the press: *Negro Americans, What Now?* (1935, Johnson's rebuttal to Du Bois's series of controversial articles published in the *Crisis* in 1934 promoting separatism as the most promising social model for black advancement), *God's Trombones*, and *Along This Way*.[2] May 1931 found Johnson presiding over a "small group meeting" at millionaire businesswoman and arts promoter A'lelia Walker's home "to hear in advance a talk on the plans and program of an important Negro Theatre which will soon be opened in New York."[3] And since the early 1930s he had been called upon to preside over literary circles that would result in the *Challenge* (later, the *New Challenge*), a magazine showcasing the best writing by black authors, including Dorothy West, Richard Wright, and others.[4] He was also invited to participate in the *African: A Journal of Literary and Social Progress*, to which his mentee Claude McKay, describing the "takeover" of the journal's editorship, wished to name Johnson and W. E. B. Du Bois "Honorary Editors."[5] Johnson was also asked to guide what McKay called the Negro Writers Guild, "a purely cultural organization. Its aim is to further . . . literary aspirations and assist youthful talents," including McKay, Zora Neale Hurston, Countee Cullen, Romare Bearden, Jessie Fauset, Sterling Brown, Augusta Savage, Dorothy Peterson, and others.[6]

By the early to mid-1930s Johnson had cultivated warm interracial friendships with Eugen Boissevain and Edna St. Vincent Millay, Alfred A. and Blanche Knopf, E. George and Anna Payne, and Carl Van Vechten and Faunia Marinoff, among others. These friendships included stays in each other's homes—still a rare occurrence in a racist and segregated nation where one's reputation was easily contaminated by interracial mingling of any sort, in physical proximity or intellectual discourse—attesting to the sincerity and commitment of all parties involved. In 1937 the Johnsons' garden at Five Acres in Great Barrington was featured as Millay's own in *Vanity Fair*'s magazine feature of her estate at Steepletop in upstate New York. A gleeful Boissevain wrote that he had provided the magazine with a photograph taken by Johnson of Millay in their western Massachusetts retreat when urged to send a photo immediately.[7] For the Paynes, as well as for the Knopfs and others, Johnson was the point man on political and cultural issues concerning race in America, and their personal friendship with the Johnsons was both intimate and symbolic of racial progressivism.

On June 28, 1938, the Johnsons were traveling by car through coastal Maine, returning from a visit to the Paynes' summer home. Traveling through a driving rainstorm in Wiscasset, Maine, on the way to their own summer home in Great Barrington, Massachusetts, the Johnsons crossed a bridge over the Sheepscot River, at the end of which was a poorly marked railroad crossing. The train was upon them before they knew it. James was killed instantly, and Grace was severely injured. The coroner's report described Johnson suffering two broken legs and a fractured skull. Grace's father's nurse, Lucille V. Miller, rushed to tend to her in the Maine hospital and assisted Grace by taking her dictation and filing the insurance report for the accident.

Johnson's accidental death is recounted the same way, over and over: the "driving rainstorm," the "poorly marked railroad crossing," and Johnson's "instant" death from the impact of the train-and-automobile crash.[8] I have repeated this description to emphasize the rigidity of the narrative of Johnson's life at the point of his death. The repetitious narrative is derived from the insurance report Grace was obligated to file just a day after the accident. What's missing from this narrative is the agency of the driver: Grace drove the Johnsons' car on that fateful day, as she did every time they traveled by car; for many years, Johnson had "preferred to leave the driving" to his wife, as he confided to his friend Carl Van Vechten. Whether or not Johnson died immediately or suffered an excruciating and slow death is in fact open for debate. The way the event is remembered successfully erases public awareness of the crushing guilt she must have felt for the accident, even if it was not her fault.

Arrangements were made to hold Johnson's burial service in New York City while Miller stayed in Maine with Grace, who could not attend her husband's funeral service.[9] She remained a convalescent in the Lincoln County Memorial Hospital in Maine for two months. When she returned to Harlem she was in the care of a family nurse, Ollie Jewell Sims (who later adopted the surname Okala through marriage), who became Grace's caregiver and companion until her death in 1974.[10] The trauma and grief Grace endured was crippling, but she at last overcame it, focusing her efforts on preserving her husband's legacy. That legacy could prove at times to be overwhelming. As she wrote H. L. Mencken in 1940, she was left with "a little house full of its record."[11] And yet she rose to the challenge of becoming Johnson's curator, the custodian of his name and legacy. She became Johnson's tireless advocate and promoter, constantly encouraging the republication of his works and even proposing the posthumous publication of his Fisk and New York University lectures on black literature and culture in America, the latter of which, since he had delivered them in 1934, were widely considered to be groundbreaking, his very presence at NYU emblematic of a changing, more diverse, and more tolerant atmosphere of learning and leading.[12] Johnson's memory soon became a commodity, with textual, visual, recorded, and performed representations of him emerging from responses to his unexpected loss.

While his body lay in state in New York City, a death mask was made of Johnson—a fairly uncharacteristic practice of the day but an act that demonstrates the rituals of grieving that shaped Johnson's remembrance and the way we think about his works (fig. 6). Created by sculptor Augusta Savage, Johnson's death mask manipulates emotion, time, and memory by substituting a single image as the totality of his person, erasing and re-creating a new memory based on a single instance of representation. To paraphrase Roland Barthes, the existential Johnson had been erased and substituted with the infinite reproduction of an event that had only occurred once, only in this case it is Johnson's death and its representation, emblematized by the death mask, that erase and re-create that which has gone before.[13] What has been rendered infinite, permanent is his loss. This loss, represented in the ritual acts of remembrance enacted by his mourners, is an appeal made to the feeling

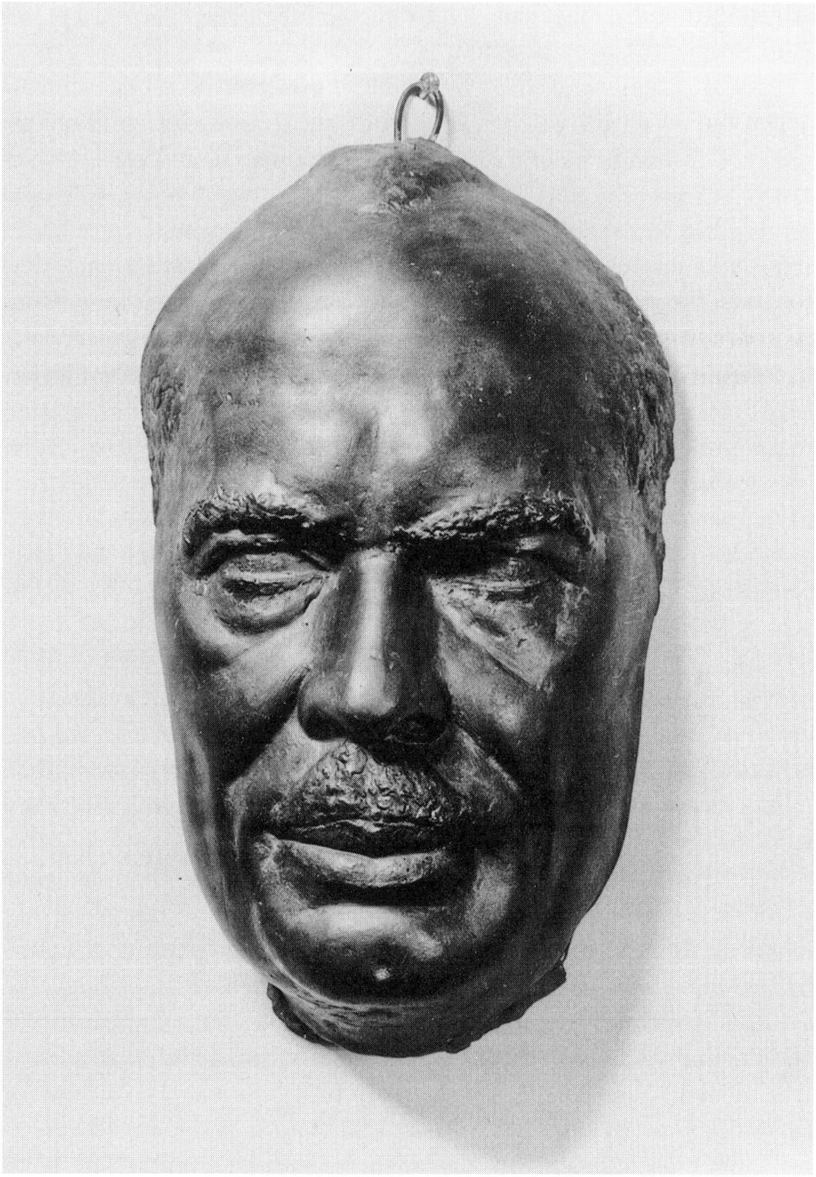

6. James Weldon Johnson. Death mask by Augusta Savage, 1938. Savage made a death mask of Johnson while his body lay in state in a New York City funeral home. Two molds of Savage's death mask were made, but her name was all but erased from them. Photograph courtesy of Fabry Studio for the James Weldon Johnson Papers, Special Collections, Fisk University Franklin Library.

self to sufficiently represent loss and mourning, yet it also conveys the anxiety of failing to do just that.

As Karen Sánchez-Eppler has pointed out, rituals of bereavement depend upon individual, intimate emotions that are also commodifiable. The death mask both is and is not the deceased; it functions as an idealized likeness that must contain more of the viewer's emotional projection than the deceased, inanimate subject's likeness and spirit. Johnson's death mask, a ritual of bereavement, reveals the ambivalences and contradictions of memorialization and commodification. These ritual acts of remembrance—visually tangible, textually biographical, and archival—made Johnson into a memorial object in which a viewer could locate, and cherish, loss.[14] The loss of Johnson was immediately connected to his widely accepted status as a hero of civil rights on whom hope for racial equality and justice hung. Johnson's death mask, a realistic, static, and confrontational image, is unconventionally idealized in order to inspire certain emotions in its viewers as he and they bear the weight of a public life of confronting wrongs. The individualized emotions that the death mask seems to privilege are also used for its commodification: Johnson's personal misfortune is made into a public trauma. In projecting the totality of his person—his existential being—onto his body for commodification, this death mask advances the uneasy claim to possession of and feeling for Johnson through his body.

It is an act of mourning to miraculously make a deceased, mutilated body whole.[15] Johnson's body was restored, dressed according to his wishes in his writing attire of "lounging robe" and trousers, a copy of *God's Trombones* placed on his chest, effectively making his very body a national symbol as an author, at once personal and private, and public.[16] Funeral orations have been observed to function as an opportunity to publicly invent and rehearse into being a founding history of a place and its civic values.[17] Johnson as mourned subject was rehearsed into being by the funeral orations of him by Theodore Roosevelt Jr., Gene Buck, and the Reverend Frederick Asbury Cullen, which were then extended by the many additional outpourings of remembrance of him. Johnson as mourned subject was pointed toward the nation and toward an assessment of the nation's moral unity. In this enormous, public act of mourning for Johnson, the deceased was perceived to be the unifier of diverse groups of people of the American nation who otherwise appeared to possess no common thread of connection.

Johnson's physical commodification had begun in his lifetime with the attribution of one or another of his bodily attributes with his charismatic leadership of the race cause. In *Portraits in Color*, NAACP founder Mary White Ovington remarked upon the grace and dignity of Johnson manifested in his hands; a reporter interviewing Johnson in Great Barrington associated Johnson's shrewd social acuity with his "grey-green eyes," as did others.[18] These synecdochal representations of Johnson presume the correspondence of inner and outer selves as well as the intimacy of relation between Johnson's viewers and his "actual" self. Where Johnson may have maintained celebrity as a protective distinction from what he termed his "inner life," spectators assumed a familiarity with the man they decided Johnson really was, dissolving any distinction between public and private selves.[19] These practices were replicated in the wide-scale enactment of public mourning of Johnson.

Esther Schor writes:

> Sympathy . . . results from our tendency to imagine ourselves in the place of the suffering. If we seem to experience "true grief" for those beyond our circle, it is because we habitually imagine "the objects of public love and admiration and gratitude" as our familiars; in order to sympathize with them (or grieve for them) we identify ourselves with *an imaginary figure erected in the place of those close enough to warrant our sympathy.* This phenomenon, which we might call "celebrity," is actually a second-order sympathetic identification. This phenomenon calls forth intense affections for remote figures, even to the point where our sympathy rivals the "true grief" we bear for "the circle of those especially dear to us." Shelley's theory of celebrity is that "public mourning" is simply mourning for the imaginary, intimately known simulacrum of a public figure.[20]

The construction of Johnson's effigy inevitably propelled forth the question of who could control his image, legacy, publications, compositions, and overall meaning. Partly in an effort to distinguish Johnson's greatness from mere popularity, Grace Nail Johnson devoted the rest of her life to preserving and extending Johnson's legacy through the continued request to reissue his works, the development of scholarship awards, and the housing projects named after him. She carefully guarded Johnson's name and the use of his literary works by others through copyright protection, a concern initiated by Johnson himself as a charter member of the American Society of Composers, Authors and Publishers. Grace, who lived until 1973, devoted the rest of her life to preserving Johnson's memory. She sanctioned monuments to Johnson erected each decade following his death, from the housing projects renamed in his memory on New York City's 112th Street and Park Avenue, to the yearlong exhibition on Johnson mounted at the Smithsonian Institution from June 15, 1970, to June 1, 1971.[21] A succession of children's books highlighted Johnson's exemplary life, simplifying his memory and clarifying its purpose to his survivors. Following Johnson's death, Grace became known as "the widow Mrs. James Weldon Johnson," and she made rare appearances for the release of these works. Overwhelmed with her circumstance immediately following the accident, she had had no say in the funeral arrangements for her late husband, nor had she been able to attend. Her only consolation was knowing that, as the couple had arranged, following her death, her ashes and her husband's would be buried alongside each other in the family plot of her father, John B. Nail, in Brooklyn's Green-Wood Cemetery.

On June 30, 1938, crowds of mourners—over two thousand—spilled out of Salem Methodist Episcopal Church at 129th Street and Seventh Avenue in Harlem. The Reverend Frederick Asbury Cullen, pastor of the church and a fixture of Harlem, presided over the funeral service for James Weldon Johnson as mourners attempted to comprehend the tragic accident that had cut short his life. The body had lain in state for one day, and, according to the *Call*, "among the heaps of flowers banked around the casket was a wreath from Mrs. Franklin D. Roosevelt."[22] On this day, officials from the National Urban League and the NAACP, members of the American Society of Composers, Authors and Publishers, New York–based authors and artists (most of whom Johnson knew not only professionally but also personally), and the everyday Harlemite demonstrated the wide and interracial cast of Johnson's net over the worlds of art, education, civil rights, and the media despite the sometimes vigorous differences professed by each group's members.

Johnson's pallbearers composed a veritable who's who list of locally and nationally recognized figures in art and politics: New Negro Renaissance artists, civil rights advocates, New York politicians, nationally renowned composers, actors, musicians, authors, and their publishers. The long list of honorary pallbearers included Rabbi Stephen S. Wise of *Scottsboro* fame; W. C. Handy, known as the "father of the blues";

Arthur B. Spingarn, vice president of the NAACP; Col. Theodore Roosevelt; New York mayor Fiorello LaGuardia, represented ex officio by his secretary, Stanley Howe; railroad tycoon William H. Baldwin; Marshall Best of Viking Press; composer and performer Eubie Blake of *Shuffle Along* fame; composer, performer, and author Harry T. Burleigh; composer and lyricist Irving Caesar; Elmer Anderson Carter of *Opportunity* magazine; and Dr. John Lovejoy Elliott of the New York Society for Ethical Culture.[23] Johnson's brother, John Rosamond Johnson, was in attendance with his wife, Nora Floyd, as were Mary White Ovington, Countee Cullen, Langston Hughes, Aaron Douglas, W. C. Handy Jr., Mr. and Mrs. Lewis Gannet, Mrs. W. E. B. Du Bois, and Arthur Garfield Hays (defense lawyer in landmark civil liberties cases such as *Sweet* and *Scottsboro*).[24] Many more had been sent telegrams but could not attend because of the short notice and their distance from New York, such as William Pickens of the NAACP and Max Eastman of the *Liberator*. As Carl Van Vechten, also an honorary pallbearer, wrote to Grace Nail Johnson of her deceased husband's memorial service, "Could any one else bring out such a strange combination of people united in love?"[25]

Reverend Cullen made an appropriate and meaningful choice as spiritual leader of this funeral service. Reverend Cullen, foster parent to Countee Cullen, served as president of the Harlem branch of the NAACP for many years and was also James Weldon Johnson's friend. As pastor of Salem Methodist Episcopal Church, Reverend Cullen headed "one of the most powerful, socially active, and committed institutions in the black community."[26] Cullen's direction of the memorial harked back to the collaborative civic and national front the two men, with Du Bois and others, mounted in 1917, when Johnson used Manhattan as the site for protesting the East Saint Louis massacre. This collaboration was extended in February 1918, when Cullen "accompanied Johnson to Washington after the Houston affair in which a black regiment of soldiers on rather scant evidence was accused of shooting several white people in a melee."[27] Cullen's presiding over Johnson's memorial service appropriately marks the spiritual passing of a man committed to worldly justice. Johnson, a self-professed agnostic with "little patience with the zealot . . . [who] forever tr[ies] to prove to others that they do not need religion" as well as with the "religionist" (*ATW*, 413–14), appreciated the friendship and community of a like-minded man focused on youth ministry and social activism rather than on the practice of judging others.[28]

Reverend Cullen opened the services by reading from the scriptures and delivering a prayer. The Southernaries, an all-male black quartet, sang "Abide with Me" and then "Sence You Went Away"—one of Johnson's first musical collaborations with his brother, John Rosamond, and one of their most popular compositions. The Reverend Shelton Hale Bishop read the scripture lesson, and the Hall Negro Choir recited one of Johnson's hallmark poetic sermons: "Go Down, Death," from *God's Trombones*. Three people gave keynote eulogies of Johnson: Col. Theodore Roosevelt; Gene Buck, president of the American Society of Composers, Authors and Publishers; and the Reverend Cullen. Following the services, Johnson was interred in Green-Wood Cemetery's mausoleum, awaiting his wife. Johnson was interred as he had requested, dressed in his "work clothes" for writing—his lounging robe and trousers—and holding a copy of *God's Trombones* in his hands.

Close associates, remote acquaintances, and the everyday people of Harlem whose lives surrounded this era of the New Negro packed the church, crowded the entrance, and filled the streets. Traffic was stopped; a special squad of ten policemen was required to keep the crowd that overflowed the church from blocking traffic. Regular movement at the intersection of the church was interrupted for several hours while onlookers paid tribute to Johnson and his legacy.[29]

Johnson's memorial service in Harlem appropriately dramatized his lifelong calling and contributions as a lyricist, poet, and author. His memorial service recalled a great, multitalented man who could unite those traditionally divided by difference, but it also initiated the acts of remembrance that form the Johnson archive—reductive tendencies that diminish not just the magnitude and complexity of his works but the innovative complexities of the man himself.[30] As Salomé Voegelin writes, "The visual object is the permanence of melancholia and history. Sound by contrast is the permanence of production . . . simultaneity."[31] Locating Johnson's memory in his body, the memorial service unwittingly obscured the subtle "swing" of Johnson's works and his investment in "play"—between forms of blackness, between individual and collective representations of the black artist, between sound and text—substituting instead the rigid progress- and archive-oriented Johnson. This version of Johnson is what has survived, whether he is regarded as a perfect success or as a self-aggrandizing traditionalist in American letters and politics.

This archiving of Johnson began almost immediately. Two weeks after the funeral service, on July 14, 1938, the radio station WNYC broadcast five addresses delivered in memory of James Weldon Johnson. They were delivered by Mayor Fiorello LaGuardia, Col. J. E. Spingarn (brother of Arthur B. Spingarn), Ada Scott Dunbar, Walter White, and William Pickens.[32] LaGuardia described Johnson as "a fighter for the rights of his people and the rights of all" who "played an important part in the historic developments of his span of life." "James Weldon Johnson wrote 'Under the Bamboo Tree,'" LaGuardia continued, "but he didn't lie lazily under it. He went out and worked and fought. He won respect and admiration in every field of endeavor in which he engaged." As LaGuardia observed, the struggle for citizenship and equality in his political work was tied to his art, making the art not an end in itself but one tied to "historical developments" in America.[33]

Fisk University, where Johnson had held an endowed professorship since 1931, held its own memorial service in February 1939. Arthur B. Spingarn, Carl Van Vechten, and Sterling Brown gave addresses in memory of Johnson; those addresses were published by the Fisk University Department of Publicity in 1940 as *James Weldon Johnson: A Biographical Sketch* (Spingarn's contribution is titled "James Weldon Johnson: An Appreciation"; Van Vechten's is "James Weldon Johnson: My Friend"; and Brown's is "The Negro in American Literature"). Following the direct advice of Grace Nail Johnson, Luanna J. Bowles, director of publicity, assembled the publication.[34] Fisk University president Thomas Elsa Jones described it to letter writers offering their condolences as "a permanent memorial to James Weldon Johnson," emphasizing biographical practice—Johnson's construction in words—as an act of remembrance and also a commodity, functioning as a fundraiser for the university.[35]

New York University and Columbia University, both of which had hired Johnson to teach in their Teachers Colleges, held their own memorial services in 1938. E. George Payne, dean of New York University's Teachers College, whom the Johnsons had visited just prior to his fatal accident, directed NYU's service, at which Sterling Brown, Oswald Garrison Villard, and fellow professor Hughes Mearns spoke. Columbia University titled its August 3, 1938, memorial service "James Weldon Johnson: Eminent American." New York University continued the course of instruction that Johnson had designed and taught since 1934—Negro Contributions to American Culture—by inviting a series of guest speakers: Johnson's brother, Rosamond, to lecture on music and theater; Sterling Brown to lecture on contributions to literature; and Walter White to lecture on political factors in court and history as well as prejudicial treatment of blacks in textbooks.[36]

The NAACP also organized its own memorial, intended to contribute a permanent record of Johnson's life. By September 30, 1938, the NAACP had announced the sale of a recording of Johnson reading his poetic sermons from *God's Trombones*—first recorded in 1929—in the *Crisis*, the literary organ of the association. The announcement claimed that the record would "keep alive the voice of James Weldon Johnson for posterity" through the recordings of Johnson's voice reading four of his sermons: "The Creation," "Go Down, Death," "The Prodigal Son," and "Listen Lord—a Prayer." Here again we see the combination of memorial with commodity, as Johnson's recorded voice is presented as a living archive, the source of the man, which can be purchased to perpetuate his memory (while also raising revenue for the organization).

As early as one and a half weeks after Johnson's death proposals for memorials in sculpture were taking shape, too. Carl Van Vechten wrote Grace Nail Johnson on July 9, 1938 (while she was convalescing in Maine), that the sculptor and educator "Augusta Savage is making a bust of Jim (from photographs and a death mask) to be cast in bronze and I went to see it today. It is not yet finished but it is most promising" (fig. 7).[37] Soon that sculpture would become part of a competition over which sculptor would be authorized by Johnson's widow to create a monument of him. As Savage formed her sculpture of Johnson, Grace Nail grew to dislike it and expressed as much to Van Vechten. He in turn proposed that the sculptor Richmond Barthé do the memorial sculpture of Johnson. Van Vechten wrote to Grace Nail just one week later: "Augusta Savage's bust is progressing but isn't finished. I am invited to inspect it with Rosamond soon, that is Rosamond told Miss S he wanted ME to be there when he saw it. Richmond Barthé who has just returned from New Orleans is going to do one too and I am SURE his will be the better one. As you know he had long desired to do Jim's hands and Jim had promised to go there this fall."[38]

Van Vechten photographed Savage's work in progress and sent the pictures to Grace Nail for inspection. By the beginning of November, she had written Van Vechten expressing her disapproval of Savage's work and her fear that the bust would be purchased and displayed in

7. James Weldon Johnson. Sculpture by Augusta Savage, 1939. Savage created a sculpture of Johnson as a memorial based on the death mask that she had made. Johnson's widow, Grace Nail Johnson, disliked the portrayal, and it was not selected for use as a memorial to Johnson. It was later displayed in the Arthur A. Schomburg Library, the Harlem branch of the New York Public Library. Photograph courtesy of the James Weldon Johnson and Grace Nail Johnson Papers, Collection of American Literature, Beinecke Rare Book and Manuscript Library, Yale University.

some public place or, worse yet, reproduced. Van Vechten shared her concern and proposed a different sort of sculpture in response to her concerns "in the idea of 'O Black and Unknown Bards.'"[39] Savage's bust remains in the Johnson Collection at Yale University, purchased, one suspects, so that it would not be displayed.

Grace Nail Johnson's struggle over ownership and dissemination of her late husband's image, shown in her concern for and domination over Augusta Savage's sculpture of Johnson as the widow's property, was reflected in nearly every institution's deliberations over suitable memorials to Johnson. Organizations and individuals who felt that they had had personal contact with Johnson argued about the importance and ownership of the projects and disputed the appropriate kind and place of the memorial. These disputes culminated in the James Weldon Johnson Memorial Committee, a list of members handpicked by Grace Nail Johnson to assist her in plans for a memorial. Carl Van Vechten played an influential role in directing the committee's plans, turning their attention away from a scholarship fund and toward a sculpture. He reasoned that a scholarship fund would be an unsuitable way of remembering Johnson both because it was too modest and because it risked allowing Johnson's importance to pass into obscurity, he suggested to Grace Nail. A scholarship recipient might not know the significance of Johnson's name.[40] Van Vechten authored the final proposal of the committee, published in *Opportunity*, the journal of the National Urban League, thus temporarily breaking with the NAACP's *Crisis* and the influence of its executive secretary, Walter White, who initially supported the idea of a scholarship fund.[41] In the final proposal of a memorial, Van Vechten sealed off Savage's participation in shaping it by stating, "The committee further agreed to intrust the creation of this work to Richmond Barthé, the Negro sculptor."[42]

In February 1940 "The Proposed James Weldon Johnson Memorial" was not only published in *Opportunity* but also reprinted and mailed directly to potential supporters and financers of the plan. Van Vechten did more than simply propose a monument; he described its visual presentation and the story that it would tell. Van Vechten stated that he could not imagine Johnson "standing stiffly in a frock coat." Both in location and form, Van Vechten's monument would evoke motion and resound with its location, establishing Johnson as a modern connected to all those who encountered him: "The particular site which the committee would prefer is the island in the center of Seventh Avenue, immediately above One Hundred and Tenth Street, the monument facing the entrance to Central Park, so that anyone who emerged from the Park at that point—and many thousands in the course of one week—would meet the statue face to face." The statue would face and address Johnson's ideal community of "Black Manhattan" emanating outward to the whole of New York. The monument would enhance the city's symbolic geography and attest to Johnson's significance as a poet-prophet in an interracial American history. It would be "a monument in bronze, not *of* James Weldon Johnson, but *to* his Black and Unknown Bards, the creators of the Spirituals. On the marble base of this Memorial would appear on one side a bas-relief of Mr. Johnson's head, while on the other would be carved a stanza from the verses of the poet which had inspired the monument."[43]

Here at Seventh Avenue and 110th Street, Johnson's name and image would meet the masses; his name would evoke an originary past of black culture in America. From the unnamed creators of the spirituals would spring Johnson, the artist with a name who memorialized them. This monument would present itself to those traversing Central Park and traveling to and from Harlem, offering, through its Romanesque evocation of the ancient and original civilization in bas-relief, a narrative of black cultural foundations similar to that advanced by Johnson in his social history of New York, *Black Manhattan.* In Van Vechten's visual representation of mourning, Johnson's physical presence—his head—and his poetry—a stanza—dramatically claimed his history.

A press release dated February 16, 1940, "First Lady Heads List of National Sponsors for James Weldon Johnson Memorial Statue," names Mrs. Franklin D. Roosevelt as leading "the list of prominent persons included in a nation-wide sponsoring committee of persons in all walks of life, who will raise $20,000 to erect a memorial to James Weldon Johnson in New York City, the National Association for the Advancement of Colored People announced today." The release grasped at the fleeting possibility of making the sculpture memorial materialize on the brink of the outbreak of World War II with concrete, descriptive language, authenticating Johnson as a New Yorker through his poetry: "The memorial . . . will be erected on a plot of ground at 110th Street and Seventh Avenue, facing Central Park. The ground will be donated by the City of New York, where Mr. Johnson wrote his poem 'My City,' and where he spent most of his life." The release continued: "The statue will be executed by Richmond Barthé, the internationally famous sculptor," eliminating the possibility that any other sculptor might claim the opportunity. Mayor Fiorello LaGuardia was named "honorary chairman," with Col. Theodore Roosevelt as chairman.[44]

Augusta Savage had had a closer relation to Johnson's deceased body than anyone else, certainly Barthé, as she revealed in a letter of correction she addressed to the Johnson Memorial Committee. It seems that the *Opportunity* article announcing Barthé as the executing sculptor had mistakenly included a photograph of Savage's work-in-progress, misattributed to the other sculptor, thus erasing her hand in the creation of his memorial. She made plain to the committee that her sculpture "of the head of Mr. Johnson [was] created by me from a death mask which I made in the Universal Funeral Chapel, 597 Lexington Avenue, where Mr. Johnson lay in state." She continued: "Inasmuch as the idea was originally mine, I feel it cruelly unjust of Mr. Van Vechten to use my head of Mr. Johnson, which was executed under such trying circumstances, to sell the talents of Mr. Barthé."[45] Walter White's response on behalf of the committee was unabashedly cruel. He wrote Savage: "Mr. Van Vechten not only had nothing to do with the use of your head as an illustration but was very much annoyed by the error."[46]

Despite Van Vechten's enthusiasm and influential reach in the world of New York arts, his sculpture never materialized. LaGuardia's secretary, and the mayor himself, ignored correspondence from Van Vechten and from Walter White, who, sensing that the opportunity to secure the proposed city property was passing, used an increasingly insistent tone in his letters of inquiry.[47] There is little to explain LaGuardia's silence on the matter of the proposed site after his eloquent eulogy of Johnson, except that, perhaps, the symbolism of city land devoted to a black leader's memory was too generous a gesture for a local politician, even of LaGuardia's stature, to make. The outbreak of World War II sealed off any remaining possibility that the city land would be given for the monument.

Even as the committee pressed LaGuardia and his parks commissioner, Robert Moses, for the land, Richmond Barthé had produced the first version of his sculpture, *Birth of the Spirituals* (fig. 8). It features a nude male subject reaching his hands to the sky, his mouth opened in song as his ankles are shackled. Those on the committee who viewed it suggested that the shackles be broken, making the metaphor

8. Birth of the Spirituals. *James Weldon Johnson Memorial Sculpture by Richmond Barthé. Largely due to the influence of Carl Van Vechten, Barthé became the artist chosen to create a memorial of and to Johnson, which the James Weldon Johnson Memorial Committee hoped would be placed at 110th Street and Seventh Avenue in New York City. Because of the statue's representation of a nude man, New York City parks commissioner Robert Moses forbade its location in this space. Photograph by Carl Van Vechten. Photograph courtesy of the Carl Van Vechten Papers, Collection of American Literature, Beinecke Rare Book and Manuscript Library, Yale University.*

more powerful. Barthé's statue was never placed in this location, and the sculpture, now in the Smithsonian, has since lost its affiliation with Johnson's memory.

Sidney Bremer explains why Barthé's sculpture never became a monument to Johnson:

> New York City's powerful parks commissioner, Robert Moses, jammed the whole works. In 1941 he rejected the proposal to site Barthé's allegorical nude at Seventh Avenue and 110th Street—because, he proclaimed, the statue would be a bad influence on the children of Harlem. In 1942 Moses suggested placing the statue inside Central Park—near a Puerto Rican and black area where "no white man or dicty Negro has ever set foot," Van Vechten objected. Then Moses suggested saving the statue for a proposed postwar housing project deep inside Harlem, since World War II had made it impossible to divert metal from guns to statues anyhow. When Moses finally did agree to the original proposal in late 1945, the costs of casting had increased far beyond the funds that had been raised before the war. That blow sounded the death knell for the statue. It would have been the first public monument to a black person in the city of New York.[48]

To silence Walter White and the NAACP's increasingly persistent inquiries about the monument, LaGuardia and the New York City Housing Authority arranged for the construction of a low-income housing project located between East 112th and 115th Streets and Park and Third Avenues, including an already existing low-income area called Hillside, to be renamed the James Weldon Johnson Houses in 1945. The already-existing apartments were condemned, their tenants evicted; months later, with little alteration, they were reopened bearing Johnson's name.[49]

Grace Nail Johnson was an active shaper of her husband's image after his death. Indeed, she was actively pursuing many avenues for the remembrance of her husband, including an archival repository for his poetry manuscripts—at the Library of Congress, not the Schomburg Center for Research in Black Culture at the New York Public Library in Harlem, which might have affirmed Johnson's civic legacy. Johnson's papers and a host of other black writers' papers are a significant addition to Yale's collection not just in the reasoning of Van Vechten but in that of Johnson, too: they are *like* Black Manhattan, the foundation of *national* culture based on black letters, labor, and agency. Much as Johnson strategized his autobiography *Along This Way*'s inclusion in the Presidential Library shortly after its publication, establishing Johnson's papers as an archive at Yale guaranteed—even forced—national acknowledgment of black letters as a foundation of American cultural practices.

In place of the monument, Van Vechten established the James Weldon Johnson Memorial Collection of African American Arts and Letters at Yale University's Manuscript and Archives, now at the Beinecke Rare Book and Manuscript Library. Beginning in 1941 with the deposit of Johnson's papers in the archive, much of the next ten years were spent by Van Vechten soliciting contributions from writers whom Johnson had known or with whom he had corresponded, including Langston Hughes, Zora Neale Hurston, Nella Larsen, Claude McKay, and many others. Johnson's brother, Rosamond, remained adamantly opposed to the establishment of an archive and was strongly in favor of a memorial statue placed in New York's Harlem; he reluctantly joined those on the James Weldon Johnson Memorial Committee in favor of the archive. The dedication of the memorial collection in January 1950 marked the formal recognition of Van Vechten's alternative memorial to Johnson. The founding of this archive perpetuates the foundation-building narrative so closely linked to Johnson's body—one that reduced his literary works to his life, in effect silencing the narrative play that forms his sound-based aesthetic, and that can be seen even in Johnson's wish to bear *God's Trombones* on his chest in death.

The Yale collection wasn't the only archive named after Johnson. According to notes that Grace Nail sent Luanna Bowles at Fisk, Joseph Auslander at the Library of Congress had expressed an interest in creating a repository of Johnson's papers, especially his manuscripts of poetry, at the Library. Speaking of herself in the third person (in her own act of biography), Grace Nail wrote: "His widow has been invited by Mr. Auslander to participate in establishing an archives of Negro Poetry within the Poetry Room of the Library of Congress—to which he adds, 'I would consider the Manuscripts of James Weldon Johnson the very foundation stone of such a collection.'"[50]

It is impossible to miss the importance of Johnson's role in this highly symbolic placement of Negro poetry "within" the Poetry Room. It's an interracialism Johnson himself would have appreciated, as he would have the figure of the "foundation stone" representing both his oeuvre of writing and the history that he repeatedly asserted of American culture's foundation on black cultural roots. Here again we have the "Black and Unknown Bards" invoked alongside Johnson. Much like the memorial that Van Vechten had proposed, Johnson stood as the individual counterpart to his "Black and Unknown Bards," the poet who would memorialize the unnamed creators of the spirituals and in turn name the origins of black art in America and American art in black culture. This symbolic meaning of Johnson's writing as representing a larger accomplishment was again emphasized by Grace Nail when she wrote in the same memo to Bowles that Johnson was the only Negro author besides Booker T. Washington whose work was included in the Presidential Library. The proposed Library of Congress Memorial seeks to archive Johnson's writing as an essential, building component of American culture and politics.

All of these memorials located Johnson's posterity in his body: head, eyes, hand, voice, archive. Moreover, they explicitly and implicitly linked Johnson's memory with commodity. All of the memorials demanded public acknowledgment of Johnson's intellectual and cultural value as a figure in history and emphasized a particular meaning to Johnson's life and the use to which his example could be put in a variety of causes, all of which he had participated in. At the same time, these monuments attempted to reach into the future, to define posterity.[51]

The breadth of Johnson's participation in wide-ranging fields resulted in many contradictory and stultifying acts of memorialization initiated by his mourners. A tension emerged between popular, mass-culture claims to the memory of Johnson and elite claims to him through institutions such as the archive. The ambivalence of Johnson's class affiliations and commitments is derived largely from these competing claims rather than from Johnson's practices. Critical reception of his significance has repeated this ambivalence. In his death, Johnson became a symbol through which hopes and frustrations far larger than he could be articulated.

In 1938, the year of his death, the issue of the control of media images of African Americans intensified, as Barbara Diane Savage has observed. In response to anxiety over national cohesiveness as involvement in the European war seemed increasingly likely, "the U.S. government used radio to construct and popularize an expanded narrative of American history that acknowledged the contributions of immigrants, African Americans, and Jews," concluding that "it was politically necessary to continue to foster a broader notion of acceptance and inclusiveness for the sake of national unity."[52] LaGuardia's broadcast was used to this end. While he couldn't permit the construction of a memorial statue, he could use Johnson as a symbol in his radio address to argue for a national cohesion, taking Johnson's example of art and leadership to showcase the nation's progress and possibility.

Eulogies by those who knew him in some way were gathered into a sort of composite biography as a testament to his lifetime of works. Grace Nail Johnson attempted to erase her traumatic memory of the accident by telling, retelling, and resituating Johnson in permanent textual memorials—children's books, the projects of the James Weldon Johnson Literary Guild after his death, the reissue of his works to her specifications, her choice and presentation of certain of his photographs for publicity (fig. 9), and her contextualization of Johnson's papers, the record of his life. Johnson was already a public figure, so controlling his reputation and effigy as presented by his mourners/survivors would never be possible. But she could preserve the public's presumed intimacy with him by making all of his works, and subsequent ones about him, a biographical testament. Grace Nail's biography of her late husband and his legacy attempted to replace Johnson's mutable concept of writing and self. In warring against an already constructed public image, the outcome of her efforts was a simplified rendering of Johnson's oeuvres and self, presenting a repetitive, unchanging mythology in place of repetitive, perpetually mutating works and self. These are very different ideas of repetition, with different perceptions of the work that words do. Where Johnson created a poetics of form attached to "swing" as an antiessentialist, modernist notion of self—one that offered creative possibilities while conveying the dissonant realities of black modern life—Grace's actions, and those of his mourners as they rushed to preserve his memory, reverted to romantic mythologies of the hero—clear relations, a simple landscape of strong feeling, a morally right hero insulated from his corrupt world, expressing his nobility in his very physical presence (an arresting handsomeness) as well as his actions. Paradoxically, while seeming to present his organically whole and pure self, these very forms of remembrance dismembered Johnson's body, using his eyes, hands, or face synecdochally. The processes by which James Weldon Johnson was remembered served to erase his modernist outlook and substituted in its place a Victorian romantic in a modern age, making modernism and the modern world separate and

9. James Weldon Johnson. Publicity photo for the American Society of Composers, Authors and Publishers, 1937. Photograph by Irving Chidnoff. In all subsequent publicity following Johnson's death, widow Grace Nail Johnson asked that this photograph of Johnson be used, for he "looks directly into the camera." Photograph courtesy of the James Weldon Johnson and Grace Nail Johnson Papers, Collection of American Literature, Beinecke Rare Book and Manuscript Library, Yale University.

irrelevant to his life, where Johnson perceived himself as immersed in modernism and modernity. While it may never be possible to tell a life like Johnson's fully, we can at least reflect on the appropriative practices that create our stories of him, the silences and gaps that can only record his ambiguities, while continuing his song.

Notes

INTRODUCTION

1. On Johnson's hands, see Carl Van Vechten's correspondence with Grace Nail Johnson, box 37, folder 240, Johnson and Johnson Papers (Correspondence and Manuscripts), BRBL (hereafter cited as either JWJ Corr. or JWJ MSS, BRBL); on Johnson's hands and eyes, see Ovington's chapter on Johnson in *Portraits in Color*. See also Richetta Randolph, later Johnson's secretary at the NAACP, on her first sight of Johnson, recorded in her memorial speech, provided in a letter to Carl Van Vechten: "I raised my eyes and saw walking up and down the room across the hall as if lost in deep thought a man who appeared to me to be one of the most distinguished Negroes I had ever seen" (Randolph to Van Vechten, December 1, 1942, box 21, folder 507, JWJ Corr., BRBL). See also note 26.

2. Oswald Garrison Villard, untitled obituary, *Nation*, July 9, 1938, 44.

3. Alfred A. Knopf, uncredited obituary, *New York Herald Tribune*, June 28, 1938.

4. Jackson, "Letters to a Friend," 191.

5. Knopf, uncredited obituary.

6. While James Sr. held one of the highest social positions available to African Americans, he was functionally illiterate until middle age. Johnson saw his father lose several real estate endeavors in the years just before his death in 1912 as a result of being swindled by those who knew more than he did.

7. A portion of this discussion can be found in my introduction to Johnson's *Autobiography of an Ex-Colored Man and Other Writings*.

8. See Johnson's description of Ike Hines and Jimmy Marshall in *Along This Way*, chap. 16.

9. See "The Czar of Czam," box 74, folders 438–39, JWJ MSS, BRBL.

10. Cole and Johnson Brothers' songs made several appearances in films, many of those appearances uncredited. Their wildly successful "Under the Bamboo Tree" appears in *Suzy* (1936), *Lillian Russell* (1940), *White Cargo* (1942), *Meet Me in St. Louis* (1944), and *Bowery to Broadway* (1944), to name but a few. The Johnsons' original football anthem, "Oh! Didn't He Ramble," appears in *Sunny* (1930) uncredited. The lyrics to "Under the Bamboo Tree" also made it into T. S. Eliot's *Sweeney Agonistes*.

11. Berlin, "Cole and Johnson Brothers."

12. For the insertion of arias into ragtime, see Riis, *Just before Jazz*, 84.

13. Johnson, *Along This Way*, 173–74.

14. I am indebted to Gerald Early's interpretation of the New Negro Renaissance in Black Bohemia and the centrality of Jack Johnson as an icon of social

change for black culture and an emblem of racial tensions nationwide, which Early discusses in his introduction to *My Soul's High Song*, 4–25.

15. See Johnson's *New York Age* editorial "Dealing with Mobs," October 11, 1919, in Wilson, *Selected Writings*, 1:71–72. See also "The Riots: An NAACP Investigation" (1919), in Andrews, *James Weldon Johnson*, 655–59.

16. Early, introduction, 27, 29.

17. Biers, "Syncope Fever."

18. Harlan and Smock, *The Booker T. Washington Papers*, 7:141n2.

19. Osofsky, "Race Riot, 1900." As Mark Anthony Neal writes, this riot "politicize[d] the black community within New York's urban spaces in ways that would impact black political and social discourse for three decades" (*What the Music Said*, 10).

20. Johnson, *Black Manhattan*, 126–30.

21. Quoted in Knopf publicity circular for *Black Manhattan*, October 29, 1931, Author Files, 718.10, Knopf Papers, HRC, emphasis added.

22. James Weldon Johnson, commencement address, Georgia State Industrial College for Colored Youth, June 1916, box 2, folder 35, Johnson Papers, MARBL.

23. Johnson's autograph annotations; see Anonymous, *The Autobiography*, copy 2, MARBL.

24. James Weldon Johnson, "'The Poor White Musician,'" *New York Age*, September 23, 1915, in Wilson, *Selected Writings*, 1:285.

25. James Weldon Johnson, "Writers of Words and Music," *New York Age*, March 2, 1918, in Wilson, *Selected Writings*, 1:289.

26. Radano, *Lying Up a Nation*, 104.

27. Ibid., xii, xiii.

28. James Weldon Johnson, "American Music," *New York Age*, January 13, 1916, in Wilson, *Selected Writings*, 1:287.

29. Knopf, uncredited obituary.

30. Villard, untitled obituary.

31. "Rhythm" and "tonal harmony" are from Herman J. D. Carter, "My Teacher," *Pulse Magazine* (1948); "Half-closed eyes of the visionary" is from Georgia Douglas Johnson, "A Reminisence [*sic*]," *Pulse Magazine* (1948). See also note 1.

32. William E. Clark, "Johnson's Loss Blow to Theatre," *Negro Actor*, July 15, 1938, clipping in Author Publicity File, James Weldon Johnson, Knopf Papers, HRC.

33. Voegelin, *Listening*, 4.

34. Johnson, "The Story of Ragtime," "The Origin and Development of Ragtime," and "The Contents of a Name: Mozart Jackson, Composer," Writings, box 67, folder 303, and box 73, folder 368, Series II, JWJ MSS 49, BRBL.

35. See Berlin, "Cole and Johnson Brothers."

36. See Ellison, "Hidden Name," in which he references his friend Albert

Murray's coinage of "Franklin Delano Jones": "'Franklin D. Roosevelt Jones might sound like a clown to someone who looks at him from the outside,' said my friend Albert Murray, 'but on the other hand . . . he might just lie back in all that comic juxtaposition of names and manipulate you deaf, dumb and blind—and you not even suspecting it, because you're so thrown out of stance by his name! There you are, so dazzled by the F. D. R. image—which you *know* you can't see—and so delighted with your superior position that you don't realize that it is *Jones* who must be confronted'" (194).

37. Many of these recordings are available on the University of California at Santa Barbara's excellent cylinder preservation and digitization project Website, including Arthur Collins, "Oh Didn't He Ramble" (cylinder 8081), "Under the Bamboo Tree" (cylinder 8215), with Byron G. Harlan, "Run, Brudder Possum, Run!" (cylinder 301), Corinne Morgan and Frank C. Stanley, "Nobody's Looking but the Owl and the Moon" (cylinder 8577) (http://cylinders.library.ucsb.edu). National Jukebox, in the Digital Collections of the Library of Congress, also has available several early recordings of Cole and Johnson Brothers' compositions (http://www.loc.gov/jukebox).

38. Lynn Sweet, "Rev. Lowery Inauguration benediction. Transcript," transcript courtesy of Federal News Service, *Chicago Sun Times*, January 20, 2009, 1:04 p.m. (blogs.suntimes.com/sweet/2009/01/rev_lowery_inauguration_benedi.html).

1. BIOGRAPHY OF THE RACE

1. Johnson, *Along This Way*, 163. Hereafter cited in the text as *ATW*.

2. James Weldon Johnson, "Brothers" (1917), in Johnson, *Autobiography of an Ex-Colored Man and Other Writings*, 137.

3. Sundquist, *Hammers of Creation*, 22–23.

4. See the trio's "theory" of popularity leading to the composition of Cole and Johnson Brothers in Johnson, *Along This Way*, 179–80.

5. Riis, *Just before Jazz*, 65–66.

6. As David Suisman notes, "Printing the picture of a well-known performer on the cover of the sheet music took advantage of the performer's existing popularity; for performers, having their image on the cover of such sheet music enhanced their reputations" (*Selling Sounds*, 31n1.3).

7. Ibid., 26n1.2.

8. Riis, *Just before Jazz*, 60–61.

9. Ibid., 61.

10. Ibid., 88.

11. Ibid., 138. He writes: "The appearance of such written details in light-comedy songs was quite special and reveals the unusual conscientiousness for a musical show composer of this era" (140).

12. Ibid., 140.

13. Weheliye, *Phonographies*, 32.

14. "Musical quotation" and "outright parody" quoted from Riis, *Just before Jazz*, 63, 65.

15. See Southern, *Music of Black Americans*, 281.

16. Johnson, *Autobiography*, 3. Hereafter cited in the text as *AECM*.

17. Jackson, "Letters to a Friend," 189.

18. *New Orleans Picayune*, July 21, 1912.

19. Stepto, *From behind the Veil*.

20. February 7, 1912, box 18, Series I, JWJ Corr., BRBL.

21. Henson, *Truth Stranger than Fiction*; Henson, *Autobiography*.

22. Johnson, New York University lecture notes, 1934–37, JWJ MSS +478–+479, BRBL.

23. Johnson, "*Uncle Tom's Cabin* and the Clansman," *New York Age*, March 4, 1915, in Wilson, *Selected Writings*, 1:12–13.

24. Ibid.

25. Little et al., "Syncope."

26. Johnson's autograph annotations in Anonymous, *Autobiography*, copy 2, p. 97, MARBL.

27. Suisman, *Selling Sounds*, 9.

28. Ibid., 14.

29. Biers, "Syncope Fever."

30. Suisman, *Selling Sounds*, 13.

31. Thompson, *Soundscape of Modernity*, 131. Thompson describes the 1921 case of Mrs. Richard T. Wilson, who was taken to court by her downstairs neighbor for her late-night gatherings, at which "a great deal of the music was of a jazz character," according to one witness, and was described as "ragtime. I should say cacophony" by another. Wilson argued that "the music performed was of the best 'artistic character,' and therefore could not constitute noise at any time of day or night" (129–30).

32. As Christine Stansell puts it, "Fear of the immigrants, the black masses, and the labor movement blended with dislike of the New Woman, promoting appeals to restore traditional hierarchies in family and class relations . . . to . . . subdue the threat of anarchic sexual modernism" (*American Moderns*, 31–32). Johnson links the sexual modernism of the New Woman to interracialism and black masculinity in *Autobiography of an Ex-Colored Man*.

33. Johnson would write in *Along This Way* that "in the decade ending in 1899, according to the records printed in the daily press, 1665 Negroes were lynched, numbers of them with a savagery that was satiated with nothing short of torture, mutilation, and burning alive at the stake" (*Along This Way*, 158).

34. Suisman, *Selling Sounds*, 31, note to figure 1.3.

35. See Stepto's chapter on Johnson's work, "Lost in a Quest," in *From behind the Veil*; Smith, "Privilege and Evasion"; Skerrett, "Irony and Symbolic Action." See also Price and Oliver, *Critical Essays*.

36. For example, Jacqueline Goldsby claims that Johnson's literary focus in *Autobiography of an Ex-Colored Man* is engaged with realism while offering a critique of it (*Spectacular Secret*, 164–213); Michael North describes Johnson's 1912 work as modernist in his chapter "Du Bois, Johnson, and Recordings of Race" (*Camera Works*, 164–86).

37. Affect studies and the theoretical concept of phonography offer useful ways of reading Johnson's novel and inform my discussion here of sound. I will address phonography more fully in chapters 5 and 7.

38. Goldsby, *Spectacular Secret*; North, *Camera Works*.

39. See especially "Our Bodies, Our/Selves: Racial Phantasmagoria and Cultural Struggle" (14–65) and "Alien/Nation: Re-imagining the Black Body (Politic) in Williams and Walker's *In Dahomey*" (207–80), both in Brooks, *Bodies in Dissent*.

40. Brooks, *Bodies in Dissent*, 14.

41. Suisman, *Selling Sounds*, 7.

42. Roach, *Cities of the Dead*, 5.

43. Suisman, *Selling Sounds*, 9.

44. Roach, *Cities of the Dead*, 6.

45. North, *Camera Works*, 179.

46. Biers, "Syncope Fever," 123n62.

47. See especially 179–80 of North, *Camera Works*.

48. See Ruotolo, "James Weldon Johnson"; Pfeiffer, "Individualism."

49. Riis, *Just before Jazz*, 64.

50. Suisman, *Selling Sounds*, 13.

51. Tim Brooks dates this song to 1907 (*Lost Sounds*, 397).

52. Johnson, *Black Manhattan*, 127. Hereafter cited in the text as *BM*.

53. "Faust" is mistakenly identified as referring to the overture of Berlioz's *The Damnation of Faust* in the notes provided in William Andrews's 1990 Penguin edition of Johnson's novel. The reference is actually to Gounod's opera, which contains a brother-and-sister duet such as the narrator references in his moment of crisis—"Avant de quitter ces lieux"—in C minor.

54. Ellison, "Homage," 79.

55. Parakilas, "Nuit plus belle," 205–6.

56. Kielian-Gilbert, "*Chopiniana*," 190.

57. Parakilas, "Nuit plus belle," 213.

58. Kielian-Gilbert, "*Chopiniana*," 190.

59. Ibid., 192.

60. John Rosamond Johnson was the uncredited composer and musical and vocal arranger in Dudley Digges's *The Emperor Jones* (1933), starring Paul Robeson. Later he used his performance as a lawyer in the original production of George Gershwin's *Porgy and Bess* (1935) as a springboard to screenwriting and acting in film. He coauthored with Marcy Klauber the boxing film *Keep Punch-*

ing (1939), the story of Henry Jackson ("Little Dynamite"). Rosamond plays the minister. Two uncredited musical numbers in the film were possibly authored by him.

61. Johnson to Broun, May 2, 1924, box 4, folder 62, Series I, JWJ Corr., BRBL.

2. CULTURES OF TALK

1. See Stansell's discussion of Bohemian transnationalism forming in relation to New York City's Lower East Side immigrant population in the 1890s (*American Moderns*, 21–26).

2. Mikhail M. Bakhtin, "Discourse in the Novel," in Bakhtin, *The Dialogic Imagination*, 271–75.

3. Berlin, "Cole and Johnson Brothers," 21–39, 30.

4. "New Spectacular Show," *New York Times*, December 3, 1903, 6, quoted in ibid., 26, 31n23.

5. Ibid., 24.

6. Ibid., 27.

7. Ibid.

8. Ibid.

9. On intentional digressions, see Edwards, *Practice of Diaspora*. I will engage Edwards's important argument more fully in chapters 5 and 7.

10. The chapter "Those Ebony Offenbachs" in Levy, *James Weldon Johnson*, references Rosamond's dismissal of the use of the spirituals as a basis of modern composition, feeling it beneath him, and his preference for art songs. It is well to remember that the trio was composed of three voices, three artists, with occasionally divergent attitudes toward the art that they collectively produced.

11. Johnson to Washington, August 30, 1906, Washington Papers.

12. Reprinted in Jackson, "Letters to a Friend," 184.

13. Some scholars have mistakenly identified Nicaragua as the diplomatic post at which Johnson composed most of *The Autobiography of an Ex-Colored Man*. See, for example, Henry Louis Gates Jr.'s introduction to Johnson's *Autobiography of an Ex-Coloured Man*, vii.

14. Johnson to Washington, June 6, 1906, Washington Papers.

15. Ibid.

16. Johnson to Washington, August 30, 1906, Washington Papers.

17. A version of the following discussion can be found in my introduction to Johnson's work in *The Autobiography of an Ex-Colored Man and Other Writings*.

18. Johnson to Washington, August 30, 1906.

19. See Stansell, *American Moderns*.

20. Nicaragua, Register 84, vol. 308, Diplomatic Records.

21. James Weldon Johnson, "Why Latin-America Dislikes the United States" (1913), in Wilson, *Selected Writings*, 2:195–97.

22. Ibid.

23. Ibid., 197.

24. Ibid.

25. Venezuela, Register 125.3, vol. 024, letters to the Brunswick-Balke-Collender Company dated June 22, 1906, July 20, 1906, and December 31, 1906, Diplomatic Records.

26. Johnson to Washington, August 30, 1906.

27. Kellogg, *NAACP*, 281, 284–86.

28. "Haiti—Special Report (NAACP) Notes," JWJ MSS 300, BRBL.

29. James Weldon Johnson, "Self-Determining Haiti," in Wilson, *Selected Writings*, 2:211, Johnson's emphasis.

30. Ibid., 211, 216–17.

31. Du Bois, "Of Our Spiritual Strivings," in *The Souls of Black Folk*, 3–12.

32. On "intentional digressions" in Johnson's preface to *The Book of American Negro Poetry*, see Edwards, *Practice of Diaspora*, 38–50.

3. THE INTERPOLATED BODY

1. A study awaits of Grace Nail Johnson's activities in racial and gendered crossovers. Grace was a member of the radical and feminist Heterodoxy Club of Greenwich Village—its first black member, joining in 1918. Judith Schwarz describes the group's activities as one with "few formalities: the biweekly luncheons, talks, and debates were occasions for freewheeling, frank yet supportive discussions that were 'off the record'": "Among its 110 active members during its thirty-year history were such notable feminists and radicals as Charlotte Perkins Gilman, Rose Pastor Stokes, Crystal Eastman, and Elizabeth Gurley Flynn. The roster included leading women doctors, educators, actresses, playwrights, psychologists, writers and radio performers—a cast of the accomplished women of the day" (*Radical Feminists*, 119). As a member of the club, Grace arranged to be photographed for its records. She wears a man's suit.

2. See Harper, "Gender Politics."

3. Ibid., 112.

4. Ibid., 108.

5. Ibid., 110.

6. Ibid., 112.

7. Johnson to Washington, August 30, 1906.

8. A version of this discussion appears in my introduction to Johnson's work, *The Autobiography of an Ex-Colored Man and Other Writings*.

9. Skerrett, "Irony and Symbolic Action," established this important fact.

10. "Autobiographical Notes," box 45, folder 87, JWJ MSS 49, BRBL.

11. Photographs of James Weldon Johnson, box 142 oversize, folder 1163, BRBL.

12. Last Will & Testament of J. Douglas Wetmore, December 18, 1903, folder 18, MARBL.

13. *School Life in Paris*, 1897, private printing, HQ 462 S36 1897, MARBL.

14. Ann Douglas uses the phrase "conspicuous theater" to describe the way in which art and politics were linked during the Harlem Renaissance period in ways that defined national culture as a whole: "Both parade and renaissance turned protest into something like organized and conspicuous theater; both advertised their precarious psychological location between justified rage and creative restraint" (*Terrible Honesty*, 327–28).

15. For accounts of the Silent Protest Parade, see Johnson, *Along This Way*, 319–21; and Ovington, *Walls Came Tumbling Down*, 180–81. See also Lewis, *When Harlem Was in Vogue*, 8–10.

16. Suisman, *Selling Sounds*, 12.

4. COSMOPOLITAN TRAVELS

1. Lambert, *Music Ho!*, 76.

2. Suisman, *Selling Sounds*, 10. Suisman writes: "In its primary markets music was produced, marketed, and sold directly to consumers. In ancillary markets, it circulated as capital that could be used by other industries, either as a supplement or as indispensable raw material for other 'producers,' including vaudeville, dance halls, department stores, cafes, radio, and movies. A complete account of the rise of the music business and its consequences must integrate both dimensions of the new musical culture and recognize the dynamic interrelations between them" (10).

3. Ibid., 11.

4. Johnston, *Negro in the New World*, 391.

5. This series of events is recounted in Johnson's autobiography, *Along This Way*, 276–89, esp. 284. It is also related in a profile of Johnson for the *New Yorker*, September 30, 1933, 23.

6. Venezuela, vol. 123, Diplomatic Records. An April 18, 1907, letter of acknowledgment from Johnson states: "I beg to acknowledge the receipt of the Department's cablegram, by mail by way of Trinidad; and, the confirmation of the same; appointing me Consul at Goree-Dakar, Senegal." However, Johnson maintained his position in Venezuela and in June 1909 accepted a promotion to the post at Corinto, Nicaragua. A June 24, 1909, letter to the US consulate states: "I have the honor to acknowledge the receipt of the Department's confirmation of telegram of the 10th instant informing me that I have been promoted Consul at Corinto, Nicaragua, and that I should take the oath and proceed there after July first. The confirmation reached me on the 21st; the cablegram, owing I suppose, to the irregular communications between all West Indian ports and Venezuela, did not reach me until the 23rd."

7. Letter dated January 31, 1911 (acknowledged February 25, 1911), Nicaragua, vol. 201, Diplomatic Records.

8. Goldsby, *Spectacular Secret*, 175.

9. Johnson wrote his mentor, William Stanley Braithwaite, on November 22, [1915]: "I'm hard at work on a few 'pot boilers.' Some of those shameless popular songs. However, even poets must eat." He wrote Braithwaite again on October 21, n.d. (1916?): "I am plugging away doing some musical numbers. I sent in 3 short stories to *Life*" (MSS Am. 1444, Braithwaite Papers, Houghton Library).

10. See especially letters received by James Weldon from Grace Nail Johnson, box 40, folders 4 and 5, 1910–13 and 1914, Family Correspondence, JWJ MSS 49, BRBL.

11. Box 74, folders 436, 437, and 439, and box 75, folder 461, JWJ MSS 49, BRBL.

12. Rudolph P. Byrd and others have speculated that the drafts are from 1894. See Byrd, *Essential Writings*, 3. "Do You Believe in Ghosts? A Darkey Comedy" contains an autograph note of the date of delivery to Lubin: July 9, 1914. "Aunt Mandy's Chicken Dinner" contains a newspaper clipping with the date Saturday, July 11, 1914, and the film short listed under the name Lubin, with Johnson's autograph note stating, "sold to Lubin June 25, 1914." The scripts of the other dramatic works are uniform in appearance and contain the same address for the author, 138 Lee Street, Jacksonville, Florida.

13. "A Plantation Sunday," box 60, folder 213, JWJ MSS 49, BRBL.

14. Nora Holt, music editor for the *Chicago Defender* at the time of *The Autobiography of an Ex-Colored Man*'s anonymous, serialized reissue in its pages, may have had some influence in its appearance. During this same period of its reissue, the newspaper published editorials on the "Red Summer" of US racial violence and intervened in black migration to the North by publishing train schedules and fares from southern locations to Chicago.

15. Johnson to Braithwaite, February 21, 1925, MSS Am. 1444, Braithwaite Papers, Houghton Library.

16. Johnson to Mencken, June 7, 1923, reel 31 (microfilm), Mencken Papers.

17. Johnson to Broun, May 2, 1924, box 4, folder 62, Series I, JWJ Corr., BRBL.

18. Van Vechten referred to his friendship with Johnson as one of his "closest and most-lasting" with an African American. See Huggins, *Harlem Renaissance*, 99.

19. Johnson to Broun, February 21, 1925, box 4, folder 62, Series I, JWJ Corr., BRBL.

20. Huggins, *Harlem Renaissance*, 99.

21. Van Vechten to Johnson, March 23, 1925, box 21, folder 497, Series I, JWJ Corr., BRBL. The letter reveals that Johnson lent Van Vechten his father-in-law's copy of the book and that Van Vechten was interested in acquiring "a copy for [him]self."

22. Van Vechten to Johnson, May 3, 1926, box 21, folder 497, Series I, JWJ Corr., BRBL.

23. Van Vechten to Johnson, March 23, 1925, box 21, folder 497, Series I, JWJ Corr., BRBL.

24. Johnson to Van Vechten, March 25, 1925, CVV Corr. JOHN., BRBL (Van Vechten's correspondence is uncataloged).

25. Van Vechten, "Introduction," xxiv, xxxv–xxxvi.

26. Ibid., xxv.

27. Huggins, *Harlem Renaissance*, 102–3.

28. The spelling "Coloured" was used in the title of the 1927 edition, which adopted British spellings then in vogue.

29. Johnson to Blanche Knopf, April 29, 1926, box 12, folder 267, Series I, JWJ Corr., BRBL.

30. "Louis Gruenberg," www.schirmer.com, accessed February 17, 2011. Gruenberg would go on to write an opera score based on Eugene O'Neill's *The Emperor Jones* (1921) that was performed to "great critical acclaim" at the Metropolitan Opera House eleven times during the 1933 and 1934 seasons and was also featured on the cover of *Time* magazine.

31. Rebecca West to Johnson, February 14, 1931, box 23, folder 534, Series I, JWJ Corr., BRBL.

32. Lambert, *Music Ho!*

33. Johnson, *God's Trombones*, copy 4, MARBL.

34. Johnson to Marshall Best, April 8, 1936, box 22, folder 510, Series I, JWJ Corr., BRBL.

35. Gwendolyn Bennett to Johnson, January 4, 1938, box 3, folder 44, Series I, JWJ Corr., BRBL.

36. The practice of most publishing firms was to negotiate for translation rights with individual publishing houses or to dispose of translation rights as they wished. Authors and individual translators had very little say in this process. Johnson had an active interest in the translations of his works that took place during his lifetime, including "Lift Ev'ry Voice and Sing" into Japanese, *The Book of American Negro Poetry* into French, and *God's Trombones* into French, German, Norwegian, and Dutch. *God's Trombones* also appeared in Braille in 1937. See Johnson's correspondence with his three major publishers, Knopf, Harcourt Brace, and Viking: Johnson to Blanche W. Knopf, box 12, folders 267–68; Johnson to Harcourt Brace, box 9, folders 192–93; and Johnson to Viking, box 22, folders 508–15, all in Series I, JWJ Corr., BRBL.

37. Jeff Driggers, "Zu Johnson's Buch: A Forgotten Literary Piece by Frederick Delius," *Delius Society* 126 (1999): 23–29. Translation from German by Lionel Carley and Evelin Gerhardi (26).

38. Lambert, *Music Ho!*, 77.

39. Ibid., 76.

40. Ibid., 77.

41. Ibid., 78.

42. Ibid., 80.

43. Johnson, preface to *The Book of American Negro Spirituals*, 35.

44. Ibid., 29.

45. "List of books in the Johnsons' library at their home in Nashville and a list of books in the Francis Collection/1934," box 91, folder 745, JWJ MSS 49, BRBL.

46. Schulz, "Restaging," 34, 33.

47. Ibid., 35. Schulz cites page 190 of another edition of *ATW.*

48. Ibid., 34.

5. FRAMING BLACK EXPRESSIVE CULTURE

1. Much of my work on Johnson's anthologizing and experimentation with form is indebted to Brent Edwards's innovative critical treatment of Johnson's works; see his *Practice of Diaspora*, 38–50, and "Seemingly Eclipsed Window." See also O'Meally, *Jazz Cadence*.

2. I will return to theories of phonography in chapter 7, where I discuss James Weldon Johnson's use of phonographic voice in his autobiographical monographs, *Black Manhattan* and *Along This Way*.

3. Mackey, *Discrepant Engagement*, 252–53.

4. Ibid., 21.

5. Early, introduction, 3–73. Also cited in Sanders, *Afro-Modernist Aesthetics*, 177n21.

6. A significant example of this internationalism encompassing linguistic and cultural translation is the publication of some of the poems of Johnson's *God's Trombones* into French in the journal *Cahier du sud* in 1927. See Marshall Best to Johnson, June 9, 1931, box 22, folder 510, Series I, JWJ Corr., BRBL.

7. Early, introduction, 34.

8. Biers, "Syncope Fever," 118.

9. Johnson, preface to *God's Trombones*, 10. Hereafter cited in the text as *GT.*

10. Edwards, "Seemingly Eclipsed Window."

11. Ibid., 591.

12. Ibid., 592, emphasis in original.

13. Ibid., 592–93, emphasis in original.

14. Ibid., 595.

15. Ibid.

16. Ibid., 598.

17. In effect, Brent Edwards's treatment of *The Book of American Negro Poetry* and *The Book of American Negro Spirituals* in separate critical works needs to be integrated in order to fully theorize Johnson's poetics.

18. Mencken to Johnson, January 10, n.d. (1922), reel 31, Mencken Papers.

19. Brent Edwards calls attention to this in *Practice of Diaspora*, 47–49.

20. Ibid., 50.

21. Sanders, *Afro-Modernist Aesthetics*, 5.

22. Ibid., 6.

23. Johnson indicated he was reading Mencken's *Prejudices* to Spencer. See Johnson to Anne Spencer, April 16, 1919, box 19, folder 447, Series I, JWJ Corr., BRBL. Johnson to Spencer, January 9, 1920, recommends Millay's "Renascence," "a study of which will be invaluable to you."

24. Johnson to Anne Spencer, December 15, 1919, box 19, folder 447, Series I, JWJ Corr., BRBL.

25. Ibid.

26. See Williams, "Invisible Partnership"; Szefel, "Encouraging Verse"; Szefel, "Beauty."

27. Szefel, "Encouraging Verse," 47–49; Williams, "Invisible Partnership," 521.

28. Johnson, preface to *The Book of American Negro Poetry*, 9.

29. Ibid.

30. Johnson, "Negro's Creative Genius," 10.

31. Hutchinson, *Harlem Renaissance*, 119.

32. Ibid.

33. Johnson, "Negro's Creative Genius," 41–42.

34. Ibid., 13.

35. Ibid., 13–14.

36. Johnson, preface to *The Book of American Negro Spirituals*, 31. Hereafter cited in the text as *BANS*.

37. See "Krehbiel Controversy," box 15, folder 369, Series I, JWJ Corr., BRBL.

38. Krehbiel's study is titled *Afro-American Folksongs: A Study in Racial and National Music*.

39. Raboteau, *Slave Religion*, 245.

40. Ibid., 246.

41. Ibid.

42. Ibid., 247.

43. Johnson, preface to *The Second Book of American Negro Spirituals*, 11–12. Hereafter cited in the text as *SBANS*.

44. Louis Untermeyer to Johnson, July 16, 1930, box 21, folder 490, Series I, JWJ Corr., BRBL.

45. Box 17, folder 420, Series I, JWJ Corr., BRBL.

6. "The Creation"

1. North, *Camera Works*, 11.

2. Monroe, *A Poet's Life*, 393; Lindsay, *The Congo*, 1–11.

3. Monroe, introduction to *The Congo*, ix.

4. Ibid.

5. Monroe, introduction to *The New Poetry*, vi.

6. See North, *Dialect of Modernism*.

7. Sterling Brown to Johnson, December 14, 1930, box 4, folder 66, Series I, JWJ Corr., BRBL.

8. Sterling Brown to Johnson, December 16, 1931, box 4, folder 66, Series I, JWJ Corr., BRBL.

9. Johnson to Braithwaite, January 15, 1919, MSS Am. 1444, Braithwaite Papers, Houghton Library.

10. Johnson to Braithwaite, January 18, 1919, MSS Am. 1444, Braithwaite Papers, Houghton Library.

11. Sterling Brown to Johnson, January 6, 1930, box 4, folder 66, Series I, JWJ Corr., BRBL. Mark Sanders finds that, "despite Brown and Johnson's differences over the possibilities of dialect, *God's Trombones* provides the closest, most instructive model for Brown's sense of Afro-modernism" (*Afro-Modernist Aesthetics*, 31).

12. Scruggs, *Sage in Harlem*, 171.

13. Scruggs observes that Jean Toomer's *Cane* was the great Negro novel that all the critics were looking for but none recognized (ibid., 170).

14. Ibid., 170–71, 204n102.

15. Sanders, *Afro-Modernist Aesthetics*, 31, 29.

16. Mencken to Johnson, April 29, n.d. (1919), reel 31, Mencken Papers.

17. Mencken, "Prejudices," 36, 38.

18. Ibid., 36–37.

19. Monroe to Johnson, May 5, 1919, box 35, folder 12, Monroe Papers.

20. Monroe to Mencken, May 5, 1919, reel 47, Mencken Papers.

21. Mencken to Monroe, May 7, 1919, box 38, folder 6, Poetry Magazine Papers.

22. Monroe to Mencken, May 9, 1919, reel 47, Mencken Papers.

23. Mencken to Monroe, May 12, 1919, box 38, folder 6, Poetry Magazine Papers.

24. "I am sending you a couple pages out of my Preface [to *God's Trombones*] which contain the paragraphs in which I discuss my reasons for not doing the poems in dialect" (Johnson to Mencken, January 13, 1927, reel 31, Mencken Papers).

25. Hutchinson, *Harlem Renaissance*, 118.

26. Ibid., 188.

27. Ibid., 119.

28. Hutchinson observes that the diversity of modernisms has been hammered into a singular and simplistic definition by "the selective academic definition of modernism," which "ignores the asymmetries of power that effected different modes of expressive modernity. Modernism should not be identified with a single position on language in the avant-garde" (ibid., 119).

7. FROM NOUN TO VERB

1. Box 45, folder 88, JWJ MSS 49, BRBL. See Morrissette, "Past Performances."

2. W. E. B. Du Bois, "James Johnson Sings Praise of Negroes' Mecca—a Zestful History of Harlem, That Glamorous City within New York," *New York Evening Post*, July 12, 1930, clipping, Johnson Papers, FUFL.

3. De Man, "Autobiography."

4. See Mackey, *Discrepant Engagement*; Weheliye, *Phonographies.*

5. Mackey, *Discrepant Engagement*, 19–21, 183–90.

6. Biers, "Syncope Fever."

7. Edwards, "Seemingly Eclipsed Window."

8. Ibid., 596.

9. Mackey is quoted in ibid., 597.

10. Johnson to Edwin R. Embree, June 11, 1930, Rosenwald Fund Papers, FUFL.

11. Johnson to Edwin R. Embree, June 18, 1929, box 424, folder 10, Rosenwald Fund Papers, FUFL.

12. Johnson to Edwin R. Embree, June 11, 1930, box 424, folder 10, Rosenwald Fund Papers, FUFL.

13. Knopf publicity announcement, James Weldon Johnson's Black Manhattan, n.d., Author Files, 718.10, Knopf Papers, HRC.

14. Edwin R. Embree to Johnson, July 28, 1930, box 424, folder 10, Rosenwald Fund Papers, FUFL.

15. Johnson to Edwin R. Embree, August 4, 1930, box 424, folder 10, Rosenwald Fund Papers, FUFL.

16. Du Bois, "James Johnson Sings Praise."

17. John Chamberlain, "The Negro on Manhattan Island: James Weldon Johnson Tells the Story of Three Centuries of Struggle, Failure and Success, Culminating in the Harlem Movement," *New York Times Book Review*, July 27, 1930, FUFL.

18. Du Bois, "James Johnson Sings Praise."

19. Carl Van Vechten to Johnson, September 15, 1930, box 21, folder 499, Series I, JWJ Corr., BRBL.

20. Derrida, *Archive Fever.*

21. Biers, "Syncope Fever," 110.

22. Appiah, *In My Father's House*, 71.

23. "John B. Nail," biographical note by Lucille Miller, folder 16, MARBL.

24. Harry Salpeter, "Harlem Historian," *Book World*, July 20, 1930, FUFL.

25. Harry Hansen, "The First Reader," *New York City World*, July 11, 1930, FUFL.

26. Edwards, "Seemingly Eclipsed Window"; Benston, *Performing Blackness*, 2–5.

27. Edwards, "Seemingly Eclipsed Window," 584.

28. Ibid., 594.

29. Ibid., 598, emphasis added.

30. Johnson, "The White Witch," originally in *Fifty Years and Other Poems*, reprinted in *The Autobiography of an Ex-Colored Man and Other Writings*, 131.

31. Ibid., 587.

32. Ibid., 588.

33. Johnson, "Preface to the Revised Edition," 3.

34. Ibid., 8.

35. "Autobiographical Notes," JWJ MSS 110, BRBL.

8. NOT THE STORY OF MY LIFE

1. Edwards, "Seemingly Eclipsed Window."

2. Biers, "Syncope Fever"; Edwards, "Seemingly Eclipsed Window."

3. Lewis, *When Harlem Was in Vogue*, 143.

4. Ibid., 147.

5. Ibid., 146–47, 148.

6. Boyle, *Arc of Justice*, 198.

7. Johnson, *Along This Way*, 84–88, 165–70, 291–93. Jacqueline Goldsby suggests that Johnson's near lynching was mirrored by a second, similar experience: Johnson's denial of advancement in the consulate by President Woodrow Wilson. Oddly, she does not mention Johnson's earlier experience with personal violation on a Jim Crow train. See *Along This Way*, 291–93, for Johnson's description of his experience with the consulate under Wilson's administration, and Goldsby, *Spectacular Secret*.

8. The word "roseate" is from Boyle, *Arc of Justice*, 199.

9. Authors who praise or vilify Johnson for being tied to the past as foundation and for fostering a tradition of letters construed as either negative or positive include Haki Madthubuti (Don L. Lee), Addison Gayle, and Amiri Baraka (LeRoi Jones); see also Eugene Levy and John Hope Franklin. See Lee, "Voices of the Seventies"; Gayle, *Way of the New World*, especially the discussion of "sycophants" versus "the 1970s aesthetic" on page 382; Baraka, "Revolutionary Tradition"; Levy, *James Weldon Johnson*; and Franklin, *Three Negro Classics*.

10. Early, introduction, 33n40.

11. De Man, "Autobiography."

12. See Gilroy, *Black Atlantic*.

13. Edwards, "Seemingly Eclipsed Window," 45. Edwards's work has been tremendously important to studies of Johnson in that his operating principle of *décalage*—a spatial and temporal concept indicating discrepancy, gap, difference of angle, displacement—propels Johnson, "verbs" him, in a way that no one else has. Edwards also has done important work in drawing attention to Johnson's theory of the body rather than locating the "truth" of Johnson in the author's body, as past critics have.

14. Ibid., 580–81.

15. Biers, "Syncope Fever."

16. Mercer, "Romare Bearden," 125–26. Mercer discusses the appropriateness of collage as expressive of African American identity, "something that has itself been 'collaged' by the vicissitudes of modern history." Facilitating the representation of this contradiction, "the cut" becomes the creative, formal response to historical practice. Mercer aptly formulates its political as well as aesthetic importance: "The 'cut' is a formal interval in which structural conventions are decentred by the controlled agency of negativity" (142). See also Snead, "Repetition."

17. Edwards, *Practice of Diaspora*, 47.

18. These generic limitations have been observed by Gilroy, *Black Atlantic*, 36; and Mercer, "Romare Bearden," 142. Gilroy observes the "inappropriate" model of text, while Mercer finds the vocabulary limited to text-based, and not visual, tropologies such as "signifyin'" and others that are emphasized as the major tropes of black identity.

19. "Miscellaneous Notes," JWJ MSS 110, BRBL; and "Autobiographical Notes," JWJ MSS +111, BRBL. The latter collection contains notes that appear in final form in *Black Manhattan* or *Along This Way.*

20. Fisk University lecture notes, creative literature and writing, 1932, JWJ MSS 222, BRBL.

21. Fisk University lecture notes, contemporary American literature, lectures 2–5, JWJ MSS 220, BRBL.

22. Fisk University lecture notes, lecture 9, JWJ MSS 221, BRBL.

23. Fisk University lecture notes, lectures 16–21, JWJ MSS 222, BRBL.

24. Skerrett, "Irony and Symbolic Action"; Smith, "Privilege and Evasion."

25. Skerrett, "Irony and Symbolic Action," 73.

26. Ibid., 76.

27. Ibid., 85.

28. Smith, "Privilege and Evasion," 90.

29. Ibid., 93.

30. Ibid., 100.

31. Fleming, "Johnson's *Along This Way*," 226.

32. "Miscellaneous Notes," JWJ MSS 110, BRBL.

33. Ibid.; "Autobiographical Notes," JWJ MSS +111, BRBL.

34. Johnson, *Along This Way*, 293.

35. Setting typescript, chap. 18, 249, box 48, folder 106, JWJ MSS 49, BRBL.

36. Johnson to Sterling Brown, May 17, 1937, box 4, folder 66, Series I, JWJ Corr., BRBL.

37. Barthes, *Camera Lucida*, 11. Barthes writes: "It is the misfortune (but also perhaps the voluptuous pleasure) of language not to be able to authenticate

itself. . . . [L]anguage is, by nature, fictional; the attempt to render language unfictional requires an enormous apparatus of measurements . . . , but the Photograph is indifferent to all intermediaries: it is authentication itself."

38. Robert Wohlforth, "Dark Leader," *New Yorker*, September 30, 1933.

39. Johnson to Spencer, October 2, 1933, box 19, folder 447, Series I, JWJ Corr., BRBL.

40. Marshall Best to Johnson, May 11, 1933, box 22: Viking, Series I, JWJ Corr., BRBL.

41. *Along This Way*, autograph manuscript, pp. 28 and 29, box 46, folder 91, JWJ MSS 49, BRBL.

42. Johnson to Marshall Best, October 16, 1933, box 22: Viking, Series I, JWJ Corr., BRBL.

43. Carl Van Vechten to Johnson, October 14, 1933, Series I, JWJ Corr., BRBL. Johnson also cites Van Vechten's praise in a letter to his editor, Marshall Best, at Viking (October 15, 1933, box 22: Viking, Series I, JWJ Corr., BRBL).

AFTERWORD

1. Gwendolyn Bennett to Johnson, January 4, 1938, box 3, folder 44, Series I, JWJ Corr., BRBL.

2. Marshall Best to Johnson, February 8, 1938, box 22, folder 511, Series I, JWJ Corr., BRBL.

3. Invitation, n.d., postmarked May 28, 1938 (return address is McKay's *African*), box 22, folder 519, Series I, JWJ Corr., BRBL.

4. West to Johnson, October 23, 1933, and n.d. (1937), box 23, folder 533, Series I, JWJ Corr., BRBL.

5. McKay to Johnson, May 14, 1938, box 13, folder 309, Series I, JWJ Corr., BRBL.

6. McKay to Johnson, November 28, 1937, box 13, folder 309, Series I, JWJ Corr., BRBL.

7. Eugen Boissevain to Johnson, n.d. (approximately April 1938), box 14, folder 323, Series I, JWJ Corr., BRBL.

8. See, for example, Levy, *James Weldon Johnson*, 346–47, of 1973; Fleming, *James Weldon Johnson*, of 1987; and Goldsby, *Spectacular Secret*, 164, of 2007, representing the decades of this description's repetition.

9. Lucille V. Miller, Lincoln County Memorial Hospital, to Mr. Martin S. Loventhal, Insurance Company, June 27, 1938, folder 8, Johnson Papers, FUFL. Miller described the accident on behalf of Grace Nail Johnson, listing Grace's injuries and mapping out the accident. Grace Nail Johnson remained a convalescent at the hospital through the end of August.

10. Ollie Jewell Sims, later Okala through marriage to a Nigerian student of anthropology at Columbia, nursed James Weldon Johnson during a critical ill-

ness he suffered in Nashville in 1934, in which he required a blood transfusion from Rosamond. She was then a nursing student. The Johnsons, who mentored a number of young black women at Fisk in the advancement of their careers, immediately took to Sims, who became like one of the family. When Grace Nail Johnson died, Okala became literary executor of the Johnson estate. She is buried alongside Grace Nail Johnson and James Weldon Johnson in the Nail family plot in Brooklyn's Greenwood Cemetery. Her recollections of the years spent with Grace after Johnson's death can be found in Wilson, *Meet Me at the Theresa*.

11. Grace Nail Johnson to H. L. Mencken, January 1940, reel 31, Mencken Papers.

12. Grace Nail Johnson to Alfred Harcourt, October 14, 1940, and Alfred Harcourt to Grace Nail Johnson, October 17, 1940, both in box 9, folder 192, Series I, JWJ Corr., BRBL.

13. Barthes, *Camera Lucida*, 4.

14. Much of my discussion here is indebted to Karen Sánchez-Eppler's work on nineteenth-century practices of memorialization of children's deaths through the daguerreotype and the photograph. See Sánchez-Eppler, "On the Death."

15. Schor, *Bearing the Dead*, 201–6.

16. Morrissette, *Critical Fictions*, 242.

17. Schor, *Bearing the Dead*, 201.

18. "Youthport: For Juniors of the NAACP," *Crisis*, June 1930, n.p.

19. Johnson, *Negro Americans*.

20. Schor, *Bearing the Dead*, 206, emphasis in original.

21. The exhibition was mounted with the cooperation of Fisk and Howard Universities, along with Edward B. Marks Music Corporation and the heirs of Edward B. Marks. A copy of the exhibition booklet can be found in Zan J632 +970N, BRBL.

22. *Call*, July 8, 1938.

23. *New York Herald Tribune*, July 1, 1938.

24. Others in attendance were lawyer Hubert Delaney; Eugene Gordon, editor of Boston's literary magazine the *Saturday Evening Quill* and contributor to the *Messenger* and *Opportunity* magazine; James H. Hubert, head of the New York Urban League; New York publisher B. W. Huebsch; Eugene Kinkle Jones, executive secretary to the National Urban League and cofounder of the Alpha Phi Alpha fraternity; the musical score publisher E. B. Marks; Fred R. Moore of Tuskegee University; Ferdinand Q. Morton of the Negro National League (and formerly of the United Colored Democracy); R. C. McPherson (aka Cecil Mack, the lyricist); John G. Paine; Oliver Randolph (JD, Howard University); Dr. E. P. Roberts; *New York World*'s music critic and Algonquin Round Table frequenter Deems Taylor; Tin Pan alley songwriter Will Von Tilzer (younger brother of Albert, of "Take Me out to the Ball Game" fame); Judge Charles E. Toney of Manhattan District Court and also NAACP board member; William Bodery; Walter

White of the NAACP; Dr. Louis T. Wright of Harlem Hospital; and L. Hollingsworth Todd.

25. Carl Van Vechten to Grace Nail Johnson, July 2, 1938, box 37, folder 238, Series I, JWJ Corr., BRBL.

26. Early, introduction, 13. The history of Cullen discussed here is taken from Early's groundbreaking introduction.

27. Cullen "assisted James Weldon Johnson and W. E. B. Du Bois in the organizing of the famous silent protest parade of July 28, 1917" (Early, introduction, 14).

28. Early writes that "by the mid-1920s, [Salem Methodist Episcopal] could boast a membership of over 2,500 members: a large educational program that included subjects such as French, Latin, typewriting, shorthand, and math, five large choirs and a full orchestra, as well as a highly competitive youth athletic club, including a particularly notable amateur boxing program of which Dr. Cullen seemed quite proud. It was with youth that Frederick Cullen felt his ministry ought to be particularly concerned" (ibid., 13).

29. *New York Herald Tribune*, July 1, 1938.

30. Derrida, *Archive Fever.*

31. Voegelin, *Listening*, 169.

32. "In Memoriam," *Crisis*, September 1938. This issue published transcripts of the addresses.

33. Mayor Fiorello H. LaGuardia, broadcast over station WNYC, July 14, 1938, 8 p.m. Printed in *Crisis*, September 1938, 292.

34. Memo from Grace Nail Johnson to Miss Bowles, August 1939, folder 9, Johnson Papers, FUFL. Grace stated in the memo preferences for details and wording of Johnson's life and for the photograph of Johnson to be included in the publication. (She stated that Johnson himself would have wanted the photograph recently taken of him for the American Society of Composers, Authors and Publishers to be included, for he looked "directly" at the camera.)

35. Box 36, folder 7, Jones Papers, FUFL.

36. "Continue Lectures Started by James Weldon Johnson," *Philadelphia Independent*, November 13, 1938.

37. Carl Van Vechten to Grace Nail Johnson, undated postcard postmarked July 9, 1938, box 37, folder 238, Series I, JWJ Corr., BRBL.

38. Carl Van Vechten to Grace Nail Johnson, July 16, 1938, box 37, folder 238, Series I, JWJ Corr., BRBL.

39. Carl Van Vechten to Grace Nail Johnson, November 4, 1938, box 37, folder 238, Series I, JWJ Corr., BRBL.

40. Carl Van Vechten to Grace Nail Johnson, August 5, 1938, box 37, folder 238, Series I, JWJ Corr., BRBL.

41. The *Crisis* had published "The James Weldon Johnson Memorial Project" in January 1940, in which, among other plans, a memorial scholarship fund had been proposed.

42. Van Vechten to Johnson, August 5, 1938.

43. Carl Van Vechten, "The Proposed James Weldon Johnson Memorial," *Opportunity*, February 1940, 2–3.

44. NAACP press release, February 16, 1940, Johnson Vertical Files, New York Public Library.

45. Augusta Savage to Walter White, April 16, 1940 (copy), JOHN Johnson Memorial Committee, 1940 March–December, Van Vechten Corr., BRBL.

46. Walter White to Augusta Savage, April 18, 1940 (dictated; copy), JOHN Johnson Memorial Committee, 1940 March–December, Van Vechten Corr., BRBL.

47. "Memorandum on conference with Mayor Fiorello LaGuardia re James Weldon Johnson Memorial," December 11, 1939, National Association for the Advancement of Colored People Collection, Library of Congress. See also Walter White to Carl Van Vechten, December 3, 1938.

48. Bremer, "Home in Harlem," 7:8.

49. See correspondence between the New York City Housing Authority and Mayor Fiorello LaGuardia, August 1945–January 1946, Mayoral Administration Records, LaGuardia Papers.

50. Grace Nail Johnson to Luanna Bowles, Fisk University Director of Publicity, August 1939, folder 9, Johnson Papers, FUFL.

51. Derrida, *Archive Fever*, 3.

52. Savage, *Broadcasting Freedom*, 21.

Bibliography

ARCHIVES CONSULTED

Braithwaite, William Stanley, Collection. Library of Congress, Washington, DC.

Braithwaite, William Stanley, Papers. Houghton Library, Harvard University, Cambridge, MA.

Diplomatic Records. National Archives II, College Park, MD.

Johnson, James Weldon, Papers. Special Collections, Fisk University Franklin Library (FUFL).

Johnson, James Weldon, Papers. Special Collections, Manuscripts, Archives, and Rare Book Library, Emory University (MARBL).

Johnson, James Weldon, and Grace Nail Johnson Papers (Correspondence and Manuscripts). Collection of American Literature, Beinecke Rare Book and Manuscript Library, Yale University (BRBL).

Johnson, J. W., Vertical Files. Schomburg Center for Research in Black Culture, New York Public Library.

Jones, Thomas Elsa, Papers. Fisk University Franklin Library Special Collections (FUFL).

Knopf, Alfred A., Papers. Harry Ransom Center, University of Texas at Austin (HRC).

LaGuardia, Fiorello, Papers. Municipal Records, City of New York.

Mencken, H. L., Papers. New York Public Library (NYPL).

Monroe, Harriet, Papers. Special Collections, University of Chicago.

National Association for the Advancement of Colored People Collection. Manuscripts Division, Library of Congress, Washington, DC.

Poetry Magazine Papers. Special Collections, University of Chicago.

Rosenwald, Julius, Fund Papers. Special Collections, Fisk University Franklin Library (FUFL).

Van Vechten, Carl, Papers. Collection of American Literature, Beinecke Rare Book and Manuscript Library, Yale University (BRBL).

Washington, Booker T., Papers. Manuscripts Division, Library of Congress, Washington, DC.

SECONDARY SOURCES

Adamowicz, Elza. *Surrealist Collage in Text and Image: Dissecting the Exquisite Corpse*. Cambridge: Cambridge University Press, 1998.

Anderson, Linda. *Autobiography*. 2001. Reprint, New York: Routledge, 2005.

Anderson, Paul Allen. *Deep River: Music and Memory in Harlem Renaissance Thought*. Durham, NC: Duke University Press, 2001.

Andrews, William L., ed. *James Weldon Johnson: Writings*. New York: Library of America, 2004.

Appiah, Kwame Anthony. *In My Father's House: Africa in the Philosophy of Culture*. New York: Oxford University Press, 1992.

Aptheker, Herbert, ed. *The Correspondence of W. E. B. Du Bois*. 2 vols. Amherst: University of Massachusetts Press, 1973.

Baker, Houston. *Modernism and the Harlem Renaissance*. Chicago: University of Chicago Press, 1989.

Bakhtin, Mikhail M. *The Dialogic Imagination*. Edited by Michael Holquist. Translated by Caryl Emerson and Michael Holquist. 1981. Reprint, Austin: University of Texas Press, 1990.

Baraka, Amiri. "The Revolutionary Tradition in Afro-American Literature." 1979. In *The Amiri Baraka Reader*, edited by William J. Harris, 311–22. New York: Thunder's Mouth Press/Avalon, 2000.

Barthes, Roland. *Camera Lucida: Reflections on Photography*. Translated by Richard Howard. New York: Hill and Wang, 1981.

Benston, Kimberly W. *Performing Blackness: Enactments of African-American Modernism*. New York: Routledge, 2000.

Berlin, Edward A. "Cole and Johnson Brothers' 'The Evolution of Ragtime.'" *Current Musicology* 36 (1981): 21–39.

Biers, Katherine. "Syncope Fever: James Weldon Johnson and the Black Phonographic Voice." *Representations* 96 (Fall 2006): 99–125.

Boyle, Kevin. *Arc of Justice: A Saga of Race, Civil Rights, and Murder in the Jazz Age*. New York: Henry Holt, 2004.

Brawley, Benjamin. *The Negro in Literature and Art in the United States*. 1918. Revised edition. New York: Duffield, 1921.

Bremer, Sidney H. "Home in Harlem, New York: Lessons from the Harlem Renaissance Writers." In *The Harlem Renaissance 1920–1940: Analysis and Assessment, 1980–1994*, edited by Cary D. Wintz, 7:1–10. 7 vols. New York: Garland, 1996.

Brooks, Daphne. *Bodies in Dissent: Spectacular Performances of Race and Freedom, 1850–1910*. Durham, NC: Duke University Press, 2006.

Brooks, Tim. *Lost Sounds: Blacks and the Birth of the Recording Industry, 1890–1919*. Urbana: University of Illinois Press, 2004.

Brown, Sterling. *Outline for the Study of the Poetry of American Negroes*. Prepared to be used with *The Book of American Negro Poetry*. Edited by James Weldon Johnson. New York: Harcourt Brace, 1931.

Butler, Judith. *Bodies That Matter*. New York: Routledge, 1993.

Byrd, Rudolph P., ed. *The Essential Writings of James Weldon Johnson*. New York: Random House, 2008.

De Man, Paul. "Autobiography as De-facement." In *The Rhetoric of Romanticism*, 67–82. New York: Columbia University Press, 1984.

Derrida, Jacques. *Archive Fever*. Translated by Eric Prenowitz. Chicago: University of Chicago Press, 1996.

Douglas, Ann. *Terrible Honesty: Mongrel Manhattan in the 1920s*. New York: Farrar, Straus and Giroux, 1996.

Driggers, Jeff. "Zu Johnson's Buch: A Forgotten Literary Piece by Frederick Delius." *Delius Society Journal* 126 (1999): 23–29.

Du Bois, W. E. B. *The Souls of Black Folk*. 1903. Reprint, New York: Penguin, 1996.

Early, Gerald. Introduction to *My Soul's High Song: The Collected Writings of Countee Cullen, Voice of the Harlem Renaissance*, 3–73. New York: Doubleday, 1991.

Edwards, Brent. *The Practice of Diaspora: Literature, Translation, and the Rise of Black Internationalism*. Cambridge, MA: Harvard University Press, 2003.

———. "The Seemingly Eclipsed Window of Form: James Weldon Johnson's Prefaces." In *The Jazz Cadence of American Culture*, edited by Robert G. O'Meally, 580–601. New York: Columbia University Press, 1998.

Ellison, Ralph. "Hidden Name and Complex Fate." In *The Collected Essays of Ralph Ellison*, edited by John Callahan, 189–209. New York: Random House, 1995.

———. "Homage to Duke Ellington on His Birthday." In *Living with Music: The Jazz Essays of Ralph Ellison*, edited by Robert G. O'Meally, 77–86. New York: Random House, 2001.

Fabi, M. Giulia. *Passing and the Rise of the African American Novel*. 2001. Reprint, Urbana: University of Illinois Press, 2004.

Feld, Steven. *Sound and Sentiment: Birds, Weeping, Poetics, and Song in Kaluli Expression*. 2nd ed. Philadelphia: University of Pennsylvania Press, 1990.

Fleming, Robert E. *James Weldon Johnson*. Boston: Twayne, 1987.

———. "James Weldon Johnson's *Along This Way*: Text and Subtext." In *Critical Essays on James Weldon Johnson*, edited by Kenneth M. Price and Lawrence J. Oliver, 223–31. New York: G. K. Hall, 1997.

Franklin, John Hope, ed. *Three Negro Classics*. New York: Avon, 1965.

Gayle, Addison. *The Way of the New World: The Black Novel in America*. New York: Anchor/Doubleday, 1975.

Gilroy, Paul. *The Black Atlantic: Modernity and Double Consciousness*. Cambridge, MA: Harvard University Press, 1993.

Gitelman, Lisa. *Scripts, Grooves, and Writing Machines: Representing Technology in the Edison Era*. Stanford, CA: Stanford University Press, 1999.

Goldberg, Halina, ed. *The Age of Chopin: Interdisciplinary Inquiries*. Bloomington: Indiana University Press, 2004.

Goldsby, Jacqueline. *A Spectacular Secret: Lynching in American Life and Literature*. Chicago: University of Chicago Press, 2006.

Harlan, Louis T., and Raymond W. Smock, eds. *The Booker T. Washington Papers*. 14 vols. Chicago: University of Illinois Press, 1979–81.

Harper, Phillip Brian. "Gender Politics and the 'Passing' Fancy: Black Masculinity as Societal Problem." In *Are We Not Men? Masculine Anxiety and the Problem of African American Identity*, 103–26. New York: Oxford University Press, 1996.

Hemenway, Robert E. *Zora Neale Hurston: A Literary Biography*. 1977. Reprint, Chicago: University of Illinois Press, 1980.

Henson, Josiah. *An Autobiography of Josiah Henson (Mrs. Harriet Beecher Stowe's "Uncle Tom")*. London: Christian Age Office, 1876.

———. *Truth Stranger than Fiction: Father Henson's Story of His Own Life*. With an introduction by Harriet Beecher Stowe. Boston: Samuel A. Eliot, 1858.

Hill, Robert A., et al., eds. *The Marcus Garvey and Universal Negro Improvement Association Papers*. 10 vols. Berkeley: University of California Press, 1983–2006.

Huggins, Nathan Irvin. *Harlem Renaissance*. New York: Oxford University Press, 1971.

Hutchinson, George. *The Harlem Renaissance in Black and White*. Cambridge, MA: Belknap Press, 1997.

Jackson, Miles, ed. "Letters to a Friend: Correspondence from James Weldon Johnson to George A. Townes." *Phylon* 29, no. 2 (1968): 182–98.

Johnson, James Weldon. *Along This Way: The Autobiography of James Weldon Johnson*. New York: Viking Press, 1933.

———. "American Music." In Wilson, *Selected Writings*, 1:288–89.

———. *The Autobiography of an Ex-Colored Man*. Boston: Sherman, French, 1912. Published anonymously.

———. *The Autobiography of an Ex-Colored Man and Other Writings*. Edited by Noelle Morrissette. New York: Fine Creative Media, 2007.

———. *The Autobiography of an Ex-Coloured Man*. Introduction by Henry Louis Gates Jr. New York: Vintage, 1989.

———. *The Autobiography of an Ex-Coloured Man*. Introduction by Carl Van Vechten. New York: Alfred A. Knopf, 1927.

———. *Black Manhattan*. New York: Knopf, 1930.

———. "Dealing with Mobs." In Wilson, *Selected Writings*, 1:71–72.

———. *Der weisse Neger*. Translated by Elisabeth Von Gans. Foreword by Frederick Delius. Frankfurt: Frankfurter Societäts-Druckerei GMBH, 1928. Translation of *The Autobiography of an Ex-Coloured Man*. New York: Alfred A. Knopf, 1927.

———. *Fifty Years and Other Poems*. Introduction by Brander Matthews. New York: Cornhill, 1917.

———. *God's Trombones: Seven Negro Sermons in Verse.* 1927. Reprint, New York: Viking Press, 1990.

———. "Harlem: The Culture Capital." 1925. In *The New Negro*, edited by Alain Locke, 301–11. Reprint, New York: Touchstone, 1997.

———. *Negro Americans, What Now?* New York: Viking, 1935.

———. "The Negro's Creative Genius." 1922. Preface to *The Book of American Negro Poetry*, edited by James Weldon Johnson, vii–xlviii. Reprinted in *The Book of American Negro Poetry*, edited by James Weldon Johnson, 9–48. New York: Harcourt Brace, 1931. Reprint, New York: Harcourt Brace, 1969.

———. "The Poor White Musician." In Wilson, *Selected Writings*, 1:284–86.

———. Preface to *The Book of American Negro Spirituals*, edited by James Weldon Johnson, 11–51. New York: Viking Press, 1925.

———. "Preface to the Revised Edition." In *The Book of American Negro Poetry*, edited by James Weldon Johnson, 3–8. New York: Harcourt Brace, 1931.

———. Preface to *The Second Book of American Negro Spirituals*, edited by James Weldon Johnson, 11–24. New York: Viking Press, 1926.

———. *Saint Peter Relates an Incident of the Resurrection Day: Selected Poems by James Weldon Johnson.* New York: Viking Press, 1935.

———. "Self-Determining Haiti." In Wilson, *Selected Writings*, 2:207–43.

———. "Uncle Tom's Cabin and the Clansman." In Wilson, *Selected Writings*, 1:12–13.

———. "Why Latin America Dislikes the United States." In Wilson, *Selected Writings*, 2:195–97.

———. "Writers of Words and Music." In Wilson, *Selected Writings*, 1:288–89.

Johnston, Sir Harry H. *The Negro in the New World.* New York: Macmillan, 1910.

Jones, LeRoi (Amiri Baraka). *Blues People: Negro Music in White America.* 1963. Reprint, New York: HarperCollins, 2002.

Kaplan, Carla, ed. *Zora Neale Hurston: A Life in Letters.* New York: Doubleday, 2002.

Kellogg, Charles Flint. *NAACP: A History of the National Association for the Advancement of Colored People.* Vol. 1, 1909–20. Baltimore, MD: Johns Hopkins Press, 1960.

Kielian-Gilbert, Marianne. "*Chopiniana* and Music's Contextual Allusions." In *The Age of Chopin: Interdisciplinary Inquiries*, edited by Halina Goldberg, 162–200. Bloomington: Indiana University Press, 2004.

Kittler, Friedrich A. *Gramophone, Film, Typewriter.* Translated by Geoffrey Winthrop-Young and Michael Wutz. Stanford, CA: Stanford University Press, 1999.

Krehbiel, Henry Edward. *Afro-American Folksongs: A Study in Racial and National Music.* New York: G. Schirmer, 1914.

Lambert, Leonard Constant. *Music Ho! A Study of Music in Decline*. New York: Charles Scribner's Sons, 1934. Project Gutenberg Canada E-book 245.

Lamothe, Daphne. *Inventing the New Negro: Narrative, Culture, and Ethnography*. Philadelphia: University of Pennsylvania Press, 2008.

Lee, Don L. "Voices of the Seventies: Black Critics." *Black World/Negro Digest*, September 1970, 24–30.

Levine, Lawrence W. "Slave Songs and Slave Consciousness: An Exploration in Neglected Sources." 1971. In *African-American Religion: Interpretive Essays in History and Culture*, edited by Timothy E. Fullop and Albert J. Raboteau, 57–87. New York: Routledge, 1997.

Levy, Eugene. *James Weldon Johnson: Black Leader, Black Voice*. Chicago: University of Chicago Press, 1973.

Lewis, David Levering. *When Harlem Was in Vogue*. 1981. Reprint, New York: Penguin Books, 1997.

Lindsay, Vachel. *The Congo and Other Poems*. New York: Macmillan, 1914.

Little, William, et al. "Syncope." In *The Shorter Oxford English Dictionary*, 2:2112. 3rd ed. Oxford: Oxford at the Clarendon Press, 1964.

Locke, Alain, ed. *The New Negro*. 1925. Reprint, New York: Touchstone, 1997.

Mackey, Nathaniel. *Discrepant Engagement: Dissonance, Cross-Culturality, and Experimental Writing*. New York: Cambridge University Press, 1993.

———. "Sound and Sentiment, Sound and Symbol." In *The Jazz Cadence of American Culture*, edited by Robert G. O'Meally, 602–28. New York: Columbia University Press, 1998.

Marek, Jayne E. *Women Editing Modernism: "Little" Magazines & Literary History*. Lexington: University Press of Kentucky, 1995.

Marks, Edward B. *They All Sang: From Tony Pastor to Rudy Valée*. New York: Viking Press, 1934.

Massa, Ann. "Form Follows Function: The Construction of Harriet Monroe and *Poetry: A Magazine of Verse*." In *A Living of Words: American Women in Print Culture*, edited by Susan Albertine, 115–31. Knoxville: University of Tennessee Press, 1995.

Mencken, Henry Louis. "Prejudices: First Series." In *Critical Essays on American Modernism*, edited by Michael J. Hoffman and Patrick D. Murphy, 36–42. New York: G. K. Hall, 1992.

Mercer, Kobena. Introduction to *Cosmopolitan Modernisms*, edited by Kobena Mercer, 6–23. Cambridge, MA: MIT Press, 2005.

———. "Romare Bearden, 1964: Collage as Kunstwollen." In *Cosmopolitan Modernisms*, edited by Kobena Mercer, 124–45. Cambridge, MA: MIT Press, 2005.

Miller, Monica L. "The Black Dandy as Bad Modernist." In *Bad Modernisms*, edited by Douglas Mao and Rebecca Walkowitz, 179–205. Durham, NC: Duke University Press, 2006.

Miller, Nancy K. "Getting Personal: Autobiography as Cultural Criticism." In *Getting Personal: Feminist Occasions and Other Autobiographical Acts*, by Nancy K. Miller, 1–30. New York: Routledge, 1991.

Monroe, Harriet. Introduction to *The Congo and Other Poems*, by Vachel Lindsay, v–ix. New York: Macmillan, 1914.

———. Introduction to *The New Poetry: An Anthology of Twentieth-Century Verse in English*, edited by Harriet Monroe. Reprinted in *Critical Essays on American Modernism*, edited by Michael J. Hoffman and Patrick D. Murphy, 25–30. New York: G. K. Hall, 1992.

———. *A Poet's Life*. New York: Macmillan, 1938.

Morrissette, Noelle. *Critical Fictions: The Prose Writings of James Weldon Johnson*. Ann Arbor, MI: University Microfilms, 2002.

———. Introduction to *The Autobiography of an Ex-Colored Man and Other Writings by James Weldon Johnson*. New York: Fine Creative Media, 2007.

———. "'Past Performances' of the Negro: James Weldon Johnson's *Black Manhattan*." *Obsidian III: Literature in the African Diaspora* 5, no. 2 (2004): 151–68.

Murray, Albert. *The Omni-Americans: Black Experience and American Culture*. 1970. Reprint, New York: Da Capo Press, 1990.

Neal, Mark Anthony. *What the Music Said: Black Popular Music and Black Public Culture*. New York: Routledge, 1998.

North, Michael. *Camera Works: Photography and the Twentieth-Century Word*. New York: Oxford University Press, 2005.

———. *The Dialect of Modernism: Race, Language, and Twentieth-Century Literature*. New York: Oxford University Press, 1994.

Olney, James. *Metaphors of Self: The Meaning of Autobiography*. Princeton, NJ: Princeton University Press, 1972.

O'Meally, Robert G., ed. *The Jazz Cadence of American Culture*. New York: Columbia University Press, 1998.

Osofsky, Gilbert. "Race Riot, 1900: A Study of Ethnic Violence." *Journal of Negro Education* 32 (1963): 16–24.

Ovington, Mary White. *Portraits in Color*. New York: Viking Press, 1927.

———. *The Walls Came Tumbling Down*. New York: Arno Press, 1969.

Parakilas, James. "'Nuit plus belle qu'un beau jour': Poetry, Song, and the Voice in the Piano Nocturne." In *The Age of Chopin: Interdisciplinary Inquiries*, edited by Halina Goldberg, 203–23. Bloomington: Indiana University Press, 2004.

Pfeiffer, Kathleen. "Individualism, Success, and American Identity in *The Autobiography of an Ex-Colored Man*." *African American Review* 30, no. 3 (1996): 403–19.

Price, Kenneth M., and Lawrence J. Oliver, eds. *Critical Essays on James Weldon Johnson*. New York: G. K. Hall, 1997.

Raboteau, Albert J. *Slave Religion: The "Invisible Institution" in the Antebellum South*. New York: Oxford University Press, 1980.

Radano, Ronald. *Lying Up a Nation: Race and Black Music*. Chicago: University of Chicago Press, 2003.

Riis, Thomas L. *Just before Jazz: Black Musical Theater in New York, 1890–1915*. Washington, DC: Smithsonian Institution Press, 1989.

Roach, Joseph. *Cities of the Dead: Circum-Atlantic Performance*. New York: Columbia University Press, 1996.

Ruotolo, Cristina L. "James Weldon Johnson and the Autobiography of an Ex-Colored Musician." *American Literature* 72, no. 2 (2000): 249–74.

Sánchez-Eppler, Karen. "On the Death of a Child and the Replication of an Image." In *Sentimental Men: Masculinity and the Politics of Affect in American Culture*, edited by Mary Chapman and Glenn Hendler, 64–85. Berkeley: University of California Press, 1999.

Sanders, Mark. *Afro-Modernist Aesthetics and the Poetry of Sterling Brown*. Athens: University of Georgia Press, 1999.

Savage, Barbara Diane. *Broadcasting Freedom: Radio, War, and the Politics of Race, 1938–1948*. Chapel Hill: University of North Carolina Press, 1999.

Schafer, R. Murray. *The Soundscape: Our Sonic Environment and the Tuning of the World*. 1977. Reprint, Rochester, VT: Destiny Books, 1994.

Schor, Esther. *Bearing the Dead: The British Culture of Mourning from the Enlightenment to Victoria*. Princeton, NJ: Princeton University Press, 1994.

Schulz, Jennifer L. "Restaging the Racial Contract: James Weldon Johnson's Signatory Strategies." *American Literature* 74, no. 1 (2002): 31–58.

Schwarz, Judith. *Radical Feminists of the Heterodoxy: Greenwich Village, 1912–1940*. Revised edition. Norwich, VT: New Victoria Publishers, 1986.

Schwarz, Judith, Kathy Peiss, and Christina Simmons. "'We Were a Little Band of Willful Women': The Heterodoxy Club of Greenwich Village." In *Passion and Power: Sexuality in History*, edited by Kathy Peiss and Christina Simmons, 118–21. Philadelphia: Temple University Press, 1989.

Scruggs, Charles. *The Sage in Harlem: H. L. Mencken and the Black Writers of the 1920s*. Baltimore, MD: Johns Hopkins University Press, 1984.

Skerrett, Joseph. "Irony and Symbolic Action in James Weldon Johnson's *The Autobiography of an Ex-Colored Man*." *American Quarterly* 32 (1980): 540–48.

Smith, Valerie. "Privilege and Evasion in *The Autobiography of an Ex-Colored Man*." In *Self-Discovery and Authority in Afro-American Narrative*, by Valerie Smith, 44–64. Cambridge, MA: Harvard University Press, 1987.

Snead, James A. "Repetition as a Figure of Black Culture." In *Black Literature and Literary Theory*, edited by Henry Louis Gates Jr., 59–79. New York: Routledge, 1990.

Southern, Eileen. *The Music of Black Americans: A History*. 3rd ed. New York: W. W. Norton, 1997.

Stansell, Christine. *American Moderns: Bohemian New York and the Creation of a New Century*. Princeton, NJ: Princeton University Press, 2010.

Stepto, Robert. *From behind the Veil: A Study of Afro-American Narrative*. 1979. Reprint, Chicago: University of Illinois Press, 1991.

Suisman, David. *Selling Sounds: The Commercial Revolution in American Music*. Cambridge, MA: Harvard University Press, 2009.

Sundquist, Eric J. *The Hammers of Creation: Folk Culture in Modern African-American Fiction*. Athens: University of Georgia Press, 1992.

Szefel, Lisa. "Beauty and William Braithwaite." *Callaloo* 29, no. 2 (2006): 560–86.

———. "Encouraging Verse: William S. Braithwaite and the Poetics of Race." *New England Quarterly* 70, no. 1 (2001): 32–61.

Thompson, Emily. *The Soundscape of Modernity: Architectural Acoustics and the Culture of Listening in America, 1900–1933*. Cambridge, MA: MIT Press, 2004.

Van Vechten, Carl. "Introduction to Mr. Knopf's New Edition." 1927. *The Autobiography of an Ex-Coloured Man*. New York: Vintage, 1989.

Voegelin, Salomé. *Listening to Noise and Silence: Towards a Philosophy of Sound Art*. New York: Continuum International Publishing Group, 2010.

Weheliye, Alexander G. *Phonographies: Grooves in Sonic Afro-Modernity*. Durham, NC: Duke University Press, 2005.

Werner, Craig. *A Change Is Gonna Come: Music, Race & the Soul of America*. Ann Arbor: University of Michigan Press, 2006.

Williams, Kenny J. "An Invisible Partnership and an Unlikely Relationship: William Stanley Braithwaite and Harriet Monroe." *Callaloo* 32 (Summer 1987): 516–50.

Wilson, Sondra Kathryn. Introduction to *Along This Way*, by James Weldon Johnson. 1933, 1990. Reprint, New York: Penguin, 2008.

———. *Meet Me at the Theresa: The Story of Harlem's Most Famous Hotel*. New York: Atria Books, 2004.

———, ed. *The Selected Writings of James Weldon Johnson*. 2 vols. New York: Oxford University Press, 1995.

Index